THE INDEPENDENT'S GUIDE TO FILM DISTRIBUTORS

EDITED BY MICHELE MEEK

A PUBLICATION BY

2

A publication of Independent Media Publications, Inc.
P.O. Box 391620
Cambridge, MA 02139
www.independent-magazine.org

As the media distribution field changes rapidly, we urge you to contact distributors directly before sending DVDs or promotional materials, to ensure that the information listed herein is accurate and up-to-date.

Independent Media Publications, a nonprofit 501(c)(3) organization, aims to inform, promote, encourage and mobilize the independent and grassroots media arts movement. For more information about Independent Media Publications, visit www.independent-magazine.org.

This book was made possible with the assistance of Independent Media Publications board and *The Independent* staff:

Board Members: John Bodt, Mike Hofman, and Michele Meek
Publisher: Michele Meek
Editor-in-Chief: Mike Hofman
Managing Editor: Erin Trahan
Associate Editor: Nikki Chase
Book Associate Editors: Matthew Quan and Vanessa Willoughby

Library of Congress Control Number: 2009929852
ISBN-13: 978-0-9840925-0-5

Table of Contents

Introduction

ABOUT THIS BOOK

This first edition of the *The Independent's Guide to Film Distributors* was inspired in part by the book *The AIVF Guide to Film & Video Distributors* originally published by the Association of Independent Film and Videomakers and acquired by our organization Independent Media Publications, Inc. For our re-envisioning of the book, we have contacted each company in order to obtain accurate information for the listings.

HOW TO USE THIS BOOK

1. **Supplement your research in this book with the company's website.** You will find much more detail about the types of films that the company handles to help you decide if it is a good fit for your film.
2. **Never send screeners or DVDs without being asked.** Companies that are listed in this book as accepting "unsolicited inquiries" typically expect filmmakers to begin with an e-mail or mail inquiry about their film. If the company is interested, they will ask you to send a DVD. There are exceptions to this, however. If in doubt, call and ask first.
3. **Check the contact information before mailing screeners.** Keep in mind that companies are always changing addresses, phone numbers, acquisition directors, etc., so be sure to call and double check contact information before you send out any queries.
4. **Read the articles on distribution to learn more.** In addition to the company listings, we have compiled several articles about distribution, some of which have been previously published at *The Independent* (www.independent-magazine.org) with tips to help you prepare your films for distribution, pitch distributors, negotiate a contract, get your films online, and even how to self-distribute, if you should decide on that option.
5. **Use the indexes.** In our indexes at the back, you can quickly find distributors that accept films of different lengths, on various subject matters, and at different stages.

We wish each of you the best of luck in seeking distribution!

ACKNOWLEDGEMENTS

Thank you to the board members of Independent Media Publications, John Bodt and Mike Hofman, as well as *The Independent's* Managing Editor Erin Trahan and Associate Editor Nikki Chase who assisted in editing the articles in this book. Thanks also to Book Associate Editors Matthew Quan and Vanessa Willoughby who assisted in updating the individual company listings, in addition to helping choose the articles for inclusion in this book. I'd also like to thank Cynthia Peters for copy editing the book and Tony Zamora for creating the cover design for the book. And of course, thanks to all the writers who contributed their work to this edition.

I would also like to extend a special thanks to the staff of the former Association of Independent Film and Videomakers (AIVF) who conceived the *AIVF Guide to Film & Video Distributors* back in the 1980s.

Michele Meek
Executive Director, Independent Media Publications, Inc.
Editor, *The Independent's Guide to Film Distributors, First Edition*
www.independent-magazine.org
michele@independent-magazine.org

ABOUT THE EDITOR

Michele Meek is a co-founder and the executive director of Independent Media Publications. In 1997, she founded NewEnglandFilm.com, the magazine, resource and community for independent filmmaking in the northeast. Soon after, she founded BuyIndies.com, an international community for buying and selling independent, educational and hard-to-find films from over 1,000 filmmakers and niche distributors. Respected as a champion of independent film, she received the 2005 Baldwin Award for Alumni Recognition in Film & Video from Boston College and the 2000 Image Award for Vision and Excellence from Women in Film & Video New England. Her most recent short narrative film *Red Sneakers* premiered at the Woods Hole Film Festival in 2008 and received second place in the children's category at the Rhode Island International Film Festival. She has written extensively on film and travel in leading publications such as *MovieMaker Magazine, The Independent, WHERE Magazine, Bonjour Paris* and *indieWIRE*. Learn more about her on her website at www.michelemeek.com.

Distributor Company Profiles

ACADEMY ENTERTAINMENT
AKA: MLR Films International
611 Cedar Lane Teaneck NJ 07666
Phone: (201) 394-1849 | Fax: (201) 357-8482
http://www.academyentertainment.net

900 titles. Est. 1991. Principals: Alan Miller, Nancy Miller

Academy Entertainment, Inc., is a worldwide film and television program distribution company. It has a library of classic movies, short subjects, documentaries, and cartoons. It also represents feature films, television programs, and series on behalf of individual producers for worldwide licensing. Customers include television stations, film distributors, video distributors, stock footage companies, individual producers, broadband Internet TV stations, and content for streaming media on the Internet.

Subjects: Action/Adventure, Aging, Animation, Archival, Arts, Literature & Music, Biography, Children's Programming, Comedy, Criminal Justice, Disability, Drama, Environmental Issues, Experimental/Avant Garde, Family, LGBT, Gender Issues, Health & Medicine, History, Human Rights, Immigration, Labor Issues, Language/Linguistics, Multicultural Perspective, Nature, Politics & Government, Psychology, Regional Profiles & Issues, Religion, Science, Sociology, Sports, Theater, Travel, Women's Issues **Markets:** Theatrical, Nontheatrical, Educational, Home Video, Cable TV, Public TV, Network TV, TV Syndication, Satelitte/DBS, Web, Airline, Foreign **Specialty:** All genres **Titles:** *The Long Way Home* **Territories:** Worldwide **Marketing:** Web Catalog

Acquisition Information: Acquires Narrative Feature, Doc Feature, Animation **Acquisition Method:** Unsolicited Inquiries, Festivals, Markets **Stage:** Script, Production **Advance:** Sometimes. **Acquisition Contact:** Alan Miller

ACORN MEDIA GROUP
8515 Georgia Avenue, Suite 650 Silver Spring MD 20910
Phone: (800) 999-0212 | Fax: (301) 608-9312
feedback@acornmedia.com
http://www.acornmedia.com

500 titles. Est. 1984. Principals: Miguel Penella, CEO; Rozanne Hakala, Executive Vice President of Operations

The Acorn Media Group provides distinctive home video products and other merchandise to the North American, U.K., and Australia markets. It caters to consumers seeking products that fall outside the mainstream with a special focus on the best of British television and mind, body, spirit programming.

Subjects: Arts, Literature & Music, Comedy, Drama, History **Markets:** Home Video **Specialty:** British **Marketing:** Web Catalog

Acquisition Information: Acquires Narrative Feature **Acquisition Method:** Unknown **Stage:** Unknown

AGEE FILMS

AKA: James Agee Film Project
6707 Wells Parkway University Park MD 20782
Phone: (301) 277-3880
jagee@cstone.net
http://www.ageefilms.org

15 titles. Est. 1974. Principals: Ross Spears, Jamie Ross

AGEE Films is a nonprofit media production and distribution organization. Founded in 1974, it has made a dozen or more award-winning films, which it distributes online. Agee Films produces and distributes award-winning documentary films on a wide range of subjects, including environmental history, American literature, American history, social justice, religion, child development, and American culture.

Subjects: Aging, Arts, Literature & Music, Biography, Environmental Issues, Family, History, Nature, Religion, Science **Markets:** Nontheatrical, Educational, Home Video, Public TV, Web, Other **Specialty:** American History, the Environment, Childhood, American Literature, Religion, Documentary Art **Titles:** *Appalachia, Tell About the South to Render a Life.* **Marketing:** Printed Catalog, Web Catalog

Acquisition Information: Acquires Doc Feature, Short Doc **Acquisition Method:** Other **Stage:** Fine Cut, Finished **Advance:** No. **Philosophy:** As our favorite filmmaker wrote many years ago: "I put my deepest hope and faith in the future of movies, in their being made of relatively little money, in actual rather than imitated places, with the binding eye, conviction, and delight in work which are fostered in good enough people by that predicament. The theme or the story needs to be passionately felt and intimately understood, and it should be a theme or story worthy of such knowledge and passion." – Jim Agee, 1909-1955 **Advice:** Patience, Perseverance, Passion **Acquisition Contact:** Ross Spears

ALIVE MIND

Parent Company: Lorber HT Digital
56 West 45th St., Suite 805 New York NY 10036
Phone: (212) 398 3112
elizabeth@lorberdigital.com
http://www.alivemind.net

20 titles. Est. 2007. 6 employees. Principals: Richard Lorber and Stuart Rekant

Alive Mind is the DVD label and online content business of Lorber HT Digital.
The company releases a selection of documentary programming in the areas of
enlightened consciousness, secular spirituality, and cultural change.

Subjects: Arts, Literature & Music, Drama, Experimental/Avant Garde, LGBT,
Gender Issues, History, Politics & Government, Psychology, Religion, Science,
Sociology, Theater, Women's Issues **Markets:** Nontheatrical, Educational, Home
Video **Specialty:** Award-winning Documentaries **Titles:** Jennifer Fox's *Flying:
Confessions of a Free Woman*; Nik Sheehan's *FLicKeR*; *Hair: Let the Sun Shine In*;
Jessica Yu's *Protagonist*. **Territories:** North America, International **Marketing:** Web
Catalog, Direct Mail, Other

Acquisition Information: 20 titles per year. Acquires Doc Feature **Acquisition
Method:** Unsolicited Inquiries, Festivals, Markets, Other **Stage:** Fine Cut, Finished
Philosophy: "Our mission is to deliver smart and stimulating work with the 'aha'
factor of a transformative experience," explains CEO & President Richard Lorber.
Advice: Don't hesitate to contact us regarding potential distribution of your film.
Acquisition Contact: Elizabeth Sheldon, Vice President (212) 398-3112
elizabeth@lorberdigital.com

ALLUMINATION FILMWORKS

21250 Califa Street, Suite 102 Woodland Hills CA 91367
Phone: (818) 712-9000 | Fax: (818) 712-9074
info@alluminationfilmworks.com
http://www.alluminationfilmworks.com

600 titles. Est. 2002. Principals: Kerry McCluggage, Chairman; Jeff Sagansky,
Chairman; Cheryl A. Freeman, Chief Executive Officer

Allumination FilmWorks (formerly Ardustry Home Entertainment) focuses on the
distribution of quality entertainment to broadcast, satellite, and cable television as
well as both the theatrical and home entertainment markets worldwide. The award-
winning company maintains a portfolio of nearly 600 theatrical films, in all major
categories, as well as over 4,000 hours of television programming, along with music
specials and kids/family feature titles for television, cable, and home video/DVD
distribution markets worldwide. With its focus on high-demand, under-served

consumer markets, Allumination will also present a roster of horror and science fiction, alternative lifestyle, and ethnic and family titles to the burgeoning digital distribution, VOD, DVD and home video sell-through retail industry. The company's release plans call for a minimum of 2-10 titles per month entering the DVD/Video sell-through marketplace.

Subjects: Action/Adventure, Children's Programming, Comedy, Drama, Family, Multicultural Perspective, Sports **Markets:** Theatrical, Home Video, Public TV **Specialty:** Music specials and Kids/family features **Titles:** *305, Evil Behind You, Call of the Wild, Baby Blues, The Secret Life of Girls* **Marketing:** Web Catalog

Acquisition Information: Acquires Narrative Feature, Doc Feature **Acquisition Method:** Solicited Only, Festivals, Markets **Stage:** Finished **Venues:** Cannes, Santa Fe Film Festival, South by Southwest (SXSW) Film Festival, Sundance **Philosophy:** "At Allumination, we are committed to the producer as well as to the programmer and retailer. We strive to pay producers respect as well as revenues, by welcoming them as hands-on business partners. In essence, our philosophy is that passion drives success – not a simple 'advance.' Allumination is built on passion, and the worldwide entertainment marketplace is responding." **Acquisition Contact:** Sam Toles, Vice President of Business Development and Acquisitions (818) 712-9000 info@alluminationfilmworks.com

ALPINE PICTURES, INC.
3500 W. Magnolia Blvd. Burbank CA 91505
Phone: (818) 333-2600 x1215
info@alpinepix.com
http://www.alpinepix.com

10 titles. Est. 1995. Principals: Roland Carroll, President; Ryan Carroll, CEO; James Jones, Executive Vice President

Founded in 1995 by brothers Ryan and Roland Carroll, Alpine Pictures, Inc., was created to develop and produce independent films and later expanded into distribution. The combined elements of the company cover film production, television production, distribution to all markets, including theatrical, cable, broadcast, and home video (DVD) markets. As the computer revolution is adding new market segments, API is preparing to enter those markets as well.
Subjects: Action/Adventure, Children's Programming, Drama, Family **Markets:** Theatrical, Home Video, Cable TV **Titles:** *The Gold Retriever, AKA Treasure of the West, An Angel on Abbey Street, The Blue Light* **Territories:** International markets, International distribution, Feature films **Marketing:** Web Catalog

Acquisition Information: Acquires Narrative Feature **Acquisition Method:** Unsolicited Inquiries, Festivals, Markets **Stage:** Script, Production, Finished **Venues:** Cannes, Sundance, Slamdance, Toronto, Berlin, Los Angeles International

Children's Film Festival, San Diego International Children's Film Festival
Acquisition Contact: (818) 333-2600 ext. 1215 info@alpinepix.com

AMAZING MOVIES

Parent Company: A Douglas Witkin Company
7471 Melrose Avenue, Suite 7 Los Angeles CA 90046
Phone: (323) 852-1396 | Fax: (323) 658-7265
amazingmov@aol.com
http://amazingmovies.biz

11 titles. Est. 1985. Principals: Douglas C. Witkins, President; Matt Giedlinski,
Director of Operations

Amazing Movies acquires the rights to genre films (action, adventure, sci-fi, thriller,
suspense, etc.) mainly to license to foreign video and television buyers. With a
broad catalog of product led by adventure, thriller and comedy titles, the company
provides a regular flow of product to buyers in all media in every territory
throughout the year.

Subjects: Action/Adventure, Comedy, Drama **Markets:** Nontheatrical, Home
Video, Foreign **Specialty:** Genre film for the foreign market **Titles:** *Alec to the
Rescue, A Dirty Little Business, Centurion Force* **Marketing:** Web Catalog

Acquisition Information: Acquires Narrative Feature **Acquisition Method:**
Unknown **Stage:** Unknown **Venues:** AFM, Cannes Market, MIFED, Sundance,
Berlin, Toronto, Outfest **Acquisition Contact:** Douglas Witkins, President/CEO
(323) 852-1396 amazingmov@aol.com

AMBROSE VIDEO PUBLISHING, INC.

145 West 45th Street, Suite 115 New York NY 10036
Phone: (800) 526-4663 | Fax: (212) 768-9282
aldohra@hotmail.com
http://www.ambrosevideo.com

1000 titles. Est. 1987. 35 employees. Principals: William Ambrose, President;
Kathy Popolani, VP of Finance

Ambrose Video is a leading producer of DVDs and digital content for education
and libraries. It has a library of over 1,000 titles that feature award-winning
materials in social studies, literature, and the sciences. The core of its collection is
broadcast quality productions from the BBC, public broadcasting, HBO, and
assorted independent producers. The titles range from the BBC Shakespeare Plays
to Public TV's Legacy to Discovery's Connection series.

Subjects: Arts, Literature & Music, Criminal Justice, Health & Medicine, History, Human Rights, Multicultural Perspective, Science **Markets:** Educational, Home Video, Cable TV, Public TV, Network TV, Foreign **Specialty:** Educational and training programs **Titles:** *LifeStories, Families in Crisis* series, *Over America*

Acquisition Information: Acquires Doc Feature, Short Doc **Acquisition Method:** Unknown **Stage:** Unknown

APOLLO CINEMA
519 Hillcrest Rd. Beverly Hills CA 90210
Phone: (323) 939-1122 | Fax: (323) 939-1133
info@apollocinema.com
http://www.apollocinema.com/default.htm

250 titles. Est. 1998. 3 employees. Principals: Carol Crowe, President; Eric Hatter, VP of Business Affairs

Apollo Cinema is an international distributor of short films of all types and genres. Apollo sells to television stations (broadcast, cable, pay-per-view, and satellite), Internet sites, airlines, theaters, military bases, home video, and DVD. Apollo was founded in 1997 by executives with experience in film and television distribution, marketing, development, and production. Apollo is dedicated to using this experience to provide each filmmaker with the broadest possible audience and maximum exposure. Accordingly, Apollo is very selective about the shorts it acquires.
By selecting only a small number of shorts each year to represent, Apollo aims to highlight quality films that will appeal to international buyers while focusing individual attention on each film and filmmaker.

Subjects: Action/Adventure, Animation, Children's Programming, Comedy, Drama, Family **Markets:** Theatrical, Nontheatrical, Home Video, Cable TV, Public TV, Network TV, TV Syndication, Satelitte/DBS, Web, Airline, Foreign **Specialty:** Shorts **Titles:** *The Accountant, For the Birds, George Lucas in Love* **Marketing:** Web Catalog

Acquisition Information: Acquires Short Narrative, Animation **Acquisition Method:** Unsolicited Inquiries, Festivals, Markets **Stage:** Finished **Venues:** Film festivals and referrals **Advice:** We welcome all submissions on DVD, NTSC, and PAL VHS tapes. Please fill out the submission form and mail it with your screener. (This will make the screening process much smoother, so we won't watch it unless you fill out the form, ok?) If you would like your tape returned, enclose a self-addressed stamped envelope (postage pre-paid). Submission form and guidelines are at http://www.apollocinema.com/submit.htm **Acquisition Contact:** Film Submissions submit@apollocinema.com

APPALSHOP FILM AND VIDEO
91 Madison Avenue Whitesburg KY 41858
Phone: (606) 633-0108 | Fax: (606) 633-1009
appalshopsales@appalshop.org
http://www.appalshop.org

100 titles. Est. 1969. 26 employees. Principals: Art Menius, Director; Beth
Bingman, Managing Director

Appalshop is a nonprofit, multi-disciplinary arts and education center in the heart
of Appalachia producing original films, video, theater, music and spoken-word
recordings, radio, photography, multimedia, and books. Each year, Appalshop
productions and services reach several million people nationally and internationally.
Appalshop is dedicated to the proposition that the world is immeasurably enriched
when local cultures garner the resources, including new technologies, to tell their
own stories and to listen to the unique stories of others.

Subjects: Arts, Literature & Music, Drama, Labor Issues, Multicultural Perspective,
Sociology **Markets:** Theatrical, Nontheatrical, Educational, Home Video **Specialty:**
Film and video on culture and social issues **Titles:** *Stranger with a Camera, The
Ralph Stanley Story, Shelter* **Marketing:** Web Catalog

Acquisition Information: Acquires Doc Feature, Short Doc **Acquisition Method:**
Unknown **Stage:** Unknown

AQUARIUS HEALTH CARE MEDIA
18 North Main Street Sherborn MA 01770-9985
Phone: (508) 650-1616 | Fax: (508) 650-1665
lkussmann@aquariusproductions.com
http://www.aquariusproductions.com

750 titles. Est. 1988. 5 employees. Principals: Leslie Kussmann, President and
Producer

Aquarius Health Care Media is a leading distributor of educational documentaries
on many major healthcare issues. Its films are winners of major international film
festivals, featured at major conferences, and reviewed by the media.

Subjects: Aging, Children's Programming, Disability, Family, LGBT, Gender
Issues, Health & Medicine, Human Rights, Nature, Psychology, Religion,
Sociology, Women's Issues **Markets:** Nontheatrical, Educational, Public TV,
Network TV, TV Syndication, Satelitte/DBS, Web **Specialty:** Educational media
on health care **Titles:** *Eternal High, Making Connections, Late Life Depression,
Caregivers Resource Library Series, A Lion in the House* series, *Abilities to the Xtreme,*

Pursuing the Dreams, Anorexia: Recognizing & Combating it in Your Child, Part of the Keeping Kids Healthy eeries **Territories:** All available **Marketing:** Printed Catalog, Web Catalog, One Sheets, Direct Mail

Acquisition Information: 100 titles per year. Acquires Doc Feature, Short Doc **Acquisition Method:** Solicited Only **Stage:** Finished **Venues:** Film festivals, web, different alternatives **Advance:** No. **Philosophy:** Aquarius believes that if you produce films that you believe in, are committed to, and have a personal attachment to, then they will be successful. The company distributes quality programs that reflect the future of health care and healing. **Advice:** Call us for details. We would love to work with you if your film is health-related and appropriate for what we are looking for at the time. **Acquisition Contact:** Leslie Kussmann, President/Producer (508) 650-1616 ext. 111 lkussmann@aquariusproductions.com and Toni Knights (508) 650-1616 ext. 110 toni@aquariusproductions.com

ARENAS ENTERTAINMENT MARKETING
3375 Barham Blvd. Los Angeles CA 90068
Phone: (323) 785-5555 | Fax: (323) 785-5560
http://www.arenasgroup.com/

300 titles. Est. 1988. Principals: Santiago Pozo, CEO; Larry Gleason, President of Distribution

Arenas is a diversified entertainment and media company specializing in products for U.S. Latino audiences. Arenas, with its unique team of experienced bilingual and bicultural executives, has worked on over 300 films and TV programs. Arenas has developed and executed Hispanic targeted campaign strategies on behalf of major studio clients such as Universal and Disney, and networks such as ABC and PBS. The services that Arenas offers include marketing strategy, creative advertising, media planning, media buying, research, publicity, and promotions.

Subjects: Animation, Children's Programming, Drama, Family, Human Rights, Immigration, Multicultural Perspective, Politics & Government, Religion **Markets:** Theatrical, Nontheatrical, Home Video, Cable TV, Public TV **Specialty:** Latino market, U.S. Hispanic market **Titles:** *Empire, Nicotina, Imagining Argentina, Culture Clash in America, Three Wise Men* **Marketing:** Web Catalog

Acquisition Information: Acquires Narrative Feature, Doc Feature, Animation **Acquisition Method:** Solicited Only **Stage:** Finished **Venues:** Sundance, Cannes **Philosophy:** Arenas believes that, in order to develop the most effective marketing campaign, client partnerships must involve an honest evaluation of the diverse, ever-changing Hispanic consumer. **Acquisition Contact:** Larry Gleason, President of Distribution (323) 785-5552 larry@arenasgroup.com and Rosy Thompson, President of Marketing (323) 785-5578 rosy@arenasgroup.com

ARROW ENTERTAINMENT, INC.
7 Givins St. Toronto Ontario M6J 2X5 Canada
Phone: (416) 516-0815 (416) 771-1721 | Fax: (416) 850-9973
steve-arroyave@arrow-entertainment.com
http://www.arrow-entertainment.com

30 titles. 2 employees. Principals: Steve Arroyave, CEO; Lars Bjorck, President

Arrow Entertainment is a worldwide sales agent of feature films and documentaries, acquiring films of all genres that have a specific and identifiable audience.

Subjects: Comedy, Drama, Religion **Markets:** Theatrical, Nontheatrical, Home Video, Cable TV, Foreign

Acquisition Information: Acquires Narrative Feature, Short Narrative **Acquisition Method:** Unknown **Stage:** Unknown **Venues:** Sundance film Festival, European Film Market, Berlin Film Festival, MIPTV, Cannes Film Festival, Toronto International Film Festival, MIPCOM and the American Film Market.
Acquisition Contact: Steve Arroyave, CEO (416) 771-1721 steve-arroyave@arrow-entertainment.com and Lar Bjorck, President (818) 359-1405 lars-bjorck@arrow-entertainment.com

ARTIST VIEW ENTERTAINMENT, INC.
4425 Irvine Avenue Studio City CA 91602
Phone: (818) 752-2480 | Fax: (818) 752-9339
info@artistviewent.com
http://www.artistviewent.com

180 titles. Est. 1991. Principals: Scott J. Jones, President; Jay E. Joyce, Vice President; Shelly Rangel, Controller

Artist View Entertainment, Inc., represents a wide variety of feature films and prides itself on the acquisition of movies with that "special marketing hook." Artist View prides itself on strong relationships with independent, self-financed production companies. Currently representing over a dozen producers from which it receives a regular stream of product, Artist View is always on the lookout for its next long-term relationship.

Subjects: Action/Adventure, Children's Programming, Comedy, Drama, Family **Markets:** Nontheatrical, Home Video, Cable TV **Titles:** *Brother War, Christmas in the Clouds, The Eleventh Hour, Safehouse, House of Fears* **Marketing:** Web Catalog

Acquisition Information: Acquires Narrative Feature **Acquisition Method:** Unsolicited Inquiries, Festivals, Markets **Stage:** Finished **Venues:** AFM, NATPE,

Berlin Film Festival, MIP-TV, Cannes Film Festival, DISCOP and MIPCOM
Philosophy: The core belief of the business is based on integrity and a mutual
respect for its investors, producers, and buyers alike. **Acquisition Contact:** Scott J.
Jones, President (818) 752-2480 scott@artistviewnet.com and Shelly Rangel,
Controller (818) 752-2480 shelly@artistviewnet.com

ARTISTIC LICENSE FILMS
250 West 57th Street, #606 New York NY 10107
Phone: (212) 265- 9119 | Fax: (212) 262-9299
artlic@aol.com
http://www.artlic.com

38 titles. Est. 1994. 3 employees. Principals: Sande Zeig, President; Steve Fagan,
Theatrical Sales Manager; Nora Coblence, Financial Director

Artistic License Films is a full-service theatrical distributor that works
collaboratively with filmmakers on all creative aspects of distribution. As a booking
agent, Artistic License Films provides filmmakers, producers, and distribution
companies with individualized services to ensure the successful theatrical release of a
film.

Subjects: LGBT, Gender Issues, Multicultural Perspective, Women's Issues
Markets: Theatrical **Specialty:** Art house film **Titles:** *Troublesome Creek: A*
Midwestern, Who Does She Think She Is? **Marketing:** Printed Catalog, Web Catalog

Acquisition Information: Acquires Narrative Feature, Doc Feature **Acquisition**
Method: Unsolicited Inquiries, Festivals, Markets **Stage:** Finished **Acquisition**
Contact: szeig@artlic.com

ARTS ALLIANCE AMERICA
AKA: Hart Sharp Video
304 Hudson Street, 7th floor New York NY 10013
Phone: (212) 475.2888 | Fax: (212) 475.5487
joe@artsallianceamerica.com
http://www.hartsharpvideo.com

200 titles. Est. 2003. Principals: Joe S. Amodei, President; Craig Van Gorp,
Executive Vice President

Arts Alliance America, formerly known as Hart Sharp Video, is a full-service home
entertainment company that develops, acquires, markets, and distributes DVDs in
the film, documentary, special interest, and sports genres. Arts Alliance America has
successfully built partnerships with TV Guide, E! Entertainment Television,
Sundance Channel Home Entertainment, ESPN, MLB Productions, Bombo
Sports and Entertainment, NESN, and other high profile entertainment brands.

Subjects: Action/Adventure, Children's Programming, Comedy, Drama, Politics & Government, Sports **Markets:** Theatrical, Nontheatrical, Educational, Home Video **Titles:** *Chalk, Bad Meat, Never Forever, Admissions, Book of Love, Soho Square* **Territories:** Sundance Channel **Marketing:** Web Catalog

Acquisition Information: Acquires Narrative Feature, Doc Feature **Acquisition Method:** Festivals, Markets **Stage:** Finished **Venues:** Sundance, Cannes, Tribeca, Rome International Film Festival, Toronto Film Festival **Acquisition Contact:** Camille Perretti-Fiato, Vice President of Operations (212) 475-2888 camille@artsallianceamerica.com and Lauren Diamond, Operations Coordinator (212) 475-2888 lauren@artsallianceamerica.com

ATOM ENTERTAINMENT, INC.
AKA: AtomFilms.com and AtomShockwave
Parent Company: MTV
2049 Century Park East, Suite 4000 Los Angeles CA 90067
Phone: (206) 264-2735 | Fax: (206) 264-2742
info@atomfilms.com
http://www.atomfilms.com

300 titles.

Formerly known as AtomFilms.com, Atom Entertainment, Inc., (now owned by MTV Networks) is a leading entertainment provider for businesses and consumers in emerging media channels. It distributes world-class entertainment properties across the Internet, broadband services, and mobile devices, as well as traditional outlets such as television, theaters, and airlines. Atom Entertainment's extensive catalog of game, film, and animation content is supported through advertising, sponsorship, syndication, and e-commerce. It offers several ways for great videos to get noticed: Atom Studio funds/develops original comedy programming; the Atom Content Team scours the Internet for content to license; and it receives hundreds of uploads per day from budding talent across the Web.

Subjects: Action/Adventure, Animation, Children's Programming, Comedy, Drama **Markets:** Web **Specialty:** Web film **Marketing:** Web Catalog

Acquisition Information: Acquires Short Narrative, Short Doc, Animation **Acquisition Method:** Unsolicited Inquiries, Festivals, Markets, Other **Stage:** Finished **Advice:** We're a full-blown digital entertainment network that has paid millions of dollars to creators and distributed content to just about every screen that plays video. Now, thanks to a partnership with Comedy Central, we've got a weekly TV series, and we're funding more Atom Originals than ever. Upload a video, animation, or game now. If the Atom audience or staff like it, you could earn Pro Video status, and the exposure, dollars, and distribution that come with it. More information at http://www.atom.com/creators

AVATAR FILMS
150 West 28th Street, Suite 1803 New York NY 10001
Phone: (212) 675-0300 | Fax: (212) 675-1960
info@avatarfilms.com
http://www.avatarfilms.com

15 titles. Est. 1999.
Based in New York City, Avatar Films is an independent film distribution company specializing in art house films and documentaries that "push the envelope." Founded in 1999, its mission is to bring films of a certain caliber and transcendence to a much deserved audience. Avatar provides a hands-on approach towards marketing and distribution to ensure a successful reception of films in the marketplace and offer innovative and flexible distribution deals that aim to be results-oriented and filmmaker-friendly.

Subjects: Arts, Literature & Music, Comedy, Drama, History, Multicultural Perspective, Politics & Government **Markets:** Theatrical, Nontheatrical, Educational, Home Video, Cable TV, Public TV, Network TV, Foreign **Specialty:** Art house film **Titles:** *After Midnight, Kandahar, Nico and Dani, New York in the Fifties, Tosca*

Acquisition Information: Acquires Narrative Feature, Doc Feature **Acquisition Method:** Unsolicited Inquiries, Festivals, Markets **Stage:** Rough Cut, Fine Cut, Finished **Venues:** Cannes, Sundance, Toronto, Montreal, Berlin, Rotterdam **Philosophy:** Avatar Films adheres to a profound sense of belief in the ability of film to inspire and transform. It provides a hands-on approach towards marketing and distribution to ensure a successful reception of films in the marketplace. **Advice:** In order for us to consider viewing your film please first e-mail us a synopsis of your film, a cast list, production details (format, etc.), any awards it may have received, whether it has been viewed in any festivals, and any other relevant information. Please send this information to acquisitions@avatarfilms.com. Once we have reviewed this material we will contact you if we feel that we can effectively distribute your film. At this time, we do not accept unsolicited material. **Acquisition Contact:** Jason Leaf, Co-President, jason@avatarfilms.com

BALCONY RELEASING
26 Mill Lane Amherst MA 01002
http://www.balconyfilm.com

20 titles.

Balcony Releasing designs and implements theatrical distribution strategies for independently produced documentary features. Founder Connie White recognized, particularly through her work programming film festivals, that many worthy films don't find their way to movie theaters. Together with her husband, Greg Kendall, they developed this niche film distribution service.

Subjects: Aging, Biography, Gender Issues, Health & Medicine, History, Human Rights, Multicultural Perspective, Politics & Government, Sociology, Women's Issues **Markets:** Theatrical **Titles:** *King Corn, Enlighten Up!* **Marketing:** Web Catalog

Acquisition Information: Acquires Doc Feature **Acquisition Method:** Unsolicited Inquiries **Stage:** Unknown **Acquisition Contact:** Connie White, Founder (413) 253-6781 connie@balconyfilm.com and Greg Kendall, Founder (413) 253-6783 greg@balconyfilm.com

BAUER MARTINEZ STUDIOS
801 West Bay Drive, Suite 800 Largo FL 33770
Phone: (727) 582-9939
karinne@bauermartinez.com
http://www.bauermartinez.com

20 titles. Est. 1999. Principals: Philippe Martinez, Chairman and CEO

Bauer Martinez Studios (BMS) is a U.S. film production and acquisition company led by its Chairman and CEO, veteran producer/director Philippe Martinez. With alliances to some of Hollywood's most renowned companies, Bauer Martinez focuses on producing, acquiring, and marketing high quality commercial films from respected directors, such as Amy Heckerling and Andrew Lau, and featuring world famous actors, such as Andy Garcia, Richard Gere, and Michelle Pfeiffer. Having both directed and produced his own movies, Martinez aims to establish a personal connection with his filmmakers that sets the tone for a collaborative working arrangement.

Subjects: Action/Adventure, Children's Programming, Comedy, Drama, Family **Markets:** Theatrical, Nontheatrical, Home Video **Titles:** *I Could Never Be Your Woman, Harsh Times, The Flock* **Territories:** Feature films **Marketing:** Web Catalog

Acquisition Information: Acquires Narrative Feature, Doc Feature **Acquisition Method:** Festivals, Markets **Stage:** Finished **Venues:** Cannes, Sundance, Toronto Film Festival, Tribeca Film Festival, Newport Beach Film Festival **Acquisition Contact:** Philippe Martinez, Chairman/CEO (727) 582-9939

BAXLEY MEDIA GROUP
510 W. Main Urbana IL 61801
Phone: (217) 384-4838
baxley@baxleymedia.com
http://www.baxleymedia.com/

100 titles. Est. 1983. Principals: Carolyn Baxley, President; Karen Krusa, Director of Operations

Baxley Media Group is a small, woman-owned business, which began operations in August 1983, distributing films and videos on psychological and ethical issues in health care primarily to hospitals and colleges. Since that time it has expanded its line to include programs for schools and businesses as well.

Subjects: Aging, Health & Medicine, Politics & Government, Women's Issues **Markets:** Nontheatrical, Educational, Foreign **Specialty:** Educational media on health care **Titles:** *Living with AIDS, Heavy Load, Thin Dreams* **Marketing:** Web Catalog

Acquisition Information: Acquires Doc Feature, Short Doc **Acquisition Method:** Unknown **Stage:** Unknown

BERKELEY MEDIA, LLC
2600 Tenth Street, Suite 626 Berkeley CA 94710
Phone: (510) 486-9900 | Fax: (510) 486-9944
info@berkeleymedia.com
http://www.berkeleymedia.com

160 titles.

Berkeley Media, LLC is one of America's foremost distributors of independently produced documentaries and educational media. Its collection of some 160 titles has won more than 720 awards and honors at major festivals and at screenings by academic associations worldwide. Berkeley Media's collection consists of titles that are notable both for their educational utility and merit and for their high production values and creative artistry.

Subjects: Aging, Arts, Literature & Music, Biography, Criminal Justice, Disability, Environmental Issues, Family, LGBT, Gender Issues, Health & Medicine, History, Human Rights, Immigration, Labor Issues, Language/Linguistics, Multicultural Perspective, Nature, Politics & Government, Psychology, Regional Profiles & Issues, Sociology, Women's Issues **Markets:** Educational **Titles:** *Anonymously Yours, Flag Wars, You Don't Know Dick* **Marketing:** Printed Catalog, Web Catalog

Acquisition Information: Acquires Doc Feature **Acquisition Method:** Unsolicited Inquiries **Stage:** Unknown **Advice:** If you have a new documentary with strong educational usefulness and merit, professional technical standards, and creative originality and vision, please contact us regarding its distribution to the educational marketplace. We can put more than 35 years of educational media marketing experience to work for you.

BULLFROG FILMS
P.O. Box 149 Oley PA 19547
Phone: (610) 779-8226 (800) 543-FROG | Fax: (610) 370-1978
info@bullfrogfilms.com
http://www.bullfrogfilms.com

614 titles. Est. 1973. 9 employees. Principals: John Hoskyns-Abrahall, Winifred Scherrer, Partners

Bullfrog Films is the oldest and largest publisher of videos and films about the environment in the United States. Founded in 1973, it has been honored with a retrospective screening at the Museum of Modern Art in New York and with a special award from Medikinale International in Parma, Italy. Its producers include the National Film Board of Canada, CBC, Television Trust for the Environment, BBC-TV, Australian Broadcasting Corporation, and leading independent producers from around the world.

Subjects: Aging, Animation, Arts, Literature & Music, Children's Programming, Environmental Issues, Gender Issues, Health & Medicine, History, Human Rights, Immigration, Labor Issues, Multicultural Perspective, Nature, Politics & Government, Science, Sociology, Theater **Markets:** Nontheatrical, Educational, Home Video, Cable TV, Public TV, Satelitte/DBS, Foreign **Specialty:** Educational media **Titles:** *Affluenz, Toast, Coming to Light* **Marketing:** Printed Catalog, Web Catalog, One Sheets, Direct Mail

Acquisition Information: Acquires Doc Feature **Acquisition Method:** Unsolicited Inquiries, Festivals, Markets **Stage:** Finished **Venues:** Festivals: DoubleTake, Taos, MountainFilm, Hot Docs, Hot Springs, San Francisco **Philosophy:** To bring together programs that point the way to a new paradigm for living happily, healthily, and sustainably. **Advice:** We are happy to give advice at any stage of production, but normally acquire finished programs. Contact us to make sure we are interested in the subject matter. When you send a program, include background information on the production. We usually won't take anything with a copyright date more than two years old, or that has already been in distribution. Most importantly, we want exclusive rights – at least in the nontheatrical market – to every program we distribute. We usually acquire home video rights as well, and if the producer is not willing to give home video rights, we usually require a 3-year window in which no one else will exploit those rights. **Acquisition Contact:** John

Hoskyns-Abrahall john@bullfrogfilms.com and Winifred Scherrer
winnie@bullfrogfilms.com

BUREAU FOR AT-RISK YOUTH
P.O. Box 1246 Wilkes-Barres PA 18703-1246
Phone: (800) 999-6884 | Fax: (800) 262-1886
info@at-risk.com
http://www.at-risk.com

100 titles. Est. 1991. Principals: Edward Werz, President

The Bureau for At-Risk Youth provides award-winning guidance and prevention
materials for K-12 schools, and juvenile justice organizations.

Subjects: Children's Programming, Criminal Justice, Health & Medicine,
Multicultural Perspective, Psychology, Sociology **Markets:** Educational, Home
Video **Specialty:** Educational media **Marketing:** Printed Catalog, Web Catalog

Acquisition Information: Acquires Doc Feature, Short Doc **Acquisition Method:**
Unknown **Stage:** Unknown

CALIFORNIA NEWSREEL
500 Third Street, Suite 505 San Francisco CA 94107
Phone: (415) 284-7800 | Fax: (415) 284-7801
contact@newsreel.org
http://www.newsreel.org

225 titles. Est. 1968. Principals: Lawrence Daressa, Laurence Adelman, Cornelius
Moore, Co-Directors

California Newsreel produces and distributes cutting edge, social justice films that
inspire, educate, and engage audiences. Founded in 1968, Newsreel is the oldest
nonprofit, social issue documentary film center in the country, the first to
intertwine media production and contemporary social movements. It is a leading
resource center for the advancement of racial justice and diversity, and the study of
African American life and history, as well as African culture and politics. In 2006,
California Newsreel launched a new thematic focus for its work: the Global
Economy, with an emphasis on the international division of labor. In the years
ahead it looks forward to continuing traditions of innovation and responsible
advocacy by providing films that help inform, educate, and organize.

Subjects: Human Rights, Labor Issues, Multicultural Perspective, Sociology
Markets: Educational, Public TV **Specialty:** Educational video on African
American life **Titles:** *Long Night* **Marketing:** Web Catalog

Acquisition Information: Acquires Doc Feature **Acquisition Method:** Unknown
Stage: Unknown

CAMBRIDGE DOCUMENTARY FILMS

P.O. Box 390385 Cambridge MA 02139-0004
Phone: (617) 484-3993 | Fax: (617) 484-0754
mail@cambridgedocumentaryfilms.org
http://www.cambridgedocumentaryfilms.org

17 titles. Est. 1974. Principals: Carol Belding, President

Cambridge Documentary Films aims to create new perspectives on important social
issues. It produces, directs, and distributes documentaries about advertising's image
of women, domestic violence, trauma, rape, eating disorders, self esteem, media
literacy, homophobia, the labor movement, gender roles, career counseling, nuclear
war, reproductive health hazards, the women's health movement, gay and lesbian
parenting, and other social issues.

Subjects: Criminal Justice, LGBT, Gender Issues, Health & Medicine, History,
Human Rights, Labor Issues, Multicultural Perspective, Sociology **Markets:**
Educational **Specialty:** Documentaries on social issues **Titles:** *Rape is ..., Defending
Our Lives, Killing Us Softly, Strong in Broken Places* **Marketing:** Printed Catalog,
Web Catalog

Acquisition Information: Acquires Short Doc **Acquisition Method:** Solicited Only
Stage: Unknown **Philosophy:** Cambridge Documentary Films is designed to
influence public opinion and foster social change. Documentaries are most
effective when presented in a setting that includes discussion and the exchange of
ideas. This is a different experience from passive viewing and enables audiences to
make the ideas their own and engage their potential activism. Because this
experience requires time, Cambridge Documentary Films aims for films that are
less than 40 minutes. **Acquisition Contact:** Margaret Lazarus
margaret@cambridgedocumentaryfilms.org and Renner Wunderlich
renner@cambridgedocumentaryfilms.org

CANADIAN FILMMAKERS DISTRIBUTION CENTER

401 Richmond St. West, Suite 119 Toronto Ontario M5V 3A8 Canada
Phone: (416) 588-0725 | Fax: (416) 588-7956
director@cfmdc.org
http://www.cfmdc.org

2600 titles. Est. 1967. 18 employees. Principals: Lauren Howes, Executive
Director; Jeffrey Crawford, Festival Officer

The CFMDC is Canada's foremost non-commercial distributor and resource for
independently produced film. The CFMDC's collection is diverse, ranging from
the 1950s to the present, and continues to grow steadily. CFMDC is artist-driven
and dedicates itself to distributing films that operate not simply outside of the
mainstream, but that are innovative and diverse in their origins and expressions.
CFMDC believes that works gain historical and cultural value over time and that
an evolving body of work by an individual artist is important to preserve. Films are
in all genres including drama, documentary, experimental, animation, and
installation by a wide range of local, national, and international artists, both
established and emerging.

Subjects: Animation, Archival, Arts, Literature & Music, Comedy, Environmental
Issues, Experimental/Avant Garde, LGBT, Gender Issues, Women's Issues
Markets: Nontheatrical, Educational, Home Video, Public TV, Network TV,
Web, Foreign **Specialty:** Short experimental / lesbian & gay cinema **Titles:**
Wavelength **Territories:** Worldwide, non-exclusive **Marketing:** Web Catalog

Acquisition Information: 100 titles per year. Acquires Short Narrative, Short Doc,
Animation, Experimental **Acquisition Method:** Unsolicited Inquiries, Festivals
Stage: Finished **Venues:** Ann Arbor Film Festival, Michigan, Festival du Nouveau
Cinema, Montreal, Berlin International Film Festival, the Melbourne Queer Film
Festival, the Jerusalem International Film Festival, Tate Modern Gallery, London
UK, Museum of Modern Art, New York **Advance:** No. **Philosophy:** Give the
filmmaker and the client the best service we can possibly provide. **Advice:** Bring
film to a distributor before a filmmaker starts submitting film on their own.
Acquisition Contact: Jeff Crawford, Festival Officer (416) 588-0725
bookings@cfmdc.org and Lauren Howes, Executive Director (416) 588-0725
director@cfmdc.org

CANYON CINEMA
145 Ninth Street, Suite 260 San Francisco CA 94103
Phone: (415) 626-2255
films@canyoncinema.com
http://www.canyoncinema.com

3500 titles. Principals: Dominic Angerame, Executive Director; Mark Toscano, Assistant Director and Film Traffic Controller

Canyon Cinema's collection of more than 3,500 films traces the history of the experimental and avant-garde filmmaking movement from the 1930s to the present. Canyon's primary activity is the distribution of 16mm films, videotapes, and DVDs by independent film artists. More than 40% of Canyon's gross income is returned directly to the filmmakers.

Subjects: Arts, Literature & Music, Experimental/Avant Garde **Markets:** Nontheatrical, Educational, Home Video **Specialty:** Independent and experimental film **Titles:** *Scorpio Rising, Castro Street, Wavelength, Window Water Baby Moving, Fuses, Mujer de Milfuegos* **Marketing:** Web Catalog

Acquisition Information: Acquires Experimental **Acquisition Method:** Unknown **Stage:** Unknown **Acquisition Contact:** Dominic Angerame, Executive Director, dominic@canyoncinema.com and Lauren Sorensen, Assistant Director/Film Traffic, lauren@canyoncinema.com

CAPITAL COMMUNICATIONS
2357-3 South Tamiami Trail Venice FL 34293
Phone: (941) 492-4688 (800) 822-5678 | Fax: (941) 492-4923
cap5678@isp.com
http://labtrainingvideos.com/

600 titles. Est. 1966. Principals: James Springer

Capital Communications distributes broadcast programming, as well as nontheatrical programming worldwide.

Subjects: Arts, Literature & Music, Biography, Disability, Health & Medicine, History, Multicultural Perspective **Markets:** Nontheatrical, Educational, Airline, Foreign, Other **Specialty:** Documentaries **Territories:** Worldwide **Marketing:** One Sheets

Acquisition Information: Acquires Doc Feature, Short Doc **Acquisition Method:** Solicited Only **Stage:** Unknown **Venues:** Monte Carlo, MIP-TV **Advice:** Take a long look. Will it sell in Detroit as well as in New Orleans? **Acquisition Contact:** Jim Springer (941) 492-4688 cap5678@isp.com

CASTLE HILL PRODUCTIONS
AKA: Castle Hill Films
36 West 25th St., 2nd Floor New York NY 10010
Phone: (212) 242-1500 | Fax: (212) 414-5737
mm@castlehillproductions.com
http://www.castlehillproductions.com/

350 titles. Est. 1978. 14 employees. Principals: Julian Schlossberg, Owner; Mel Maron, President of Marketing and Distribution

Castle Hill Productions is a multifaceted corporation that distributes, produces and represents motion pictures and producers. Founded in 1978 by Julian Schlossberg, the company has offices located in New York and Florida. Castle Hill Productions is entering its 26th year of business and now owns a library of more than 400 motion pictures. It specializes in distributing first-run, classic, and reissue movies to theaters, pay TV, and basic cable, home video, TV syndication, and all other motion picture outlets worldwide.

Subjects: Action/Adventure, Archival, Comedy, Drama, Family **Markets:** Theatrical, Home Video, Cable TV, Network TV, Foreign **Specialty:** Art house film **Titles:** *A Great Day in Harlem, The Line King: The Al Hirschfeld Story, Left Luggage, The Next Best Thing* **Marketing:** Web Catalog

Acquisition Information: 8 titles per year. Acquires Narrative Feature **Acquisition Method:** Unsolicited Inquiries, Festivals, Markets **Stage:** Unknown **Venues:** NATPE, AFM

CENTER FOR ASIAN AMERICAN MEDIA
145 Ninth Street, Suite 350 San Francisco CA 94103
Phone: (415) 552-9550 | Fax: (415) 863-7428
distribution@asianamericanmedia.org
http://www.distribution.asianamericanmedia.org

250 titles. Est. 1986. 14 employees. Principals: Stephen Gong, Executive Director

The Center for Asian American Media (CAAM) is a premier distributor of Asian American film and video works to educational institutions and community organizations nationwide. Some of its major buyers are professors, teachers, librarians, and student groups in Asian American and Asian studies, ethnic studies, sociology, history, women's studies, art and film departments, media centers, and museums.

Subjects: History, Multicultural Perspective, Psychology, Sociology, Women's Issues **Markets:** Nontheatrical, Educational **Specialty:** Asian American Film and

Video **Titles:** *Bittersweet Roots: The Chinese in California's Heartland, A Dream in Doubt, Little Manila* **Marketing:** Web Catalog

Acquisition Information: Acquires Doc Feature **Acquisition Method:** Unsolicited Inquiries **Stage:** Unknown **Advice:** We welcome submissions of work that are appropriate for classroom use, screening on campus, other school or library use, and for other public educational screenings. The films in our collection provide insight into the rich and diverse cultures, histories, current events and issues, personal identities, and experiences of Asians and Asian Americans. Guidelines at http://distribution.asianamericanmedia.org/about-us/submissions/

CHIP TAYLOR COMMUNICATIONS
2 East View Drive Derry NH 03038
Phone: (603) 434-9262 (800) 876-CHIP | Fax: (603) 432-2723
chip.taylor@chiptaylor.com
http://www.chiptaylor.com

2500 titles. Est. 1985.

Chip Taylor Communications is the exclusive distributor of over 2,500 programs, with a focus on educational and documentary programming.

Subjects: Arts, Literature & Music, Children's Programming, Criminal Justice, Drama, Family, Health & Medicine, Science, Sports **Markets:** Nontheatrical, Educational, Home Video, Cable TV, Public TV **Specialty:** Educational video and television **Marketing:** Web Catalog, One Sheets, Direct Mail

Acquisition Information: Acquires Narrative Feature, Doc Feature, Short Narrative, Short Doc **Acquisition Method:** Unsolicited Inquiries, Festivals, Markets **Stage:** Fine Cut, Finished **Advice:** We prefer a series of titles. Educational titles should be curriculum-oriented. Special interest films and videos should be on contemporary subject matter. Producers should send a copy of the film and an SASE.

CHOICES, INC.
3740 Overland Ave., Suite F Los Angeles CA 90034
Phone: (310) 839-1511 | Fax: (310) 839-1511
getinfo@choicesvideo.net
http://www.choicesvideo.net

32 titles. Est. 1998. 10 employees. Principals: Larry Rattner

Choices, Inc., is a specialty distributor of quality documentaries, educational programming, and independent feature films targeted to schools, colleges, and libraries. Its award-winning documentaries are produced by filmmakers from around the world on topics tailored for the educational marketplace. Guidebooks and lesson plans that accompany the documentaries are available for download on their website. Choices, Inc. distributes titles to both the United States and Canada.

Subjects: Arts, Literature & Music, Children's Programming, Criminal Justice, Environmental Issues, Family, History, Human Rights, Multicultural Perspective, Nature, Politics & Government, Religion, Science, Theater, Travel, Women's Issues **Markets:** Nontheatrical, Educational, Home Video, Web **Specialty:** Documentary and Educational Media **Titles:** *Daughters of Afghanistan, Checkpoint, Elie Wiesel Goes Home, In the Tall Grass, City of Bees, The Perfect Life, Beyond Beijing* **Marketing:** Web Catalog, Direct Mail

Acquisition Information: 6 titles per year. Acquires Doc Feature, Short Doc **Acquisition Method:** Unsolicited Inquiries, Festivals, Markets **Stage:** Finished **Venues:** L.A. Film Festival, Tribeca Film Festival, IDFA, Silverdocs **Philosophy:** Company goal and philosophy is to expand knowledge through film and assist filmmakers in reaching as wide an audience as possible. **Advice:** We are only acquiring documentaries, educational films/videos and/or series. Short films are fine as long as they are 20 minutes or longer. Films will be considered if they meet the following criteria: North American (U.S. and Canada) Rights are available (including Home Video, Nontheatrical, Digital/Internet Rights) and Films must be 95-100% completed. We do not provide finishing funds or post-production funding. Our submission guidelines: "Know who the audience for your film is, especially for a documentary. That core audience will be the ones most interested and most likely to watch and buy a copy of your film. Having a website is not enough. Be able to answer the question, 'What makes this film unique?' and 'What new perspective/voice does it bring to the issue or subject you are presenting?' Finally, make sure your music is cleared and remember to take as many still photographs as possible while filming as they will be used for marketing and promotion later on." **Acquisition Contact:** John Gruber (310) 839-1500 getinfo@choicesvideo.net

CINEMA GUILD
115 West 30th Street, Suite 800 New York NY 10001
Phone: (800) 723-5522 (212) 685-6242 | Fax: (212) 685-4717
info@cinemaguild.com
http://www.cinemaguild.com

900 titles. Est. 1975. Principals: Philip Hobel, Chairman; Mary-Ann Hobel, Chairman; Gary Crowdus, General Manager

The Cinema Guild is one of America's leading distributors of films and videos. For over 30 years, The Cinema Guild has distributed both documentary and fiction films (narrative features and shorts), offering producers full-service distribution in all markets, including educational, nontheatrical, theatrical, television, cable, Internet, and home video. It distributes award-winning films and videos, representing the work of many of the leading filmmakers in the world, including such prestigious organizations as The American Film Institute, The British Broadcasting Corporation, The National Film Board of Canada, and The United Nations.

Subjects: Aging, Animation, Arts, Literature & Music, Children's Programming, Criminal Justice, Family, LGBT, Gender Issues, Health & Medicine, History, Multicultural Perspective, Politics & Government, Psychology, Regional Profiles & Issues, Religion, Science, Sociology, Women's Issues **Markets:** Theatrical, Nontheatrical, Educational, Home Video, Cable TV, Public TV, Network TV, Satelitte/DBS **Specialty:** Documentaries and fiction features **Titles:** *The Charcoal People, Little Man, From a Ball of Clay* **Marketing:** Web Catalog, One Sheets, Direct Mail

Acquisition Information: Acquires Narrative Feature, Doc Feature, Short Narrative, Short Doc, Animation, Experimental **Acquisition Method:** Unsolicited Inquiries, Festivals, Markets **Stage:** Fine Cut, Finished **Venues:** IFP, film and video festivals **Philosophy:** Good working relationships with their producers is the most important consideration for Cinema Guild. **Advice:** Contact them first with information on your programs before sending DVDs or tapes. **Acquisition Contact:** gcrowdus@cinemaguild.com

CINEQUEST ONLINE
Phone: (408) 995-5033 | Fax: (408) 995-5713
customerservice@cinequest.org
http://www.cinequestonline.org

57 titles.

Cinequest Distribution presents a collection of films that include audience and jury award winners from the top festivals. The company offers direct DVD and Internet downloads, plus Cinequest works with an array of additional DVD retailers and Internet partners to maximize the reach of its titles in the U.S. and worldwide.

Subjects: Comedy, Drama **Markets:** Theatrical, Home Video **Titles:** *Full Moon, On The Road With Judas, A Model Employee* **Marketing:** Web Catalog

Acquisition Information: Acquires Narrative Feature **Acquisition Method:** Festivals, Markets **Stage:** Finished

CINEVOLVE STUDIOS
11950 Riverside Drive Los Angeles CA 91607-3725
Phone: (310) 295-1088 | Fax: (310) 388-5476
info@cinevolvestudios.com
http://cinevolvestudios.com

25 titles. Est. 2007. Principals: Arik Treston, Co-Founder/CEO; Nicole Ballivian, Co-Founder/President

Cinevolve Studios, based in Los Angeles, CA, was formed in 2007 by a collective of independent filmmakers and entertainment industry professionals with a common goal: Fill that niche in the market as the truly filmmaker-friendly distributor and offer compelling, critically-acclaimed, and entertaining feature films and documentaries to the public. Cinevolve Studios was formed as a full-service distribution model, encompassing theatrical, home entertainment, foreign sales, and TV sales. Cinevolve's distribution titles are a blend of independent feature films and documentaries. Cinevolve's distribution involves theatrical releases in theatres across the nation, distribution of DVDs into major retailers and wholesalers in the U.S. and Canada, sales to foreign territories, and sales to domestic television.

Subjects: Action/Adventure, Arts, Literature & Music, Comedy, Drama, LGBT, History, Human Rights, Regional Profiles & Issues **Markets:** Theatrical, Nontheatrical, Home Video **Titles:** *Goodbye Baby, The Line, Scab, The F Word, Homefront* **Territories:** National, International **Marketing:** Web Catalog

Acquisition Information: Acquires Narrative Feature, Doc Feature **Acquisition Method:** Unsolicited Inquiries, Festivals, Markets **Stage:** Production, Finished **Venues:** Sundance, Cannes, Tribeca, Southwest by Southwest **Advance:** Yes. **Philosophy:** To create an environment that enables our films and filmmakers to flourish. **Acquisition Contact:** Mary Keeler, Distribution Manager (310) 295-1088 and Orion Martindale, Distribution Coordinator (310) 295-1088

CONCEPT MEDIA
2493 Du Bridge Avenue Irvine CA 92606
Phone: (800) 233-7078 | Fax: (949) 660-0206
info@conceptmedia.com
http://www.conceptmedia.com/

250 titles. Est. 1969. 25 employees.

Concept Media produces and distributes award-winning educational media for colleges, healthcare institutions, social service agencies, and counseling centers throughout North America, Europe, and the South Pacific. Most programs come in VHS, DVD, and CD formats. Concept Media is best known in the area of professional nursing education and represented in more than 95 percent of the nation's nursing school media libraries. Concept Media has also developed partnerships with leading nursing education institutions including Brigham Young University, Drexel University, and ICN/ Washington State University College of Nursing. Additionally, Concept Media is well-respected in the field of human development and mental health, receiving numerous awards for programs on human development, mental health, substance abuse, counseling, and addiction.

Subjects: Health & Medicine **Markets:** Educational **Specialty:** Educational media on health care **Titles:** *Pain Management, The Vulnerable Young Child, Young Children with Developmental Challenges* **Marketing:** Printed Catalog, Web Catalog

Acquisition Information: Acquires Doc Feature, Short Doc **Acquisition Method:** Unsolicited Inquiries **Stage:** Unknown

CRITERION COLLECTION
AKA: Janus Films
215 Park Ave South New York NY 10003
Phone: (212) 756-8850
suggestions@criterion.com
http://www.criterion.com

1000 titles. Est. 1984.

Since 1984, the Criterion Collection, a continuing series of important classic and contemporary films, has been dedicated to gathering the greatest films from around the world and publishing them in editions that offer the highest technical quality and award-winning, original supplements. The foundation of the collection is the work of such masters of cinema as Renoir, Godard, Kurosawa, Cocteau, Fellini, Bergman, Tarkovsky, Hitchcock, Fuller, Lean, Kubrick, Lang, Sturges, Dreyer, Eisenstein, Ozu, Sirk, Buñuel, Powell, and Pressburger. Each film is presented uncut, in its original aspect ratio, as its maker intended it to be seen. Their supplements enable viewers to appreciate Criterion films in context, through audio commentaries by filmmakers and scholars, restored director's cuts, deleted scenes, documentaries, shooting scripts, early shorts, and storyboards. To date, more than 150 filmmakers have made their library of Director Approved DVDs, Blu-ray discs, and laserdiscs the most significant archive of contemporary filmmaking available to the home viewer.

Subjects: Arts, Literature & Music, Comedy, Drama, Experimental/Avant Garde **Markets:** Educational, Home Video **Specialty:** Classic films and restorations **Titles:** *Overload, The Shop on Main Street, Equinox Flower* **Marketing:** Web Catalog

Acquisition Information: Acquires Narrative Feature **Acquisition Method:** Unknown **Stage:** Unknown

CURB ENTERTAINMENT INTERNATIONAL CORP.
3907 West Alameda Avenue Burbank CA 91505
Phone: (818) 843-8580 | Fax: (818) 566-1719
cpeterson@curb.com
http://www.curbentertainment.com

100 titles. Est. 1984. Principals: Mike Curb, Chairman; Carole Curb Nemoy,
President

Curb Entertainment formed in 1984 to concentrate on film production and
distribution.

Subjects: Action/Adventure, Comedy, Drama **Markets:** Theatrical, Foreign
Specialty: Feature film **Titles:** *Oxygen, Kill Me Later*

Acquisition Information: Acquires Narrative Feature **Acquisition Method:**
Unsolicited Inquiries, Festivals, Markets **Stage:** Finished **Venues:** American Film
Market (AFM), CANNES Film Festival, MIPCOM, MIP-TV, MIP-ASIA,
NATPE, AFM Regional Markets, and MIFED **Advice: For** finished features, please
send screening DVDs or screening invitations to the attention of Christy Peterson,
Head of Acquisitions (cpeterson@curb.com).

DIRECT CINEMA LIMITED, INC.
P.O. Box 10003 Santa Monica CA 90410-1003
Phone: (310) 636-8200 | Fax: (310) 636-8228
info@directcinemalimited.com
http://www.directcinema.com

300 titles. Est. 1974. 8 employees. Principals: Mitchell Block, President

Direct Cinema Limited was created in 1974 to serve independent filmmakers. Its
films have won 54 Academy Award nominations and 15 Oscars – more than any
other collection of short films and documentaries in the world. In addition, Direct
Cinema Limited has won hundreds of Emmy, Cable Ace Awards, Peabody's,
Dupont's, and other awards.

Subjects: Action/Adventure, Aging, Animation, Archival, Arts, Literature & Music,
Biography, Children's Programming, Comedy, Criminal Justice, Disability,
Drama, Environmental Issues, Family, LGBT, Gender Issues, Health & Medicine,
History, Human Rights, Immigration, Labor Issues, Language/Linguistics,
Multicultural Perspective, Nature, Politics & Government, Psychology, Regional
Profiles & Issues, Religion, Science, Sociology, Sports, Theater, Travel **Markets:**
Theatrical, Nontheatrical, Educational, Home Video, Cable TV, Public TV, Web,
Airline, Foreign **Specialty:** Educational media **Titles:** *Einstein on the Beach, The*

Changing Image of the Opera, The Life and Times of Rosie the Riveter, Marx Brothers in a Nutshell, Promise of Play **Marketing:** Web Catalog

Acquisition Information: Acquires Narrative Feature, Doc Feature, Short Narrative, Short Doc, Animation **Acquisition Method:** Unsolicited Inquiries, Festivals, Markets **Stage:** Rough Cut, Fine Cut, Finished **Venues:** The staff does not locate work at festivals. They prefer to be involved in the idea stage or whenever a filmmaker contacts them. **Philosophy:** We are interested in works that have both home and educational markets, that have a long shelf life, and represent the best there is in their subject matter. Excellence is the priority, and profit secondary. **Advice:** We do not accept unsolicited tapes or DVDs. If you have a finished film idea or film in production that you think would be of interest to us (you can see the kind of films we distribute by browsing our website), you can send us a short description of your film via e-mail. Send it to acquisitions@directcinema.com. If the description interests us, we will contact you to find out how we could see your film. But please bear in mind that we distribute only a handful of new films each year. They can be animation, live action fiction, and documentaries.

DISCOVER FILMS VIDEO
Parent Company: Discover Films, Inc.
616 E. Rutland Street Covington Louisiana 70433
Phone: 985-892-7571 | Fax: 985-893-7556
aml@discover-films.com
http://discover-films.com

52 titles. Est. 1989. 2 employees. Principals: Angelique LaCour

An award-winning, health education video publishing company since 1989, Discover Films Videos targets the school market, middle and high school teachers, college student affairs departments, counselors, alcohol and drug prevention specialists, state departments of health, law enforcement (school resource officers, DARE officers, DEA and FBI prevention programs), district attorneys, and drug courts.

Subjects: Health & Medicine **Markets:** Educational, Public TV **Titles:** *Tobacco Horror Picture Show, This Is Your Brain On Alcohol, Keep Off The Grass, Rape Under The Influence* **Marketing:** Web Catalog

Acquisition Information: Acquires Narrative Feature, Short Narrative **Acquisition Method:** Unsolicited Inquiries **Stage:** Finished **Advance:** No. **Philosophy:** Our films use a peer education, "kids teaching kids," model and incorporate a social norms approach to help young people understand how dangerous substances and certain situations can tragically change their lives forever. **Advice:** Know your market even better than you know your audience. If you would like to consider

Discover Films Video as a distributor of your film, please visit our web site first to determine if your film is a fit for our collection. **Acquisition Contact:** Angelique LaCour, President/Producer (985) 635-9436 aml@discover-films.com

DISCOVERY EDUCATION

Parent Company: Discovery Communications, LLC
1560 Sherman Avenue Suite 100 Evanston IL 60201
Phone: (800) 323-9084 | Fax: (847) 328-6706
http://www.discoveryeducation.com

5000 titles.

The leader in digital video-based learning, Discovery Education produces and distributes high-quality digital resources in easy-to-use formats in all core-curricular subject areas. Discovery Education is committed to creating scientifically proven, standards-based digital resources for teachers, students, and parents that make a positive impact on student learning. Through solutions like Discovery Education streaming, Discovery Education Science, Discovery Education Health and more, Discovery Education helps over one million educators and 35 million students harness the power of broadband and media to connect to a world of learning.

Subjects: Arts, Literature & Music, Children's Programming, Environmental Issues, Health & Medicine, History, Language/Linguistics, Nature, Politics & Government, Science, Sociology **Markets:** Nontheatrical, Educational, Home Video, Cable TV, Web

Acquisition Information: Acquires Doc Feature, Short Doc **Acquisition Method:** Unknown **Stage:** Unknown **Philosophy:** Discovery Education provides engaging digital resources to schools and homes with the goal of making educators more effective, increasing student achievement, and connecting classrooms and families to a world of learning.

DOCUMENTARY EDUCATIONAL RESOURCES, INC.

101 Morse Street Watertown MA 02472
Phone: (617) 926-0491 (800) 569-6621 | Fax: (617) 926-9519
docued@der.ord
http://www.der.org

900 titles. Est. 1968. 8 employees. Principals: Cynthia Close, Executive Director; Peter Dow, Board Chairman

Since 1968, Documentary Educational Resources has been distributing some of the most unique documentary films made by both national and international filmmakers to a worldwide broadcast, educational, and consumer marketplace. In addition to over 900 titles, it also has an historically important stock footage archive and acts as a fiscal sponsor for over 40 projects currently in production.

Subjects: Aging, Animation, Archival, Arts, Literature & Music, Biography, Disability, Environmental Issues, Experimental/Avant Garde, Family, LGBT, Gender Issues, History, Human Rights, Immigration, Labor Issues, Multicultural Perspective, Nature, Politics & Government, Psychology, Religion, Science, Sociology, Women's Issues **Markets:** Nontheatrical, Educational, Home Video, Cable TV, Public TV, Network TV, Satelitte/DBS, Web, Airline, Foreign **Specialty:** Documentary **Titles:** *Tehran Has No More Pomegranates, The Ballad of Esequiel Hernandez, Standing Silent Nation, Balkan Rhapsodies: 78 Measures of War, Dead Birds, The Hunters* **Territories:** Worldwide **Marketing:** Printed Catalog, Web Catalog, One Sheets, Direct Mail

Acquisition Information: 30 titles per year. Acquires Doc Feature, Short Doc, Animation, Experimental **Acquisition Method:** Unsolicited Inquiries, Festivals, Markets, Other **Stage:** Fine Cut, Finished, Other **Venues:** Hot Docs, Silver Docs, Tribecca **Advance:** Sometimes. **Philosophy:** DER's mission is to cultivate community engagement with the peoples and cultures of the world in which we live through media that is both entertaining and educational. **Advice:** Know who you are talking to! Do your research before you approach a distributor. See what films are in their catalog and try to decide if yours would be a good fit before calling. **Acquisition Contact:** Cynthia Close, Executive Director (617) 926-0491 cclose@der.org and Erin Carney (617) 926-0491 erin@der.org

DREAM ENTERTAINMENT
8489 West 3rd Street, Suite 1038 Los Angeles CA 90048
Phone: (323) 655-5501 | Fax: (323) 655-5603
dream@dreamentertainment.net
http://www.dreamentertainment.net

50 titles. Est. 1993. Principals: Yitzhak Ginsberg, President; Moshe Peterburg, Partner

Los Angeles-based Dream Entertainment has evolved over the last 13 years as one of the industry's fastest growing independent film companies. Dream has developed, funded, and produced 13 feature films. Dream currently sells dozens of titles from its library in addition to hundreds of other titles from various sources. Under the helm of Yitzhak Ginsberg, the company is developing a diverse slate of new projects geared toward theatrical, home entertainment, and television markets worldwide. In addition, Dream's extensive film library showcases a variety of genres featuring well-known talent. Dream participates in the major film and television markets and enjoys long-standing relationships with a loyal network of clients in more than 30 territories.

Dream Entertainment is constantly looking for quality feature films to produce and represent in the foreign and domestic markets. In addition to producing its own in-house projects, Dream Entertainment acts as a sales agent for acquired films and markets and presents these films to distributors worldwide.

Subjects: Biography, Comedy, Drama, History, Sports **Markets:** Theatrical, Foreign **Specialty:** Feature film **Titles:** *Inherit the Wind* **Marketing:** Web Catalog, One Sheets, Direct Mail

Acquisition Information: Acquires Narrative Feature, Doc Feature **Acquisition Method:** Unsolicited Inquiries, Festivals, Markets **Stage:** Treatment, Proposal, Script, Production, Rough Cut, Fine Cut, Finished **Advice:** If you have a finished film or a rough cut of a film in post-production, please send a DVD screener and/or screening invitation to the attention of Taly Ginsberg, or e-mail general questions to taly@dreamentertainment.net. Be sure to include genre, synopsis, cast, budget, and financing needs with any submission. Films shorter than 70 minutes in length will not be accepted. **Acquisition Contact:** Taly Ginsberg taly@dreamentertainment.net

EBS WORLD ENTERTAINMENT
3000 W. Olympic Boulevard Santa Monica CA 90404
Phone: (310) 449-4065 | Fax: (310) 229-4061
info@ebsentertainment.com
http://www.ebsla.com

20 titles.

EBS World Entertainment focuses on production, acquisition, marketing, packaging, and home distribution. Its division EBS Home Entertainment releases over 40 new video and DVD titles a year through video retailers and mass merchants as well as an online sell-through catalog. Its offices are located in Santa Monica, California and Atlanta, Georgia.

Subjects: Action/Adventure, Comedy, Drama **Markets:** Home Video, Cable TV, Satelitte/DBS **Titles:** *You Are Alone, The Celestine Prophecy, Broken Glass* **Marketing:** Printed Catalog, Web Catalog

Acquisition Information: 40 titles per year. Acquires Narrative Feature **Acquisition Method:** Unsolicited Inquiries, Festivals, Markets **Stage:** Finished **Venues:** American Film Market, Berlin Film Fetival, Cannes Film Festival, National Association of Television Program Executives **Advice:** We are dedicated to realizing the visions of independent filmmakers and the enormous potential of an increasingly sophisticated film public. Building a slate of titles from an aggressive acquisitions program and selected in-house productions, EBS Home Entertainment plans to release up to 40 new films a year. To submit:

www.ebsla.com/video_sales_submit.html   **Acquisition Contact:**
acquisitions@ebsentertainment.com

ECHO BRIDGE ENTERTAINMENT
75 Second Avenue
Suite 500 Needham MA 02494
Phone: (781) 444-6767 | Fax: (781) 444-6472
info@ebellc.com
http://www.echobridgeentertainment.com/

5000 titles. Principals: Michael Rosenblatt, President & CEO

Echo Bridge Entertainment is a premiere independent content company that
acquires and distributes motion pictures, television series, specials, and movies of
the week, home entertainment, PC games, and digital and video-on-demand
content throughout the world. With its recent acquisition of Alliance Atlantis
International Distribution Ltd. and distribution partnership with Comcast, Echo
Bridge has added over 7,500 hours of programming to its existing library – creating
a combined portfolio of more than 5,000 titles. Echo Bridge's feature film library
includes titles with stars such as Val Kilmer, Robin Williams, Matthew Perry,
Anthony LaPaglia, Sharon Stone, Will Smith, James Belushi, Robert DeNiro, Nick
Nolte, Ryan Reynolds, and John Goodman.

Subjects: Action/Adventure, Animation, Arts, Literature & Music, Biography,
Children's Programming, Comedy, Drama, Environmental Issues, History, Nature,
Politics & Government, Sports, Travel **Markets:** Theatrical, Home Video, Cable
TV, Network TV, TV Syndication, Satelitte/DBS **Titles:** *Baby Boost, Full Force
Nature, The Sender* **Marketing:** Web Catalog

Acquisition Information: Acquires Narrative Feature, Doc Feature **Acquisition
Method:** Unsolicited Inquiries, Festivals **Stage:** Finished **Advice:** We happily accept
submissions of feature length English language (not subtitled) films that are
available for either North American and/or international distribution. Please be sure
to include a letter detailing what territories are available and your pertinent contact
information. We regret that we cannot return any screeners after we receive them
unless there is a self addressed, stamped envelope included with your package.
Because of the volume of films we receive, please allow 2-3 weeks for us to get back
to you. **Acquisition Contact:** Bobby Rock, Acquisitions Consultant (323) 658-
7903 brock@echobridgehe.com and Lenny Shapiro, Acquistions Consultant (323)
658-7917 lshapiro@ebellc.com

EDUCATIONAL PRODUCTIONS
7101 Wisconsin Ave., Suite 700 Bethesda MD 20814
Phone: (800) 950-4949 | Fax: (301) 634-0826
custserv@edpro.com
http://www.edpro.com

50 titles. Est. 1982. Principals: Linda Freedman, President; Rae Latham, VP

Educational Productions specializes in award-winning training programs that quickly engage learners and gives them tools they can immediately use whether they're working in child care, pre-K, Head Start, or K-2 classrooms. Educational Productions is widely used in colleges and university early childhood and early childhood special education programs. The company has an archive of training assets, including video programs, a video clip library, CD-ROM-based training, and video-based distance learning courses. Educational Productions also provides digital video from this archive to developers of onsite and distance training.

Subjects: Children's Programming, Family, Language/Linguistics **Markets:** Educational **Specialty:** Educational video on early childhood **Titles:** *First Steps: Supporting Early Language Development, Good Talking with You: Language Acquisition Through Conversation, Bigger than Books* series, *Super Groups* series, *Play Power* series **Marketing:** Web Catalog

Acquisition Information: Acquires Short Doc **Acquisition Method:** Unknown **Stage:** Unknown **Acquisition Contact:** Linda Freedman, President, linda@edpro.com and Rae Latham, Vice President, rae@edpro.com

EDUCATIONAL VIDEO CENTER
120 West 30th Street, 7th Floor New York NY 10001
Phone: (212) 465-9366 | Fax: (212) 465-9369
info@evc.org
http://www.evc.org

63 titles. Est. 1984. 10 employees. Principals: Steven Goodman, Executive Director

The Educational Video Center (EVC) is a nonprofit youth media organization dedicated to teaching documentary video as a means to develop the artistic, critical literacy, and career skills of young people, while nurturing their idealism and commitment to social change. Founded in 1984, EVC has evolved from a single video workshop for teenagers from Manhattan's Lower East Side to become an internationally acclaimed leader in youth media education. EVC's teaching methodology brings together the powerful traditions of student-centered progressive education and independent community documentary. In 2007, building on its model of study groups and teacher institutes, EVC launched the national Youth Media Learning Network, in partnership with the Education

Development Center, to offer peer professional development opportunities to youth media practitioners in select cities across the country.

Subjects: Arts, Literature & Music, Criminal Justice, Environmental Issues, Family, LGBT, Gender Issues, Health & Medicine, Immigration, Multicultural Perspective, Politics & Government, Psychology, Regional Profiles & Issues, Religion, Sociology, Women's Issues **Markets:** Educational, Public TV, Web **Specialty:** Documentary video produced by youths **Titles:** *Through the Eyes of Immigrants; Tough on Crime, Tough on Our Kind* **Marketing:** Printed Catalog, Web Catalog

Acquisition Information: Acquires Doc Feature, Short Doc **Acquisition Method:** Solicited Only **Stage:** Unknown **Acquisition Contact:** Steve Goodman, Executive Director (212) 465-9366 ext. 10 sgoodman@evc.org and Sheila Aminmadani, Marketing & Community Engagement Manager (212) 465-9366 ext. 15 saminmadani@evc.org

EDUCATIONAL VIDEO GROUP
291 Southwind Way Greenwood IN 46142
Phone: (317) 889.8253 | Fax: (317) 888-5857
service@evgonline.com
http://www.evgonline.com

90 titles. Est. 1985. Principals: Roger Cook, President

Educational Video Group (EVG) distributes curriculum-based video for classes in speech and social and political studies. EVG's Great Speeches Textbook & Video Series preserves some of the most profound oratory of the last 70 years. Over 90 titles are offered as DVD, VHS, CD-ROM, and textbooks.

Subjects: Biography, Gender Issues, History, Language/Linguistics, Women's Issues **Markets:** Nontheatrical, Educational, Web, Foreign **Specialty:** Educational media **Titles:** *Great Speeches* series **Marketing:** Printed Catalog, Web Catalog

Acquisition Information: Acquires Doc Feature, Short Doc **Acquisition Method:** Unknown **Stage:** Unknown

ELECTRONIC ARTS INTERMIX
535 West 22nd Street, 5th Floor New York NY 10011
Phone: (212) 337-0680 | Fax: (212) 337-0679
info@eai.org
http://www.eai.org

3000 titles. Est. 1971. Principals: Lori Zippay, Executive Director; Ann Adachi, Distribution Coordinator; Rebecca Cleman, Distribution Director

Electronic Arts Intermix (EAI) is a leading resource for the international distribution of new and historical video and interactive media by artists. Founded in 1971 as a nonprofit media arts center, EAI also offers a video preservation program and a screening room and study center. Its online catalog is a comprehensive resource on the 175 artists and 3,000 works in the EAI collection. The searchable database includes biographies of artists, tape descriptions, clips and excerpts, resource materials, and online ordering.

Subjects: Arts, Literature & Music **Markets:** Nontheatrical, Home Video, Other **Specialty:** Video by artists **Marketing:** Web Catalog

Acquisition Information: Acquires Experimental **Acquisition Method:** Unsolicited Inquiries **Stage:** Finished **Advice:** EAI distributes bodies of artists' works rather than individual titles, and we are able to include only a few new artists each year in the EAI collection. EAI's collection focuses on experimental media art; we do not distribute conventional documentaries or narrative features.

EMERGING PICTURES
245 West 55th Street, 4th Floor New York NY 10019
Phone: (212) 245-6767 | Fax: (212) 202-4984
inquiries@emergingpictures.com
http://www.emergingpictures.com

20 titles.

Emerging Pictures exhibits, represents, and distributes a wide range of content for current and future delivery systems. It is highly selective in choosing the films it takes on for representation, and is only interested in films that have not yet been screened privately for distributors or publicly in any venue.

Subjects: Arts, Literature & Music, Comedy, Drama, LGBT, Multicultural Perspective **Markets:** Theatrical, Nontheatrical, Home Video, Cable TV, Web **Titles:** *Don't Stop Believin': Everyman's Journey, Amu* **Marketing:** Printed Catalog, Web Catalog

Acquisition Information: Acquires Narrative Feature **Acquisition Method:** Unsolicited Inquiries, Festivals, Markets **Stage:** Rough Cut, Fine Cut, Finished **Advice:** We will screen early rough-cuts of films to determine our interest.

ENTERTAINMENT 7

AKA: Karma Enterprises
info@karmaenterprises.com

100 titles.

Entertainment 7 is a fully operational distribution company with its domestic and international division. The Entertainment 7 domestic theatrical and home video division works in conjunction with various studios for its releases in North America including Canada. Its international division has distributed and marketed films in over 100 territories outside of North America either directly or in conjunction with affiliated companies or via distribution co-ventures.

Subjects: Action/Adventure, Arts, Literature & Music, Comedy, Drama, Gender Issues, Human Rights, Multicultural Perspective, Sports **Markets:** Theatrical, Home Video, Cable TV **Titles:** *Waco, For Love Alone, Baby on Board* **Marketing:** Web Catalog

Acquisition Information: Acquires Narrative Feature, Doc Feature **Acquisition Method:** Unknown **Stage:** Unknown **Acquisitions Contact:** Distribution ent7@karmaenterprises.com

ENVIRONMENTAL MEDIA CORPORATION

1008 Paris Avenue Port Royal SC 29935
Phone: (843) 986-9034 (800) 368-3382 | Fax: (843) 986-9093
contact@envmedia.com
http://www.envmedia.com

80 titles. Est. 1989. 2 employees. Principals: Bill Pendergraft

Environmental Media Corporation designs, produces and distributes media to support environmental education for the classroom and community.

Subjects: Environmental Issues, Nature **Markets:** Nontheatrical, Educational, Other **Specialty:** Educational media on the environment **Marketing:** Web Catalog

Acquisition Information: Acquires Short Doc **Acquisition Method:** Unknown **Stage:** Unknown **Philosophy:** To design, produce and distribute media to support education and conservation. **Acquisition Contact:** Bill Pendergraft bpendergraft@envmedia.com

FABRICATION FILMS
8701 W. Olympic Blvd. Los Angeles CA 90035
Phone: (310) 289-1232 | Fax: (310) 289-1292
http://www.fabricationfilms.com

50 titles. Est. 2003. Principals: Kjehl Rasmussen, CEO; Jodie Skalla, VP of
Acquisitions

Based in Los Angeles, Fabrication Films is dedicated to the production and
worldwide distribution of cutting edge, commercial, and independent feature films.
Established in 2003, Fabrication Films has a library of over 50 titles and is involved
in both domestic and international distribution.

Subjects: Action/Adventure, Arts, Literature & Music, Children's Programming,
Comedy, Drama **Markets:** Theatrical, Home Video, Cable TV **Titles:**
*Conversations with Other Women, Last Dispatch, La Tropical, Zombie Honeymoon,
Her Name is Carla, The Californians, Once Upon a Wedding* **Marketing:** Web
Catalog

Acquisition Information: Acquires Narrative Feature, Doc Feature **Acquisition
Method:** Festivals, Markets **Stage:** Finished **Venues:** American Film Market,
MIPCOM, MIPTV, Sundance Film Festival, Berlin Film Festival, Cannes Film
Market/Festival and the Toronto Film Festival **Acquisition Contact:** Jodie Skalla,
Vice President of – Acquisitions, Jodie@fabricationfilms.com

FACETS MUTLIMEDIA, INC.
1517 West Fullerton Avenue Chicago IL 60614
Phone: (773) 281-9075 | Fax: (773) 929-5437
http://www.facets.org

500 titles. Est. 1975. 20 employees.

Facets Multimedia, Inc., a nonprofit 501(c)3 organization and a leading national
media arts organization, preserves, presents, and distributes independent, world,
and classic film to educate adults and children in the art and legacy of film.

Subjects: Action/Adventure, Aging, Animation, Arts, Literature & Music,
Biography, Children's Programming, Comedy, Criminal Justice, Drama,
Environmental Issues, Experimental/Avant Garde, Family, LGBT, Gender Issues,
History, Human Rights, Immigration, Labor Issues, Multicultural Perspective,
Politics & Government, Religion **Markets:** Nontheatrical, Educational, Home
Video **Specialty:** Art house film **Marketing:** Printed Catalog, Web Catalog, One
Sheets

Acquisition Information: Acquires Narrative Feature, Doc Feature **Acquisition Method:** Unsolicited Inquiries, Festivals, Markets **Stage:** Unknown **Acquisition Contact:** Facets Exclusives Video Label dan@facets.org

FANLIGHT PRODUCTIONS
4196 Washington Street, Suite 2 Boston MA 02131
Phone: (617) 469-4999 (800) 937-4113 | Fax: (617) 469-3379
fanlight@fanlight.com
http://www.fanlight.com

300 titles. Est. 1981. 4 employees. Principals: Ben Achtenberg, Owner and President

Fanlight Productions is a leading distributor of film and video works on the social issues of our time, with a special focus on healthcare, mental health, professional ethics, aging and gerontology, disabilities, the workplace, and gender and family issues. Its collection includes Academy Award winners and nominees, as well as films that have been honored by the Sundance Film Festival, the DuPont-Columbia Journalism Awards, and major media festivals throughout the world. Most of Fanlight's releases represent the personal vision of independent filmmakers; others have been created by broadcast producers and by organizations in their fields of interest.

Subjects: Aging, Criminal Justice, Disability, Family, LGBT, Gender Issues, Health & Medicine, Human Rights, Labor Issues, Multicultural Perspective, Psychology, Religion, Science, Sociology, Sports, Women's Issues **Markets:** Nontheatrical, Educational **Specialty:** healthcare, mental health, professional ethics, aging and gerontology, disabilities, the workplace and gender and family issues. **Titles:** *When Billy Broke His Head, The Personals, Breathing Lessons, Code Gray: Ethical Dilemmas in Nursing* **Territories:** Worldwide **Marketing:** Printed Catalog, Web Catalog, One Sheets, Direct Mail, Other

Acquisition Information: 25 titles per year. Acquires Doc Feature, Short Doc **Acquisition Method:** Unsolicited Inquiries, Festivals, Markets, Other **Stage:** Fine Cut, Finished **Venues:** Festivals, conferences, word-of-mouth, film schools, professional journals, and other publications **Advance:** Sometimes. **Philosophy:** Founded by independent filmmakers more than 27 years ago, our goal has been to create for our clients a select collection of educational programs that are independent in their vision, emotionally and intellectually engaging in their approach, and accurate and up-to-date in their content. Our catalog strives to present contemporary cross-cultural perspectives on the issues of concern to our many audiences, and we are engaged in an ongoing effort to maximize the accessibility of our collection. **Advice:** We are looking for new films and videos that deal effectively with the issues our customers care about. While we're happy to look at projects in a wide range of styles and formats, the programs we can market most effectively include: well researched, well produced, and well edited programs; emotionally and intellectually engaging programs; reality-based programs; shorts. **Acquisition Contact:** Anthony Sweeney (617) 469-4999 ext. 12 anthony@fanlight.com and Ben Achtenberg (617) 469-4999 ext. 10 ben@fanlight.com

FILM IDEAS, INC.
308 North Wolf Road Wheeling IL 60090
Phone: (847) 419-0255 (800) 475-3456 | Fax: (847) 419-8933
info@filmideas.com
http://filmideas.com

1000 titles. Est. 1979.

Film Ideas, Inc., distributes and produces award-winning videos, DVDs, and chaptered MPEGs for a variety of public and private markets. As a content provider, Film Ideas, Inc., offers add-on digital rights for approved titles as well as MPEG video formats for digital streaming and downloading.

Subjects: Arts, Literature & Music, Criminal Justice, Health & Medicine, History, Language/Linguistics, Psychology, Science, Sociology **Markets:** Nontheatrical, Educational, Home Video, Web, Other **Specialty:** Educational media **Titles:** *North American GeoQuest, Rivers of North America, Symbols of America* **Marketing:** Web Catalog

Acquisition Information: Acquires Narrative Feature, Doc Feature, Short Narrative, Short Doc **Acquisition Method:** Unknown **Stage:** Unknown **Philosophy:** Film Ideas, Inc., looks for unique approaches and hard-to-find topics.

FILM MOVEMENT
109 West 27th Street, Suite 9B New York NY 10001
Phone: (212) 941-7744
info@filmmovement.com
http://www.filmmovement.com

100 titles.

Based in New York City, Film Movement is a full-service North American distributor of award-winning independent and foreign film. Film Movement focuses on both traditional film distribution methods like theatrical release, DVD sales, DVD rentals, and television in addition to unique film distribution techniques like its Film Festival On Demand channel and film-of-the-month-club.

Subjects: Action/Adventure, Animation, Arts, Literature & Music, Biography, Children's Programming, Comedy, Criminal Justice, Drama, Environmental

Issues, Family, LGBT, Gender Issues, Human Rights, Immigration, Labor Issues, Multicultural Perspective, Nature, Politics & Government, Regional Profiles & Issues, Women's Issues **Markets:** Theatrical, Educational, Home Video, Cable TV, Public TV, Network TV, Satelitte/DBS, Web, Airline **Titles:** *The Country Teacher, The Window, Munyurangabo, Lake Tahoe, In Love We Trust* **Marketing:** Web Catalog

Acquisition Information: Acquires Narrative Feature, Doc Feature, Short Narrative, Short Doc, Animation **Acquisition Method:** Festivals, Markets **Stage:** Finished **Philosophy:** Film Movement's mission is to put its films in front of the largest possible audience. To meet this challenge, Film Movement aggressively pursues all channels of film distribution including theatrical, institutional, television, retail, rental, in flight, on demand, and our first-of-its-kind DVD of the month club subscription service. **Advice:** Films are chosen with the aid of an Advisory Board that includes directors of some of the worlds leading film institutions, including Richard Pena from the Film Society of Lincoln Center, Christian Gaines of American Film Institute, Nate Kohn of Roger Eberts Overlooked Film Festival, Bethann Hardison of New York African Film Festival and New York Women's Film Festival, Bo Smith of the Museum of Fine Arts, Boston, Patricia Finneran of Silverdocs Documentary Film Festival, Nicole Guillemet of Miami International Film Festival, and Matt Dentler of South by Southwest Film Festival.

FILM-MAKERS' COOPERATIVE

c/o The Clocktower Gallery, 108 Leonard Street, 13th Floor New York NY 10013
Phone: (212) 267-5665 | Fax: (212) 267-5666
film6000@aol.com
http://www.film-makerscoop.com

4000 titles. Est. 1961. Principals: Jonas Mekas, Founder

The Film-Makers' Cooperative is an archive and distributor of independent and avant-garde films. The Coop was originally founded partly as a protest of the distribution system where curators and distributors would exclude certain innovative work, with little regard for the originality of these films. Many of these films are now classics of avant-garde cinema.

Subjects: Arts, Literature & Music, Drama, Experimental/Avant Garde, LGBT, Gender Issues **Markets:** Home Video, Other **Specialty:** Avant-garde film **Marketing:** Web Catalog

Acquisition Information: Acquires Narrative Feature, Doc Feature, Short Narrative, Short Doc, Experimental **Acquisition Method:** Unsolicited Inquiries **Stage:** Unknown **Advice:** The membership fee is $40 annually. You must also deposit your work at the Coop for it to be listed for distribution. The Coop is completely non-exclusive (you still own your work, you can still show your work, you can make use of other distribution as long as it is also non-exclusive or doesn't mind that your work is also in the Coop). At all times your film or video belongs to you. To facilitate rentals, your print or tape remains at the Coop. You still own this print or tape. You set the rental price (the minimum for any rental being $20). You receive 60% of your rentals, while 40% goes to the Coop for overhead.

Acquisition Contact: MM Serra, Executive Director of the Film-Makers' Cooperative (212) 267-5665 film6000@aol.com

FILMAKERS LIBRARY
124 East 40th Street New York NY 10016
Phone: (212) 808-4980 | Fax: (212) 808-4983
info@filmakers.com
http://www.filmakers.com

500 titles. Principals: Sue Oscar and Linda Gottesman, Founders; John Tebbetts, Office Manager

Filmakers Library has been distributing documentary films for almost 40 years, starting with a landmark, cinema vérité documentary called *Birth and Death*. The collections grew from life cycle films to a constantly widening perspective of issue-oriented documentaries. Gathering films from American independents as well as filmmakers from all over the world, Filmakers Library aims to present a collection of insightful documentaries.

Subjects: Action/Adventure, Aging, Animation, Arts, Literature & Music, Biography, Children's Programming, Comedy, Criminal Justice, Disability, Drama, Environmental Issues, Experimental/Avant Garde, Family, LGBT, Gender Issues, Health & Medicine, History, Human Rights, Immigration, Labor Issues, Language/Linguistics, Multicultural Perspective, Nature, Politics & Government, Psychology, Regional Profiles & Issues, Religion, Science, Sociology, Theater, Travel, Women's Issues **Markets:** Theatrical, Educational, Home Video **Specialty:** Educational film and video **Titles:** *Sound and Fury, My American Girls, Laughing Club of India* **Marketing:** Printed Catalog, Web Catalog

Acquisition Information: Acquires Doc Feature, Short Doc **Acquisition Method:** Unsolicited Inquiries **Stage:** Unknown **Venues:** MIP, Hot Docs, IFP **Philosophy:** To work cooperatively with filmmakers to reach the widest audience. **Advice:** Please send us the description, including subject matter, length, showings (if anywhere), date of completion. We will contact you for a screener if there is a reasonable chance it will fit into our collection. Hopefully, we will respond within two weeks of receipt of screener. **Acquisition Contact:** (212) 808-4980 info@filmakers.com

FILMS FOR THE HUMANITIES & SCIENCES

Parent Company: Films Media Group
200 American Metro Blvd., Suite 124 Hamilton NJ 08619
Phone: (800) 257-5126 (609) 671-1000 | Fax: (609) 671-0266
custserv@films.com
http://www.films.com

9000 titles. Est. 1971.

Films for the Humanities & Sciences (FFH&S) is a leader in North America in
distributing quality video and multimedia programs to colleges, schools, and
libraries. The FFH&S collection represents programs from some of the most
prestigious producers from around the world, including BBC, ARTE, ZDF,
RTVE, ABC News, the Discovery Channel, and others. Its sister companies
include Cambridge Educational, Meridian Education Corporation, and Shopware
Brands – all of which produce and distribute curricular video and multimedia
materials to schools, grades K-12.

Subjects: Arts, Literature & Music, Biography, Criminal Justice, Environmental
Issues, Health & Medicine, History, Nature, Psychology, Science, Sociology
Markets: Educational, Home Video **Specialty:** Educational media **Marketing:** Web
Catalog

Acquisition Information: Acquires Narrative Feature, Doc Feature, Short
Narrative, Short Doc **Acquisition Method:** Unknown **Stage:** Unknown **Venues:**
MIP, MIPCOM, NATPE **Philosophy:** To acquire and distribute programs from
the world.

FILMS MEDIA GROUP

AKA: Films for the Humanities & Sciences, Cambridge Educational, Meridian
Education, Shopware
P.O. Box 2053 Princeton NJ 08543
Phone: (800) 257-5126 | Fax: (609) 671-0266
custserv@films.com
http://ffh.films.com

10000 titles.

Films Media Group is a leading source of titles for academic and vocational use.
Films Media Group serves the education community through its four brands: Films
for the Humanities and Sciences, Cambridge Educational, Meridian Education,
and Shopware.

Subjects: Arts, Literature & Music, Criminal Justice, Environmental Issues, Family, Health & Medicine, History, Language/Linguistics, Nature, Sociology **Markets:** Educational, Home Video

Acquisition Information: Acquires Doc Feature, Short Doc **Acquisition Method:** Festivals, Markets **Stage:** Unknown

FILMS TRANSIT INTERNATIONAL, INC.
166 Second Avenue New York NY 10003
Phone: (212) 614 2808 | Fax: (212) 614 2808
http://www.filmstransit.com

125 titles. Est. 1982.

Founded 25 years ago by Jan Rofekamp, Films Transit International is a respected international sales agency of quality documentaries. With offices in Montreal and in New York, it specializes in the worldwide release and marketing of high profile, theatrical, and TV documentaries in two specific genres: Arts, Sports & Culture (which includes documentaries about arts, culture, biography, cinema, music, and sports) and Society, History & Politics (which includes documentaries about current affairs, society, politics, human interest, and history.

Subjects: Arts, Literature & Music, Criminal Justice, Gender Issues, History, Human Rights, Multicultural Perspective, Politics & Government, Sociology, Sports, Women's Issues **Markets:** Educational, Home Video **Specialty:** Documentaries **Titles:** *51 Birch Street, Cowboy Del Amor, Stealing Klimt, From Dust, My Country, My Country, The Ungrateful Dead, Belfast Girls* **Marketing:** Web Catalog

Acquisition Information: 20 titles per year. Acquires Doc Feature **Acquisition Method:** Unsolicited Inquiries, Festivals, Markets **Stage:** Finished **Venues:** Sundance, Berlin, New Directors/New Films, SXSW, Hot Docs, Full Frame, Tribeca Film Festival, Toronto, IDFA, among other **Advice:** Films Transit is generally looking for two types of documentaries: First there are the "epic" feature docs, generally with more cultural rather than social-political subjects. These are films on large international subject matters that may have a strong author signature. They can be historical or contemporary and must have a very high quality level of filmmaking and tell a story that everyone in the world can relate to. Secondly, we are looking for what will be referred to as "urgent" docs. These are generally TV-hour length films on very strong, edgy, provocative, contemporary subject matters that we feel people must see because of their political or social relevance. Some of the urgent films we handle have strong current affairs value. If your documentary matches the guidelines, e-mail a synopsis first, including if possible some background materials and filmmaker information. What we also like to know is who is already part of this (broadcasters, financiers), who has expressed interest, and to which festivals has the film been submitted/accepted. Please send the synopsis to jan@filmstransit.com and diana@filmstransit.com at the same time. **Acquisition Contact:** Diana Holtzberg, VP Acquisitions (NY Office), dianaholtzberg@filmstransit.com and Jan Rofekamp, President & CEO (Montreal Office) janrofekamp@filmstransit.com

FIRST LOOK MEDIA, INC.
Parent Company: Nu Image
2000 Avenue of the Stars, Suite 410 Century City CA 90067
Phone: (424) 202-5000
info@firstlookmedia.com
http://www.firstlookmedia.com

1400 titles.

First Look Studios, a leading independent supplier in the entertainment marketplace, acquires, markets, and distributes feature films, television series, and specialty programming.

Subjects: Arts, Literature & Music, Comedy, Criminal Justice, Drama, Experimental/Avant Garde **Markets:** Theatrical **Specialty:** Art house film **Titles:** *War, Inc., Transsiberian, Priceless, The Proposition, King of California*

Acquisition Information: Acquires Narrative Feature, Doc Feature **Acquisition Method:** Solicited Only, Other **Stage:** Unknown **Philosophy:** To distribute entertainment content with commercial appeal to consumers through any channel on any format profitably, with our current emphasis on theatrical and home entertainment channels, focusing on DVD and various forms of television as well as emerging digital platforms.

FIRST RUN FEATURES
630 Ninth Avenue, Suite 1213 New York NY 10036
Phone: (212) 243-0600 | Fax: (212) 989-7649
acquisitions@firstrunfeatures.com
http://www.firstrunfeatures.com

500 titles. Est. 1979.

First Run Features was founded in 1979 by a group of filmmakers to advance the distribution of independent film. Under the leadership of the late independent film pioneer, Fran Spielman, First Run Features quickly gained a reputation for its controversial catalog of daring independent fiction and non-fiction films. First Run remains one of the largest independent theatrical and home video distributors in the United States, releasing 12 to 15 films a year in theatres nationwide and 40 to

50 videos and DVDs annually. First Run has also formed a nontheatrical division that sells directly to the educational market.

Subjects: Arts, Literature & Music, Biography, Children's Programming, Comedy, Criminal Justice, Drama, Environmental Issues, Experimental/Avant Garde, Family, Gender Issues, Health & Medicine, History, Human Rights, Immigration, Labor Issues, Language/Linguistics, Multicultural Perspective, Nature, Politics & Government, Psychology, Religion, Science, Sociology **Markets:** Theatrical, Nontheatrical, Educational, Home Video, Cable TV, Public TV, Network TV, TV Syndication **Specialty:** Art house film **Titles:** *42 Up, Harlan County, Smithereens, The Watermelon Woman, New York in the Fifties, Petites Freres* **Marketing:** Web Catalog

Acquisition Information: 60 titles per year. Acquires Narrative Feature, Doc Feature, Short Narrative, Short Doc, Experimental **Acquisition Method:** Unsolicited Inquiries, Festivals, Markets **Stage:** Finished **Venues:** Toronto, Berlin, IFP, and other festivals and markets **Advice:** We do not accept unsolicited screeners, but we are open to hearing about your film if it has received press from a film festival or been reviewed in an industry publication. If this is the case, please send us an e-mail with a brief description of your film. Due to the number of inquiries we receive, we will respond only if we are interested in requesting a screener.

FOCUS FEATURES
Parent Company: NBC Universal
65 Bleecker Street, 3rd Floor New York NY 10012
Phone: (212) 539-4000
http://www.filminfocus.com

25 titles. Est. 2004.

Focus Features is a motion picture production, financing, and worldwide distribution company committed to bringing moviegoers the most original stories from the world's most innovative filmmakers. Focus Features is part of NBC Universal, one of the world's leading media and entertainment companies in the development, production, and marketing of entertainment, news, and information to a global audience.

Subjects: Action/Adventure, Arts, Literature & Music, Comedy, Drama **Markets:** Theatrical, Home Video, Cable TV, Network TV, Satelitte/DBS, Foreign, Other **Specialty:** Art house film **Titles:** *Eastern Promises, Reservation Road, Atonement, epic 9, Bruges, Burn After Reading, Lust, Caution*

Acquisition Information: Acquires Narrative Feature, Experimental **Acquisition Method:** Solicited Only, Festivals, Other **Stage:** Unknown **Venues:** Cannes,

Sundance, Toronto **Philosophy:** Committed to bringing moviegoers the most original stories from the world's most innovative filmmakers. **Advice:** Be sure you have a complete package. Back up all your decisions.

FOX LORBER

2166 Broadway
Penthouse New York NY 10024
Phone: (212) 787-3577
richard@lorbermedia.com
http://www.lorbermedia.com

1000 titles. Est. 1981. 40 employees. Principals: Richard Lorber, Founder

Lorber Media serves as a business development partner for small to mid-size entertainment and media companies. Its primary role is designing and implementing strategies for growth, focusing on the areas of international distribution and new market opportunities. Lorber Media aids a diverse range of firms – its client roster includes businesses in areas of international television distribution and co-production, domestic theatrical distribution financing, and DVD home entertainment distribution.

Lorber Media also provides gap financing for theatrical films and television programs, including an innovative prints and advertising fund, which provides up-front capital for film prints and advertising expenditures. In some cases, Lorber Media provides strategic financing as well as merger and acquisition guidance for select clients. In this type of relationship, Richard Lorber will take on an additional role as a member of the company's board, helping to guide the company from the boardroom, in addition to his strategic day-to-day consulting activities.

Subjects: Arts, Literature & Music, Theater **Markets:** Theatrical, Nontheatrical, Home Video, Cable TV, Public TV, Network TV, TV Syndication, Satelitte/DBS, Web, Airline, Foreign **Titles:** John Woo's *The Killer,* Jean-Jacques Beineix's *Diva,* Nagisa Oshima's *In the Realm of the Senses*

Acquisition Information: Acquires Narrative Feature, Doc Feature, Short Narrative, Short Doc, Animation, Experimental **Acquisition Method:** Unsolicited Inquiries, Festivals, Markets **Stage:** Treatment, Proposal, Rough Cut, Fine Cut, Finished **Philosophy:** Our mission is to help small to mid-size entertainment companies realize their potential in the domestic and international media marketplaces. **Acquisition Contact:** Richard Lorber, Founder, richard@lorbermedia.com

FOX SEARCHLIGHT PICTURES
Parent Company: Fox Entertainment Group, Inc.
10201 West Pico Boulevard, Building 38 Los Angeles CA 90035
Phone: (310) 369-1000 | Fax: (310) 369-2359
http://www.foxsearchlight.com

60 titles. Est. 1994.

Fox Searchlight Pictures is a filmmaker-oriented company that focuses on distinctive films helmed by renowned directors and promising newcomers. By blending specialty films with trademark art-house fare, Fox Searchlight's leadership has solidified its position in the independent film marketplace.

Subjects: Action/Adventure, Comedy, Drama, LGBT **Markets:** Theatrical, Home Video, Cable TV **Specialty:** Art house film **Titles:** *Slumdog Millionaire, The Wrestler, Notorious, My Life in Ruins, The Full Monty, Boys Don't Cry, Kissing Jessica Stein, Juno* **Marketing:** Printed Catalog, Web Catalog

Acquisition Information: Acquires Narrative Feature **Acquisition Method:** Festivals, Markets **Stage:** Unknown

FRAMELINE DISTRIBUTION
145 Ninth Street, #300 San Francisco CA 94103
Phone: (415) 703-8650 | Fax: (415) 861-1404
info@frameline.org
http://www.frameline.org

175 titles. Est. 1981. Principals: K.C. Price, Executive Director; Maura King, Distribution Director; Desiree Buford, Operations Director

Frameline is a nonprofit organization dedicated to the promotion, distribution, and exhibition of lesbian and gay film and video. Established in conjunction with the San Francisco International Lesbian and Gay Film Festival, Frameline focuses on community-based work and serves local film festivals worldwide.

Subjects: Arts, Literature & Music, Biography, Drama, Experimental/Avant Garde, LGBT, History, Human Rights **Markets:** Theatrical, Nontheatrical, Educational, Home Video **Specialty:** Film and video on gays and lesbians **Titles:** *Tongues Untied, Out at Work, Gay Cuba* **Marketing:** Web Catalog

Acquisition Information: Acquires Narrative Feature, Doc Feature, Short Narrative, Short Doc **Acquisition Method:** Unsolicited Inquiries **Stage:** Unknown **Philosophy:** To strengthen the diverse lesbian, gay, bisexual, and transgender community and further its visibility by supporting and promoting a broad array of cultural representations and artistic expression in film, video and other media arts.

Advice: Watch lots of films. Research your subject. Speak from your truth.
Acquisition Contact: Maura King, Distribution Director

FREESTYLE RELEASING

6310 San Vincente Blvd., #500 Los Angeles CA 90048
Phone: (323) 330-9920 | Fax: (323) 330-9939
http://www.freestylereleasing.com

50 titles.

Freestyle Releasing is a full-service theatrical motion picture distribution company
that specializes in representing independent companies, major studios, and mini-
major studios on a "service-deal" basis for the purpose of exhibiting their films in a
first class theatrical release.

Subjects: Action/Adventure, Comedy, Drama **Markets:** Theatrical **Titles:** *An
American Haunting, The Illusioninist, Kickin' It Old Skool, Dirty Deeds, Find Me
Guilty, The Abandoned, First Snow* **Marketing:** Web Catalog

Acquisition Information: 20 titles per year. Acquires Narrative Feature **Acquisition
Method:** Unsolicited Inquiries **Stage:** Finished

FRIES FILM GROUP

22817 Ventura Blvd., Suite 909 Woodland Hills CA 91634
Phone: (818) 888-3052 | Fax: (818) 888-3042
info@friesfilms.com
http://www.friesfilms.com

24 titles. Est. 1994. Principals: Charles Fries, President and Chief Operating
Officer

Fries Film Group, Inc., is a full-service production and distribution company.

Subjects: Action/Adventure, Arts, Literature & Music, Comedy, Criminal Justice,
Experimental/Avant Garde, Family, History **Markets:** Theatrical, Nontheatrical,
Home Video, Cable TV, Foreign, Other **Specialty:** All genres **Marketing:** Web
Catalog

Acquisition Information: Acquires Narrative Feature, Doc Feature, Short
Narrative, Short Doc **Acquisition Method:** Unsolicited Inquiries **Stage:** Unknown
Acquisition Contact: Charles Fries sales@friesfilms.com

GATEWAY FILMS/VISION VIDEO
AKA: Vision Video/Gateway Films, Inc.
P.O. Box 540 Worcester PA 19490
Phone: (800) 523-0226 (610) 584-3500
info@visionvideo.com
https://www.visionvideo.com/

3000 titles. Est. 1972. Principals: Ken Curtis, Founder and President

In its fourth decade, Gateway Films/Vision Video offers more than 3,000 Christian and family videos and DVDs for all age groups. Selections include drama, documentary, live events, curriculum, and rare historical footage among the many genres.

Subjects: Arts, Literature & Music, Children's Programming, Family, Religion
Markets: Nontheatrical, Home Video, Foreign **Specialty:** Christian film
Marketing: Printed Catalog, Web Catalog

Acquisition Information: Acquires Narrative Feature **Acquisition Method:** Festivals, Markets **Stage:** Finished **Venues:** MIP, AFM **Philosophy:** We understand our calling is to provide video resources that would allow families and churches to have an historic awareness of how God has worked among His people over the centuries.

GENIUS PRODUCTS
Parent Company: Genius Products, Inc., along with The Weinstein Company Holdings, LLC
2230 Broadway Santa Monica CA 90404
Phone: (310) 453-1222 | Fax: (310) 453-0074
info1@geniusproducts.com
http://www.geniusproducts.com

60 titles. Principals: Trevor Drinkwater, Chief Executive Officer; Ed Byrnes, Executive Vice President and Chief Financial Officer; Matthew Smith, President; Michael Radiloff, Executive Vice President of Productions and Acquisitions

Genius Products is a leading independent home-entertainment distribution company that produces, licenses and distributes a library of motion pictures, television programming, family, lifestyle and trend entertainment on DVD and other emerging platforms. Through its expansive network of retailers throughout the U.S. Genius handles the distribution, marketing and sales for such brands as Animal Planet, Asia Extreme™, Discovery Kids, Dragon Dynasty™, Dimension Films™, Entertainment Rights group companies (Entertainment Rights, Classic Media and Big Idea), ESPN®, IFC®, RHI Entertainment™, Sesame Workshop®, TLC, The Weinstein Company® and WWE®.

Subjects: Action/Adventure, Arts, Literature & Music, Biography, Comedy, Criminal Justice, Drama, Experimental/Avant Garde, Family **Markets:** Home Video, Other **Specialty:** motion pictures, television programming, family, lifestyle and trend entertainment

Acquisition Information: Acquires Narrative Feature, Doc Feature **Acquisition Method:** Unknown **Stage:** Unknown

GPN EDUCATIONAL MEDIA

Parent Company: Smarterville Productions, LLC
1407 Fleet Street Baltimore MD 21231
Phone: (800) 228-4630 | Fax: (800) 306-2330
askgpn@smarterville.com
http://www.gpn.unl.edu

3000 titles. Est. 1962.

GPN provides new technology media to the educational market. It is a service agency of Nebraska Educational Telecommunications and the University of Nebraska-Lincoln. The company pays royalties based on actual sales; for the right product it will give advances.

Subjects: Arts, Literature & Music, Children's Programming, Family, Science **Markets:** Educational, Home Video, Public TV **Specialty:** Educational media **Titles:** *Reading Rainbow, 3-2-1 Classroom Contact, Ghostwriter, Newton* **Marketing:** Web Catalog

Acquisition Information: Acquires Short Narrative, Short Doc **Acquisition Method:** Unsolicited Inquiries **Stage:** Unknown **Venues:** GPN acquires the majority of the products it distributes from leading independent producers across the country and around the world. **Advice:** GPN is looking for programming appropriate for the in-school market. Producers should submit masters on Beta, color publicity photos, and guide material to accompany the video. **Acquisition Contact:** (800) 228-4630 askgpn@smarterville.com

GUIDANCE ASSOCIATES
31 Pine View Road Mt. Kisco NY 10549
Phone: (800) 431-1242 x102 | Fax: (914) 666-5319
willg1961@gmail.com
http://www.guidanceassociates.com

300 titles. Principals: Will Goodman

Guidance Associates distributes documentaries, narratives and instructional videos.

Subjects: History, Language/Linguistics, Science **Markets:** Nontheatrical, Educational, Home Video **Specialty:** Educational media **Titles:** *A Class Divided, Eye of the Storm, The Angry Eye, What Everyone Needs to Know About Sexual Harassment* **Marketing:** Web Catalog

Acquisition Information: Acquires Doc Feature, Short Narrative, Short Doc **Acquisition Method:** Unknown **Stage:** Unknown   (914) 666-4100 x101 judiw@guidanceassociates.com

HARMONY GOLD USA
7655 Sunset Blvd. Los Angeles CA 90046

50 titles. Est. 1983.

Harmony Gold produces, acquires, and distributes international television programming, producing some of the industry's classic and history-making programs.

Subjects: Action/Adventure, Animation, Arts, Literature & Music, Children's Programming, Comedy, Drama, Family, Regional Profiles & Issues **Markets:** Theatrical **Titles:** *Robotech, The Adventure of Rin Tin Tin, Tibet: Cry of the Snow Lion, Dirt, King of the Olympics, Around the World in 80 Days*

Acquisition Information: Acquires Narrative Feature, Doc Feature, Animation **Acquisition Method:** Unknown **Stage:** Script, Finished

HIGHLAND CREST PICTURES
Parent Company: A Douglas Witkin Company
7471 Melrose Avenue, Suite 7 Los Angeles CA 90046
Phone: (323) 852-9848 | Fax: (323) 658-7265
highlandcp@aol.com
http://www.highlandcrestpictures.com

2 titles. Est. 1998. Principals: Douglas C. Witkins, President; Koing Kuoch, VP of Sales; Chris Phillips, VP of Acqustions; Jason Fox, Director of Operations

Highland Crest Pictures, one of the Douglas Witkins Companies, is the sister company of venerable Amazing Movies, an international motion picture rights licensing organization founded in Los Angeles in 1984. Whereas Amazing Movies targets video and prime-time TV buyers worldwide with product in the under-$3-million-budget range, Highland Crest Pictures concentrates more on theatrical and "all-rights" buyers with product budgets in the $3-$40 million range. In addition to acquiring already completed films, Highland Crest also initiates high-end projects and oversees their development, casting, and production to ensure a steady flow of product more specifically targeted toward the demanding world marketplace.

Subjects: Action/Adventure, Drama **Markets:** Theatrical, Home Video, Network TV, Foreign **Specialty:** Art house film **Titles:** *Six Ways to Sunday, Broken Vessels*

Acquisition Information: Acquires Narrative Feature **Acquisition Method:** Unsolicited Inquiries, Festivals, Markets **Stage:** Script, Finished **Venues:** AFM, Cannes Market, MIFED, Sundance, Berlin, Toronto, Outfest

HUMAN RELATIONS MEDIA
41 Kensico Drive Mount Kisco NY 10549
Phone: (914) 666-9151 | Fax: (914) 666-9506
Letters@hrmvideo.com
http://www.hrmvideo.com

135 titles. Est. 1976. Principals: Anton Schloat, President

Human Relations Media specializes in the production and distribution of educational video for junior and senior high school curricula with an emphasis on health, drug education, career education, science, math, and language arts.

Subjects: Aging, Children's Programming, Health & Medicine, Language/Linguistics, Science **Markets:** Nontheatrical, Educational, Home Video, Other **Specialty:** Educational video **Titles:** *Overcoming Adversity, Meth Death, Exploring Inheritance and Genetics* **Marketing:** Web Catalog

Acquisition Information: Acquires Short Narrative, Short Doc **Acquisition Method:** Unknown **Stage:** Unknown **Acquisition Contact:** Anton Schloat, President (914) 666-9151

ICARUS FILMS
32 Court Sreet, 21st Floor Brooklyn NY 11201
Phone: (718) 488-8900 | Fax: (718) 488-8642
mail@icarusfilms.com
http://www.icarusfilms.com

700 titles. Est. 1979. Principals: Jonathan Miller, President

Icarus Films is a distributor of innovative and provocative documentary films from independent producers around the world.

Subjects: Biography, Criminal Justice, Health & Medicine, History, Immigration, Multicultural Perspective, Psychology, Science, Sociology **Markets:** Nontheatrical, Educational, Home Video **Specialty:** Documentaries **Titles:** *War Photographer, Battle of Chile, A Grin Without a Cat* **Marketing:** Web Catalog

Acquisition Information: Acquires Narrative Feature, Doc Feature, Short Narrative, Short Doc **Acquisition Method:** Unknown **Stage:** Unknown **Venues:** IDFA, Berlin, Sunny Side of the Doc

IFC FILMS
11 Penn Plaza, 15th Floor New York NY 10001
Phone: (646) 273-7200 | Fax: (646) 273-7250
programming@ifctv.com
http://www.ifctv.com

200 titles. Est. 2000.

A leading theatrical film distribution company launched in 2000, IFC Films aims to bring the best of independent and specialized films to theaters. IFC is committed to realizing the visions of independent filmmakers without compromise. IFC Films releases 10-12 films per year, building a slate of titles from an acquisitions program and selected in-house productions.

Subjects: Action/Adventure, Aging, Animation, Biography, Children's Programming, Comedy, Criminal Justice, Drama, Environmental Issues, Experimental/Avant Garde, Family, LGBT, Gender Issues, History, Human Rights, Immigration, Labor Issues, Language/Linguistics, Multicultural Perspective, Nature, Politics & Government, Psychology, Regional Profiles & Issues, Religion, Sports, Theater, Women's Issues **Markets:** Theatrical, Nontheatrical, Cable TV,

Web, Other **Specialty:** Art house film **Titles:** *Our Song, Together, The Business of Strangers, Y Tu Mama Tambien, My Big Fat Greek Wedding, Lost in La Mancha* **Marketing:** Printed Catalog, Web Catalog

Acquisition Information: Acquires Narrative Feature, Doc Feature, Short Narrative, Short Doc, Animation, Experimental **Acquisition Method:** Solicited Only **Stage:** Proposal, Script, Finished **Venues:** Sundance, Toronto, Cannes, Berlin, Telluride, Seattle **Advice:** IFC Productions acts as an equity partner with established indie talent to produce low-budget ($500K to $4M total) films free of studio agendas. IFC Productions considers only fully packaged projects. Fax a 2-3 page proposal to (516) 803-4506 containing a synopsis of the script/story and with brief bios of the primary people attached to the project (producers, writer, director or other talent) along with a concise outline of your total budget and the amount of financing you are seeking. **Acquisition Contact:** sblash@rainbow-media.com

IMAGE ENTERTAINMENT

20525 Nordhoff Street, Suite 200 Chatsworth CA 91311
acquisitions@image-entertainment.com
http://www.image-entertainment.com

2500 titles. Est. 1981.

Image Entertainment, Inc., is a leading independent home entertainment company that acquires, licenses, finances and produces exclusive content for worldwide video distribution through its direct relationships with major North American retailers and foreign sublicensees such as Sony/BMG and Warner Music.

Subjects: Action/Adventure, Arts, Literature & Music, Comedy, Criminal Justice, Drama, Experimental/Avant Garde, Family **Markets:** Theatrical, Nontheatrical, Home Video, Web, Other

Acquisition Information: 30 titles per year. Acquires Narrative Feature, Experimental **Acquisition Method:** Unknown **Stage:** Unknown **Acquisition Contact:** acquisitions@image-entertainment.com

INDEPENDENT TELEVISION SERVICE
651 Brannan Street
Suite 410 San Francisco CA 94107
Phone: (415) 356-8383 | Fax: (415) 356-8391
itvs@itvs.org
http://www.itvs.org

400 titles. Est. 1991. Principals: Sally Jo Fifre, President, CEO; Judy Tam, Executive Vice President, CFO; Tamara Gould, Vice President of ITVS International Distribution;

Independent Television Service (ITVS) brings independently produced programs to public television – programs that engage creative risks, advance issues, and represent points of view not usually seen on commercial or public television. ITVS is committed to programming which addresses the needs of under-served audiences, particularly minorities and children.

Subjects: Arts, Literature & Music, Biography, Drama, Environmental Issues, Gender Issues, Human Rights, Immigration, Labor Issues, Language/Linguistics, Multicultural Perspective, Politics & Government, Regional Profiles & Issues, Sociology **Markets:** Public TV **Specialty:** Independently produced programs for public television **Titles:** *Billy Strayhorn: Lush Life, Craft in America: Landscape, Made in L.A., Operation Homecoming: Writing in the Wartime Experience*

Acquisition Information: Acquires Narrative Feature, Doc Feature, Short Narrative, Short Doc **Acquisition Method:** Unknown **Stage:** Unknown **Advance:** Sometimes. **Philosophy:** ITVS seeks to expand cultural and global awareness, advance civic participation, and creatively engage audiences as it brings new and diverse voices into the public discourse through programming. ITVS forges alliances and explores new opportunities through emerging technologies that will cultivate new audiences for independent media.

INTERMEDIA, INC.
1818 Westlake Ave N. Suite 408 Seattle WA 98109
Phone: (800)553-8336 | Fax: (800)553-1655
info@intermedia-inc.com
http://www.intermedia-inc.com

200 titles. Est. 1981. Principals: Susan Hoffman, President

Intermedia is a distributor of social interest educational program on topics such as domestic violence, sexual assault, substance abuse, teen pregnancy and workplace training.

Subjects: Aging, Health & Medicine, Labor Issues **Markets:** Nontheatrical, Educational, Home Video, Other **Specialty:** Educational media on social issues **Titles:** *I Quit: How to Stop Smoking, Facing Diversity, Small Justice, A Question of Rape* **Marketing:** Web Catalog

Acquisition Information: Acquires Short Narrative, Short Doc **Acquisition Method:** Unsolicited Inquiries **Stage:** Unknown **Philosophy:** To provide educators with effective tools to allow them to meet the needs of their clients. Whether your clients are students, adults, employees, soldiers or court-ordered treatment clients, Intermedia has a unique set of programs that you will find invaluable to your training needs. **Advice:** Intermedia is looking for high quality programs that move quickly, with a strong and clear educational message on topics of current social relevence. **Acquisition Contact:** Susan Hoffman, President (800) 553-8336

INTERNATIONAL FILM FOUNDATION
c/o Sam Bryan, #17-B 322 Central Park West New York NY 10025-7629
Phone: 212.666.2324
samkbryan@aol.com
http://www.internationalfilmfoundation.com

235 titles. Est. 1945. Principals: Sam Bryan, Executive Director

The International Film Foundation was created in 1945 as a nonprofit organization to produce and distribute documentary films that would promote better world understanding.

Subjects: History **Markets:** Nontheatrical, Educational **Specialty:** Educational film on social issues **Marketing:** Web Catalog

Acquisition Information: Acquires Doc Feature, Short Doc **Acquisition Method:** Unknown **Stage:** Unknown **Acquisition Contact:** Sam Bryan, Executive Director, samkbryan@aol.com

ITALTOONS
1375 Broadway, Floor 3 New York NY 10018
Phone: (212) 730-0280 | Fax: (212) 730-0313
info2@italtoons.com
http://www.italtoons.com

30 titles. Est. 1978. Principals: Giuliana Nicodemi, President

Italtoons is best known as a producer and distributor of award-winning children's animation, as well as for its collection of European and American animated shorts.

Italtoons is also active in worldwide distribution of live-action and animated feature films for theatrical and other media.

Subjects: Animation, Children's Programming **Markets:** Educational, Home Video **Specialty:** Animation **Titles:** *Volere Volare, The Icicle Thief, Allegro Non Troppo, The Tune* **Marketing:** Printed Catalog, Web Catalog

Acquisition Information: Acquires Animation **Acquisition Method:** Unsolicited Inquiries **Stage:** Unknown **Venues:** All major industry markets and festivals **Acquisition Contact:** Giuliana Nicodemi, (212) 730-0280

IVY VIDEO
P.O. Box 18376 Asheville NC 28814
Phone: (828) 285-9995 (800) 669-4057 | Fax: (828) 285-9997
info@ivyvideo.com
http://www.ivyvideo.com

50 titles. Est. 1972. Principals: Joshua Tager, VP

Ivy Video represents cult, foreign, classic, and hard-to-find films and videos.

Subjects: Arts, Literature & Music, Biography, History, Nature, Religion, Sports **Markets:** Nontheatrical, Educational, Home Video, Other **Specialty:** Feature films and shorts **Marketing:** Web Catalog

Acquisition Information: Acquires Narrative Feature, Doc Feature **Acquisition Method:** Unsolicited Inquiries **Stage:** Unknown **Venues:** MIPCOM, MIP, AFM, Berlin, Toronto **Acquisition Contact:** joshtager@aol.com

KINO INTERNATIONAL CORPORATION
333 West 39th Street, Suite 503 New York NY 10018
Phone: (212) 629-6880 (800) 562-3330 | Fax: (212) 714-0871
contact@kino.com
http://www.kino.com

500 titles. Est. 1977. Principals: Donald Krim, President

Kino International is a theatrical distribution company specializing in classics and foreign language art films. The collection ranges from the earliest experiments in cinema and a wide selection of silent films to the newest films from around the world.

Subjects: Action/Adventure, Archival, Arts, Literature & Music, Biography, Comedy, Drama, Experimental/Avant Garde, History **Markets:** Theatrical, Home

Video, Other **Specialty:** Art house and classic film **Titles:** *Himalaya, The Piano Teacher, Blue Angel* **Marketing:** Web Catalog

Acquisition Information: Acquires Narrative Feature, Doc Feature **Acquisition Method:** Unknown **Stage:** Unknown **Venues:** Major festivals and markets, films on tape, and screenings **Advice:** "Study our catalog." Kino does not accept unsolicited materials.

KIT PARKER FILMS
2833 N. Central Ave. #610 Phoenix AZ 85004
films@kitparker.com
http://www.kitparker.com

30 titles. Est. 1971. Principals: Kit Parker, Founder

Kit Parker Films was originally founded in 1971 as a 16mm non-theatrical motion picture distributor. In the 1980s, it expanded into theatrical distribution, and soon represented the classic libraries of major studios and independent producers. In 2000, the film distribution part of the business was phased out. Today, Kit Parker Films concentrates on locating and restoring former "orphan films" – films that never appeared on TV, cable, or home video, most which haven't been seen for decades since their theatrical release.

Subjects: Animation, Archival, Children's Programming, Comedy, Drama **Markets:** Nontheatrical, Home Video, Cable TV, Public TV, Network TV, TV Syndication, Satelitte/DBS, Web, Airline, Foreign

Acquisition Information: Acquires Narrative Feature, Doc Feature, Short Narrative, Short Doc, Animation **Acquisition Method:** Unknown **Stage:** Unknown

KITCHEN VIDEO DISTRIBUTION COLLECTION
512 West 19th Street New York NY 10011
Phone: (212) 255-5793 | Fax: (212) 645-4258
info@thekitchen.org
http://www.thekitchen.org

600 titles. Est. 1971. Principals: Elise Bernhardt, Executive Director

The Kitchen is a nonprofit, interdisciplinary organization that provides innovative artists working in the media, literary, and performing arts with exhibition and performance opportunities to create and present new work.
The Kitchen Video Collection includes the early works of artists including Vito Acconci, Lori Anderson, Richard Serra and Robert Wilson as well as newer artists such as Kristine Diekman, Van McElwee, and Andreas Troeger.

Subjects: Arts, Literature & Music **Markets:** Nontheatrical, Other **Specialty:** Documentary and experimental video

Acquisition Information: Acquires Narrative Feature, Doc Feature, Short Narrative, Short Doc, Experimental **Acquisition Method:** Unsolicited Inquiries **Stage:** Unknown **Advice:** Proposals for exhibition of media or technology-based work are reviewed twice a year. Response time is generally 6-9 months. Please do not call The Kitchen regarding your proposal. You will be notified by mail. Proposals should include the following: letter of introduction with description of recent work; résumé(s); work history documentation; related press materials; and SASE for return of materials.

KOAN, INC.
P.O. Box 982557 Park City UT 84098
Phone: (435) 645-7244 | Fax: (435) 645-8644
pmadsen@koaninc.com
http://www.koaninc.com

100 titles. Est. 1991. Principals: Gil Aglaure

Koan was founded in France in 1991 and moved to Park City, Utah in 1993. It distributes family-friendly feature films, documentaries, and series to television stations worldwide. Koan does not use sub-distributors; its alliances have enabled them to place programs directly with the buyers of television stations and video publishers. Originally a distributor of documentaries, Koan has gone on to establish itself in the fields of family entertainment and award-winning feature films. Its catalog includes over 70 films and hundreds of hours of documentary and animated programming.

Subjects: Action/Adventure, Animation, Children's Programming, Drama, Family, Religion **Markets:** Theatrical, Nontheatrical, Educational, Home Video, Cable TV, Network TV, Satelitte/DBS, Web, Airline, Foreign, Other **Specialty:** Family programs for television **Titles:** *Dog Days of Summer, The Last Winter, The Fallen, Through Your Eyes* **Territories:** Worldwide **Marketing:** Web Catalog

Acquisition Information: Acquires Narrative Feature **Acquisition Method:** Unsolicited Inquiries, Festivals, Markets, Other **Stage:** Rough Cut **Venues:** MIPCOM, AFM, Cannes Festival, NATPE **Philosophy:** We value each of the producers we work with and in order to maintain close relationships we offer honest feedback from the very beginning. Each film submitted to us is carefully examined and its potential in the international marketplace is assessed. Once we decide to include a film in our catalog we collaborate with producers to develop a customized marketing strategy that best meets the unique needs of the buyers and maximizes revenue. Our stellar sales team maintains strong relationships with buyers in virtually every territory in the world. That team also promotes films at each of the most important film markets around the world, including NATPE, AFM, MIPTV, MIPCOM, Cannes Film Festival, etc. We also inform producers of the details for each and every deal we make, to ensure they always know where their film is being sold and seen. **Acquisition Contact:** Devin, Carter Sales Department (435) 645-7244 ext. 111 dcarter@koaninc.com and Paul Madsen, Acquistions Department (435) 645-7244 ext. 133 pmadsen@koaninc.com

LANDMARK MEDIA
3450 Slade Run Drive Falls Church VA 22042
Phone: (703) 241-2030 (800) 342-4336 | Fax: (703) 536-9540
info@landmarkmedia.com
http://www.landmarkmedia.com

79 titles. Principals: Joan Hartogs, Michael Hartogs, Owners

Landmark Media is an independent family-owned company with over 25 years of experience offering educational videos and DVDs.

Subjects: Arts, Literature & Music, Children's Programming, Environmental Issues, History, Nature, Science, Sociology **Markets:** Nontheatrical, Educational, Home Video **Specialty:** Educational media **Titles:** *Atoms of Fire-An Introduction to Organic Chemistry, Bioterrorism-The Truth, Breaking the Code-The Race to Uncover the Secret of Life, An American Icon: Coca Cola-The Early Years* **Marketing:** Web Catalog

Acquisition Information: Acquires Narrative Feature, Doc Feature, Short Narrative, Short Doc **Acquisition Method:** Unsolicited Inquiries **Stage:** Unknown **Acquisition Contact:** Richard Hartogs, VP Acquisitions, richard@landmarkmedia.com and Peter Hartogs peter@landmarkmedia.com

LAS AMERICAS FILM NETWORK
1322 Hillary Street New Orleans LA 70118
Phone: (504) 866-4360 | Fax: (801) 340-7462
info@lasamericasfilms.org
http://www.lasamericasfilms.org

50 titles. Est. 2006. Principals: Brian Knighten

Las Américas Film Network is a media-arts organization that promotes and distributes high-quality, award-winning, documentary, feature and experimental films that explore the diversity and richness of Latin America.

Subjects: Action/Adventure, Aging, Animation, Archival, Arts, Literature & Music, Biography, Children's Programming, Comedy, Criminal Justice, Disability,

Drama, Environmental Issues, Experimental/Avant Garde, Family, LGBT, Gender Issues, Health & Medicine, History, Human Rights, Immigration, Labor Issues, Language/Linguistics, Multicultural Perspective, Nature, Politics & Government, Psychology, Regional Profiles & Issues, Religion, Science, Sociology, Sports, Theater, Travel, Women's Issues **Markets:** Theatrical, Nontheatrical, Educational, Home Video, Public TV **Specialty:** Films that focus on Latin American and Latino issues in the U.S. **Titles:** *Favela Rising, De Nadie, Manda Bala, Erendira* **Marketing:** Printed Catalog, Web Catalog

Acquisition Information: 12 titles per year. Acquires Narrative Feature, Doc Feature, Short Narrative, Short Doc, Animation, Experimental **Acquisition Method:** Unsolicited Inquiries, Festivals, Markets, Other **Stage:** Treatment, Proposal, Script, Production, Rough Cut, Fine Cut, Finished, Other **Advance:** Sometimes. **Philosophy:** Make available as much high-quality Latin American and Latino film as possible. **Acquisition Contact:** Brian Knighten (504) 866-4360 info@lasamericanasfilms.org

LEO FILM RELEASING
6548 Country Squire Lane Omaha NE 68152
Phone: (323) 459 5574
lustgar@pacbell.net
http://www.leofilms.com

38 titles. Est. 1991. Principals: Steve Lustgarten, President

LEO Films is a distributor of independent films to the U.S. and world market and has released over 80 feature films that run the gamut from Sundance to genre films.

Subjects: Action/Adventure, Animation, Arts, Literature & Music, Biography, Comedy, Drama, Experimental/Avant Garde, Family, Gender Issues, History **Markets:** Theatrical, Home Video, Web, Other **Specialty:** All genres **Marketing:** Web Catalog

Acquisition Information: Acquires Narrative Feature, Doc Feature, Experimental **Acquisition Method:** Unsolicited Inquiries **Stage:** Unknown **Advice:** You may send an e-mail query with information on scripts or films and we will respond if interested in proceeding **Acquisition Contact:** steve@leofilms.com

LIBRARY VIDEO
AKA: Schlessinger Media
7 E. Wynnewood Road Wynnewood PA 19096
Phone: (610) 645-4000 | Fax: (610) 645-4040
submissions@libraryvideo.com
http://www.libraryvideo.com

18000 titles. Est. 1985.

Library Video Company is a distributor of educational video, DVD and audiobook to schools and public libraries nationwide. The company stocks over 18,000 titles covering a diverse range of topics for all ages and grade levels. Each program has been carefully reviewed and selected for content that is appropriate for the classroom and public library setting.

Subjects: Arts, Literature & Music, Biography, Children's Programming, Criminal Justice, Environmental Issues, Family, Health & Medicine, History, Human Rights, Immigration, Labor Issues, Language/Linguistics, Multicultural Perspective, Nature, Politics & Government, Regional Profiles & Issues, Science, Sociology, Sports, Travel **Markets:** Educational **Titles:** Many award-winning series including *American History for Children, Ancient Civilizations for Children, Explorers of the World, Library Skills for Children, Reading for Children, Greek Mythology for Students, The Way Things Work* **Marketing:** Printed Catalog, Web Catalog

Acquisition Information: Acquires Doc Feature, Short Doc **Acquisition Method:** Unsolicited Inquiries **Stage:** Finished **Advice:** When submitting a product (Audiobook, DVD or Video) for consideration in the Library Video Company catalog, we ask that you provide us with the following information: A sample of the completed program and its packaging; Product information or sell-sheets describing your program, as well as information about any relevant awards or reviews; The product's availability date; The suggested retail price (SRP) as well as any other relevant pricing information. Please note: We do not include products that are sold at a lower SRP elsewhere and offered to the school and library market at a higher SRP; The production year or copyright date of the program and, when applicable, its running time, format, system requirements and technical support phone numbers; Complete contact information including: name, phone number, fax number and mailing address.

LIGHTNING MEDIA
301 Arizona Avenue, Suite 400 Santa Monica CA 90401
Phone: (310) 255-7999 | Fax: (310) 255-7998
http://media.lightning-ent.com

50 titles.

Lightning Media selectively targets and acquires distribution rights to commercially driven films and programs which are marketed through theatrical distribution, DVD, television, cable, Internet, VOD, PPV, electronic sell-through and emerging digital platforms in the U.S., Canada, The United Kingdom and Australia.

Subjects: Action/Adventure, Arts, Literature & Music, Comedy, Family **Markets:** Theatrical, Home Video, Cable TV, Network TV, Web **Titles:** *Columbus Day, The Devil's Ground, Skeleton Crew* **Marketing:** Web Catalog

Acquisition Information: Acquires Narrative Feature, Doc Feature **Acquisition Method:** Festivals, Markets **Stage:** Unknown **Acquisition Contact:** Joseph Dickstein, Senior Vice President, Acquisitions

LIONSGATE
AKA: Lions Gate Films, Lions Gate Entertainment
Parent Company: Lion
4553 Glencoe Avenue, Suite 200 Marina del Ray CA 90292
Phone: (310) 449-9200
http://www.lionsgatefilms.com

12000 titles. Est. 1997.

Lionsgate is an entertainment studio with a major presence in the production and distribution of motion pictures, television programming, home entertainment, family entertainment, video-on-demand, and digitally delivered content. The company leverages its content leadership and marketing expertise through a series of partnerships that include the Sony, Comcast, Viacom, Paramount Pictures, and MGM. Lionsgate also has forged partnerships with leading content creators, owners, and distributors in key territories around the world, including Televisa in the U.S. and Latin America, StudioCanal in the UK, Hoyts and Sony in Australia, and Eros International in India. Lionsgate handles a library of approximately 12,000 motion picture and television titles.

Subjects: Action/Adventure, Comedy, Drama **Markets:** Theatrical, Home Video, Foreign **Specialty:** Art house film **Titles:** *The Forbidden Kingdom,* Tyler Perry's *Meet The Browns, The Bank Job, Rambo, The Eye, Saw IV,* Tyler Perry's *Why Did I Get Married?, Good Luck Chuck*

Acquisition Information: Acquires Narrative Feature **Acquisition Method:** Solicited Only **Stage:** Unknown

LONELY SEAL RELEASING

1617 Cosmo Street, Suite #212 Los Angeles CA 90028
Phone: (323) 465-7325 | Fax: (323) 465-0504
http://www.lonelyseal.com

30 titles.

Lonely Seal Releasing is a theatrical and nontheatrical distributor as well as an international sales company founded in 2005 by Hammad Zaidi and Edward Stencel.

Subjects: Arts, Literature & Music, Biography, Children's Programming, Comedy, Drama, History, Multicultural Perspective, Politics & Government, Regional Profiles & Issues, Religion **Markets:** Theatrical, Home Video, Cable TV, Public TV, Network TV, TV Syndication, Satelitte/DBS, Web, Airline, Foreign **Titles:** *Peel: The Peru Project, Artists Off The Grid, Dalai Lama Renaissance, Fidel, Jam, Among Dead Men, Funny Valentine, The Men Who Fell* **Marketing:** Web Catalog

Acquisition Information: Acquires Narrative Feature, Doc Feature **Acquisition Method:** Unsolicited Inquiries, Festivals, Markets **Stage:** Production, Rough Cut, Fine Cut, Finished **Venues:** Sundance, Slamdance, Berlin, SWSW, Toronto, AFI Los Angeles Film Festival, Cannes, European Film Market **Advice:** We look forward to seeing newly completed movies, documentaries, and other types of specialty programing. Please send your DVD along with a letter describing the budget, format the movie was shot on (such as, video HD, SD, 35mm), cast, synopsis, and what rights you have available. Lonely Seal Releasing considers projects during their production, post-production, and completed phases for acquisition. Please do not send us unsolicited screenplays. Send films attention Edward Stencel, Partner Acquisitions & Sales. **Acquisition Contact:** Grant Raynham, VP Acquisitions and Sales, grant@lonelyseal.com and Edward Stencel, Partner, Acquisitions & Sales (323) 477-8400 ext. 269, eStencel@gmail.com

LUCERNE MEDIA

37 Ground Pine Road Morris Plains NJ 07950
Phone: (800) 341-2293 | Fax: (973) 538-0855
LM@lucernemedia.com
http://www.lucernemedia.com

1000 titles. Est. 1974.

Lucerne acquires programs for distribution from independent producers and corporations worldwide and also coproduces programming to meet the specific needs of the educational, public library, and college market communities. Lucerne prides itself on the personal attention it offers each producer. Producers deal directly with the owner of the company who has been active in marketing to the nontheatrical community for more than 30 years. Lucerne incurs all the costs involved in promotion, fulfillment, and customer service for the successful marketing of programs.

Subjects: Aging, Arts, Literature & Music, Children's Programming, Disability, Family, Health & Medicine, Language/Linguistics, Science **Markets:** Nontheatrical, Educational, Home Video, Other **Specialty:** Educational media **Titles:** *Afghanistan: State of the Taliban, Terrorism: Instrument of Fear, American Cowboys* **Marketing:** Web Catalog

Acquisition Information: 100 titles per year. Acquires Narrative Feature, Doc Feature, Short Narrative, Short Doc **Acquisition Method:** Unsolicited Inquiries **Stage:** Unknown **Acquisition Contact:** (800) 341-2293, LM@lucernemedia.com

MAGNOLIA PICTURES

49 West 27th Street, 7th Floor New York NY 10001
Phone: (212) 924-6701 | Fax: (212) 924-6742
acquisitions@magpictures.com
http://www.magpictures.com

75 titles. Est. 2002. Principals: Eammon Bowles, President; Ryan Werner, VP of Acquisitions and Distribution; John McCarron, Director of Distribution

Magnolia Pictures is the theatrical and home entertainment distribution arm of Todd Wagner and Mark Cuban's 2929 Entertainment, specializing in a unique and eclectic slate of films. Formed in 2001 by Bill Banowsky and Eamonn Bowles, Magnolia's releases have included several Academy Award nominated documentaries.

Subjects: Action/Adventure, Animation, Drama, History, Politics & Government **Markets:** Theatrical, Home Video, Cable TV **Specialty:** Art house film **Titles:** *Jesus*

Camp, 2007 Academy Award Nominated Shorts, Enron: The Smartest Guys in the Room, What Just Happened, Splinter **Marketing:** Printed Catalog, Web Catalog

Acquisition Information: Acquires Narrative Feature, Doc Feature, Short Narrative, Short Doc, Animation **Acquisition Method:** Festivals, Markets **Stage:** Unknown **Venues:** Cannes, Toronto, Sundance **Philosophy:** Magnolia looks for critically driven films of quality. **Advice:** Research the catalogs of distributors to determine where yours would be best suited.

MARYKNOLL WORLD PRODUCTIONS
P.O. Box 308, Walsh Building Maryknoll NY 10545
Phone: (914) 941- 7590 | Fax: (914) 941-5753
orbisbooks@maryknoll.org
http://www.maryknollsocietymall.org

50 titles. Est. 1911. Principals: Father Donald J. Doherty, Director; Michael Lavery, Assistant Director; Ronald E. Hines, Promotions Coordinator

Maryknoll World Productions distributes educational documentary films and videos. Maryknoll Productions produces videos for students and educators centering around global awareness with a focus on faith, hope, peace and justice issues, environmental concerns, youth and women's issues, and world cultures and religions.

Subjects: Criminal Justice, Human Rights, Multicultural Perspective, Religion, Sociology, Women's Issues **Markets:** Theatrical, Educational, Home Video, Cable TV, Public TV, Network TV, TV Syndication, Foreign **Specialty:** Documentaries on Third World issues **Titles:** *Consuming Hunger, From Sun Up, Gods of Metal, Where There is Hatred* **Territories:** International **Marketing:** Printed Catalog

Acquisition Information: Acquires Doc Feature, Short Doc **Acquisition Method:** Unknown **Stage:** Unknown

MAVERICK ENTERTAINMENT GROUP
1191 East Newport Center Drive, Suite 210 Deerfield Beach FL 33442
Phone: (954) 422-8811 | Fax: (954) 429-0565
nfo@maverickentertainment.cc
http://www.maverickentertainment.cc

300 titles. Est. 1997. Principals: Doug Schwab, President and Founder

Maverick Entertainment Group aquires and distributes independent fare to the domestic and global markets. Its mission is to be a vertically integrated entertainment company that creates, distributes, licenses, and markets all forms of entertainment and their related business platforms.

Subjects: Action/Adventure, Comedy, Drama **Markets:** Home Video **Marketing:** Web Catalog

Acquisition Information: Acquires Narrative Feature **Acquisition Method:** Unsolicited Inquiries **Stage:** Finished **Advice:** To submit a finished film for acquisition consideration: 1. Download, complete, and sign the release form (PDF document on our website) 2. Submit a DVD (no synopsis). The DVD must be able to play in a standard DVD player. Please do not send in a VHS, as we are no longer screening them. 3. We do not return materials! 4. Submit a filmmaker bio. 5. Send attention to Film Submission.

MEDFILMS, INC.
4910 W. Monte Carlo Drive Tucson AZ 85745
Phone: (520) 575-8900 (800) 535-5593 | Fax: (520) 742-6052
info@medfilms.com
http://www.medfilms.com

50 titles. Est. 1983.

Medfilms produces and distributes programs on health care topics, including training videos on safey and compliance, and productions that address JCAHO, OSHA, and FDA requirements. Its markets include hospitals and other health care facilities.

Subjects: Aging, Disability, Health & Medicine **Markets:** Educational, Home Video **Specialty:** Educational video on health care training **Titles:** *Carpal Tunnel Syndrome, Disaster Preparedness, Latex Allergy and Hand Care* **Marketing:** Printed Catalog, Web Catalog

Acquisition Information: Acquires Doc Feature, Short Doc **Acquisition Method:** Unknown **Stage:** Unknown

MEDIA EDUCATION FOUNDATION

60 Masonic Street Northampton MA 01060
Phone: (413) 584-8500 (800) 897-0089 | Fax: 413.586.8398
info@mediaed.org
http://www.mediaed.org

73 titles. Est. 1991. 15 employees. Principals: Sut Jhally, Founder and Executive Director

The Media Education Foundation, a nonprofit 501(c)3 organization, produces and distributes documentary films and other educational resources to inspire critical reflection on the social, political, and cultural impact of American mass media. From films about the commercialization of childhood and the subtle, yet widespread, effects of pornography, pop-cultural misogyny and sexism, to titles that deal with the devastating effects of rapacious consumerism and the wars for oil that it drives, The Media Education Foundation offers resources designed to help spark discussion about some of the most pressing and complicated issues of our time in the classroom. Its aim is to inspire students to think critically and in new ways about the hyper-mediated world around them.

Subjects: Gender Issues, Human Rights, Labor Issues, Multicultural Perspective, Politics & Government, Sociology, Women's Issues **Markets:** Educational, Home Video **Specialty:** Media criticism **Titles:** *Killing Us Softly 3, Tough Guise, Hijacking Catastrophe, War Made Easy, Hip-Hop: Beyond Beats & Rhymes, Dreamworlds* **Territories:** Worldwide **Marketing:** Printed Catalog, Web Catalog, Direct Mail

Acquisition Information: Acquires Doc Feature, Short Doc **Acquisition Method:** Unsolicited Inquiries **Stage:** Production, Rough Cut, Fine Cut, Finished **Advance:** Sometimes. **Philosophy: In the words of Gore Vidal:** "When Confucius was asked what would be the first thing he would do if he were to lead the state, he said, 'Rectify the language.' Words are used to disguise, not to illuminate, action. Words are used to confuse, so that at election time people will solemnly vote against their own interests. Words must be so twisted as to justify an empire that has now ceased to exist, much less make sense. Is rectification of our system possible for us?" **Acquisition Contact:** Kendra Hodgson, Director of Marketing & Distribution (413) 584-8500 ext. 2203 kendra@mediaed.org

MENEMSHA FILMS
213 Rose Ave., 2nd Floor Venice CA 90291
Phone: (310) 452-1775 | Fax: (310) 452-3740
http://www.menemshafilms.com

23 titles. Est. 1988. Principals: Neil Friedman, Founder and President

Menemsha Films, founded in 1998 by Neil Friedman, is dedicated to distributing the highest-quality art house films, hand-picked from around the globe. Menemsha Films discovered and represented five Academy Award nominees for five years in a row.

Subjects: Arts, Literature & Music, Comedy, Drama, History **Markets:** Theatrical, Home Video **Marketing:** Printed Catalog, Web Catalog

Acquisition Information: Acquires Narrative Feature **Acquisition Method:** Unknown **Stage:** Unknown

MERRIMACK FILMS
530 Concord Avenue Belmont MA 02478
Phone: (617) 489-4729 (800) 343-5540
bass@merrimack-films.com
http://www.merrimack-films.com

8 titles. Est. 1983. Principals: Henry Bass, President

Merrimack Films produces and distributes DVDs and videos on labor relations. Its products are widely used by colleges in the U.S. and worldwide, as well as by businesses, labor unions, and government agencies.

Subjects: Labor Issues **Markets:** Educational **Specialty:** DVDs and video on labor relations **Titles:** *Struggling Unions, Loose Bolts, What Happened to Saturn?, Rustbelt Phoenix* **Marketing:** Printed Catalog, Web Catalog

Acquisition Information: Acquires Short Doc **Acquisition Method:** Unsolicited Inquiries **Stage:** Unknown **Advance:** No. **Philosophy:** Good labor-management relations are the foundation of a productive economy. **Advice:** We distribute only films on labor relations. **Acquisition Contact:** Henry Bass, President, bass@merrimack-films.com

MICROCINEMA INTERNATIONAL
1636 Bush Street, Suite 2 San Francisco CA 94110
Phone: (415) 447-9750 (713) 412-5120 | Fax: (509) 351-1530
info@microcinema.com
http://www.microcinema.com

360 titles. Est. 1996. Principals: Joel S. Bachar, Founder and President, Patrick Kwiatkowski, Founder and CEO

Founded in 1996, Microcinema International is a leading international rights manager, exhibitor, and specialty markets distributor of the "moving image arts." Microcinema International specializes in the acquisition, exhibition, and distribution of independently produced works of an artistic and socially relevant nature.

Through the Blackchair Collection and Microcinema International DVD, a unique and diverse catalog of international DVD titles are distributed into retail, wholesale, online, and institutional sales channels worldwide. New delivery platforms such as mobile TV, video on demand, podcasting, and mobile telephony are also used to reach new audiences around the globe.

Subjects: Animation, Arts, Literature & Music, Biography, Experimental/Avant Garde, Family, LGBT, Politics & Government **Markets:** Nontheatrical, Educational, Home Video, Web **Specialty:** DVDs: Art and Artist, Short Subject, Experimental, Animation **Titles:** *Almond Blossoms, In Winter Still, Painted Tales Volume 1* **Territories:** Worldwide **Marketing:** Printed Catalog, Web Catalog, One Sheets, Direct Mail

Acquisition Information: Acquires Doc Feature, Short Narrative, Short Doc, Animation, Experimental **Acquisition Method:** Solicited Only, Festivals, Markets, Other **Stage:** Finished **Philosophy:** Our mission is to seek out, curate, exhibit, promote, and distribute compelling works to a broad audience via existing and emerging media. This mission is realized through exhibition-based events, web-based platforms, educational outreach, modern marketing techniques, and digital and physical distribution. **Acquisition Contact:** Joel S. Bachar, President (415) 447-9750 info@microcinema.com

MILESTONE FILM & VIDEO
P.O. Box 128 Harrington Park NJ 07640-1414
Phone: (800) 603-1104 | Fax: (201) 767-3035
milefilms@gmail.com
http://www.milestonefilms.com

150 titles. Est. 1990. Principals: Dennis Doros and Amy Heller, Co-Founders

The Milestone Film & Video collection ranges from the earliest days of the cinema, to the golden age of the silents, to the postwar foreign film renaissance, to new American independent features, documentaries, and foreign films. Some of the directors in the collection are: Alfred Hitchcock, Hiroshi Teshigahara, Luchino Visconti, Pier Paolo Pasolini, Takeshi Kitano, Jane Campion, Hirokazu Kore-eda, Manoel de Oliveira, and Charles Burnett. Because of their background in restoration and preservation, company principals Amy Heller and Dennis Doros make sure that 35mm prints always come from the best source materials and video masters are created at the best film-to-tape studios in the country and subtitles are carefully translated by native speakers.

Subjects: Archival, Arts, Literature & Music, Biography, Comedy, Drama, Experimental/Avant Garde, History, Human Rights, Immigration, Labor Issues, Multicultural Perspective, Nature, Politics & Government, Religion, Sociology, Women's Issues **Markets:** Theatrical, Home Video, Foreign, Other **Specialty:** Art house film **Titles:** *Why Has Bodhi-Dharma Left for the East?, I Am Cuba, Fireworks, I* **Marketing:** Web Catalog

Acquisition Information: Acquires Narrative Feature, Doc Feature, Short Narrative, Short Doc, Experimental **Acquisition Method:** Unknown **Stage:** Unknown **Venues:** Rotterdam, Toronto, Berlin, Vancouver **Philosophy:** We are dedicated to discovering and distributing films of enduring artistry from both yesterday and today – films that we loved and want to share. **Advice:** E-mails and phone calls must precede mailing DVD or VHS tapes and reviews. **Acquisition Contact:** milefilms@gmail.com

MIRAMAX FILMS

Parent Company: A Division of Walt Disney Company since 1993
161 Avenue of the Americas, 15th Floor New York NY 10013
Phone: (212) 219-4100 | Fax: (212) 941-3880
http://www.miramax.com

550 titles. Est. 1979. 500 employees. Principals: Harvey Weinstein, Robert
Weinstein, Co-Chairmen; Agnes Mentre, Executive VP of Acquisitions (NY
Based); Matt Brodlie, Senior VP of Acquisitions (LA Based)

Miramax Films is a motion picture production, financing, and worldwide
distribution company committed to its mission of providing audiences with high
quality, innovative, and risk-taking films from the world's best filmmakers,
established and emerging. Miramax Films is an indirect wholly owned subsidiary
of The Walt Disney Company.

Subjects: Action/Adventure, Arts, Literature & Music, Comedy, Drama, Family,
LGBT, Gender Issues, Women's Issues **Markets:** Theatrical, Home Video, Cable
TV **Specialty:** Art house film **Titles:** *Pulp Fiction, Cinema Paradiso, The Crying
Game, Shakespeare in Love, In the Bedroom, Life Is Beautiful, Red, The Importance of
Being Earnest, Bridget Jones's Diary* **Marketing:** Printed Catalog, Web Catalog

Acquisition Information: Acquires Narrative Feature **Acquisition Method:**
Festivals, Markets **Stage:** Unknown **Venues:** Sundance, Toronto, Cannes

MONARCH FILMS, INC./BEATNIK HOME ENTERTAINMENT

368 Danforth Avenue Jersey City NJ 07305
Phone: (201) 451-3770 (888) 229-4260 | Fax: (201) 451-3887
monarchfilms@aol.com
http://www.mfilms.com

300 titles. Est. 1991. Principals: Arthur Skopinsky, CEO

Monarch Films is a domestic and international entertainment sales agency that
distributes single documentaries and documentary series on Current Affairs, Crime
and Punishment, Cultural Affairs, History, Wildlife, Adventure, Reality, Science,
and Social Issues in all media around the world.

Subjects: Arts, Literature & Music, Biography, Experimental/Avant Garde, Gender
Issues, History, Human Rights, Immigration, Labor Issues, Language/Linguistics,
Multicultural Perspective, Nature, Politics & Government, Religion, Sociology,
Women's Issues **Markets:** Home Video, Cable TV, Public TV, Network TV, TV
Syndication, Other **Specialty:** Documentaries, reality and lifestyle programs
Territories: Germany, Japan, the UK, Mexico, Italy, and in the U.S.

Acquisition Information: Acquires Narrative Feature, Doc Feature, Short Narrative, Short Doc, Experimental **Acquisition Method:** Unsolicited Inquiries, Festivals, Markets **Stage:** Treatment, Proposal, Script, Production, Rough Cut, Fine Cut, Finished **Venues:** MIP-DOC, MIP., MIPCOM, AFM, ATF, DISCOP, Sundance Film Festival, Toronto Film Festival, Sunny Side of the Doc, IFFM, and NATPE **Advice:** The company welcomes direct submissions from individual producers or production companies for both international sales through Monarch Films, Inc., and/or for domestic home video and DVD through Beatnik Home Entertainment. The best way to submit programs is through the website, by filling out the Acquisition Submission Form. **Acquisition Contact:** Arthur Skopinsky

MONTEREY MEDIA, INC.
566 Saint Charles Drive Thousand Oaks CA 91360
Phone: (805) 494-7199 | Fax: (805) 496-6061
acquisitions@montereymedia.com
http://www.montereymedia.com

50 titles. Est. 1979.

Monterey Media, Inc., is a privately owned entertainment industry company specializing in the creation, acquisition, distribution, and sale of motion pictures and other programming. Monterey Media is actively engaged in all areas of domestic media, including theatrical distribution, film festivals, and other distinctive venues, television, and home entertainment markets, and is currently increasing its release slate.

Subjects: Action/Adventure, Arts, Literature & Music, Children's Programming, Comedy, Drama, Family, Science, Sports **Markets:** Theatrical, Educational, Home Video **Titles:** *10 Questions for the Dalai Lama, The Blue Butterfly, Bracelet of Bordeaux, Gooby, The Secrets, Winter of Frozen Dreams, imps, The Sensation of Sight* **Marketing:** Web Catalog

Acquisition Information: Acquires Narrative Feature, Doc Feature **Acquisition Method:** Unsolicited Inquiries, Festivals, Markets **Stage:** Finished **Philosophy:** To create a harmonious and productive work environment which services our customers, vendors, staff, and business relationships in a principled and prosperous manner. With centered leadership as our goal, we strive to keep our customers, vendors, and staff informed and serviced and to enable them to reach their full potential. **Advice:** Please visit our website to explore what types of acquisitions may be suitable for submission. Please e-mail your inquiries to acquisitions@montereymedia.com

MUSEUM OF MODERN ART-CIRCULATING FILM/VIDEO LIBRARY
AKA: MoMa
11 West 53rd Street New York NY 10019
Phone: (212) 708-9530 | Fax: (212) 708-9531
circfilm@moma.org
http://ww.moma.org

1300 titles.

The Circulating Film/Video Library of MOMA provides film and video rentals and sales of over 1,300 titles covering the history of film from the 1890s to the present. It also includes an important collection of work by leading video artists and is the sole distributor of the films of Andy Warhol.

Subjects: Arts, Literature & Music, History **Markets:** Theatrical, Other **Specialty:** Independent and classic film and video

Acquisition Information: Acquires Narrative Feature, Doc Feature, Short Narrative, Short Doc, Animation, Experimental **Acquisition Method:** Unknown **Stage:** Unknown

MYPHEDUH FILMS, INC.
2714 Georgia Ave., NW, Washington DC 20001
Phone: 202-234-4755 1-800-524-3895 | Fax: 202-234-5735
sankofa@gmail.com
http://www.sankofa.com

20 titles. Est. 1982. Principals: Haile Gerima, Shirikiana Gerima

Mypheduh Films, Inc., (MFI) was founded by filmmakers to counteract the imbalanced relationship between filmmaker and distributor. Since 1982, it has distributed films by people of African descent from around the world (including Hollywood Black classics) via nontheatrical, educational, and nonconventional routes.

Subjects: Biography, Children's Programming, Family, History, Human Rights, Immigration, Multicultural Perspective, Sociology **Markets:** Nontheatrical, Educational, Home Video **Specialty:** Film and video by people of African descent **Titles:** *Sankofa, Through the Door of No Return*

Acquisition Information: Acquires Narrative Feature, Doc Feature, Short Narrative, Short Doc **Acquisition Method:** Unknown **Stage:** Unknown **Philosophy:** We are filmmakers determined to humbly construct a means of telling our stories through film and video. **Acquisition Contact:** sankofa@gmail.com

MYRIAD PICTURES

3015 Main Street, Suite 400 Santa Monica CA 90405
Phone: (310) 279-4000 | Fax: (310) 279-4001
info@myriadpictures.com
http://www.myriadpictures.com

60 titles. Est. 1988.

Myriad Pictures is an independent entertainment company involved in the
financing, production, and worldwide sales of feature films and television
programming. Helmed by President and CEO Kirk D'Amico, the company holds
a diverse library of both art-house and mainstream commercially successful filmed
programming.

Subjects: Action/Adventure, Comedy, Drama **Markets:** Theatrical **Specialty:** Film
and television programming **Titles:** *People I Know, The Good Girl, Killing Me Softly*
Marketing: Web Catalog

Acquisition Information: Acquires Narrative Feature, Doc Feature **Acquisition
Method:** Unknown **Stage:** Unknown

MYSTIC FIRE VIDEO

P.O. Box 2330 Montauk NY 11954
Phone: (212) 941-0999 (800) 292-9001 | Fax: (212) 941-1443
acquistions@mysticfire.com
http://www.mysticfire.com

200 titles. Est. 1985. Principals: Sheldon Rochlin, Maxine Harris, Co-Founders

Mystic Fire Video specializes in works for the home video and institutional markets
concerned with the physical manifestations of mind and spirit. Subjects include
transformative visions, healing and consciousness, native peoples, relationships,
literati, ancient cultures, society in chaos, and art.

Subjects: Arts, Literature & Music, Biography, Health & Medicine, Religion
Markets: Nontheatrical, Educational, Home Video **Specialty:** Video on new age
and cultural subjects **Marketing:** Web Catalog

Acquisition Information: Acquires Narrative Feature, Doc Feature, Short
Narrative, Short Doc **Acquisition Method:** Unknown **Stage:** Unknown **Advice:**
Send a written description of your finished project via e-mail or fax. Do not send
screeners unless requested.

NATIONAL BLACK PROGRAMMING CONSORTIUM (NBPC)
68 East 131st Street, 7th floor New York NY 10037
Phone: (212) 234-8200 | Fax: (212) 234-7032
info@nbpc.tv
http://www.nbpc.tv

50 titles. Est. 1979. Principals: Jacquie Jones, Executive Director; Leslie Fields-Cruz, Director of Programming

Since 1979, NBPC has been a leading provider on American public television of quality, intelligent, and compelling programming that celebrates the cultural heritage of African Americans and the African Diaspora.

Subjects: Arts, Literature & Music, Biography, Drama, Family, Gender Issues, History, Human Rights, Immigration, Labor Issues, Multicultural Perspective, Politics & Government **Markets:** Cable TV, Public TV, Network TV, TV Syndication **Specialty:** African Americans and African Diaspora **Titles:** *Flag Wars; Daughters of the Dust; Brother to Brother; A Huey P. Newton Story; The Murder of Emmett Till; and Parliament Funkadelic: One Nation Under a Groove*

Acquisition Information: Acquires Narrative Feature, Doc Feature, Short Narrative, Short Doc, Experimental **Acquisition Method:** Unsolicited Inquiries **Stage:** Unknown **Advice:** NBPC seeks projects from producers and directors whose work have the potential for airing on the national or regional public television schedule. Previous NBPC licensed work has aired on PBS Series such as Independent Lens, POV, American Experience, American Masters, and as PBS specials or limited series. NBPC distributes programs regionally through public television distribution systems such as American Public Television (APT) and the National Educational Television Association (NETA). **Acquisition Contact:** misa@nbpc.tv

NATIONAL GEOGRAPHIC TELEVISION
Parent Company: National Geographic Society
1145 17th Street, NW, Washington DC 20036-4688
Phone: (800) 647 5463
http://www.nationalgeographic.com/tv/

200 titles. Est. 1965. 1000 employees.

National Geographic Television (NGT), a subsidiary of the National Geographic Society, focuses on documentary production and works with a number of filmmakers. It produces over 60 hours of programming each year for its National Geographic Specials (broadcast on NBC) and National Geographic Explorer (broadcast on TBS). NGT searches internationally for documentary programming that fits in with the series profile, considering a wide range of subjects including adventure and exploration films, films that tell stories of people around the world whose lifestyles or activities are particularly exotic, unusual or noteworthy, and non-fiction children's programming.

Subjects: Children's Programming, Environmental Issues, Family, Nature, Travel **Markets:** Theatrical, Nontheatrical, Educational, Home Video, Cable TV, Public TV, Network TV, TV Syndication **Specialty:** Documentary series **Titles:** *How It Was: Secrets of Mona Lisa, National Geographic Explorer: Guns in America, The Great Quake* **Marketing:** Printed Catalog, Web Catalog

Acquisition Information: Acquires Doc Feature, Short Doc **Acquisition Method:** Unknown **Stage:** Unknown

NEW & UNIQUE VIDEOS
Parent Company: Crystal Pyramid Productions
7323 Rondel Court San Diego CA 92119
Phone: (619) 644-3000 (619) 698-4336
video@newuniquevideos.com
http://www.newunique.com

25 titles. Est. 1982. Principals: Mark Schulze, CEO

New & Unique Videos specializes in TV and home video distribution, national sponsorship acquisition, direct-mail and mass marketing, and domestic and foreign rights deals. It can help package and market a broadcast-quality title internationally.

Subjects: Arts, Literature & Music, Sports, Women's Issues **Markets:** Nontheatrical, Home Video **Specialty:** Video on sports and other special interests **Titles:** *Full Cycle: A World Odyssey* **Marketing:** Web Catalog

Acquisition Information: Acquires Narrative Feature, Doc Feature **Acquisition Method:** Unknown **Stage:** Finished **Venues:** How-to's, Instructional **Advance:** No. **Philosophy:** The company believes in helping the small independent project producers make and distribute videos worldwide. **Advice:** Call first, from 9am to 6pm Pacific Standard Time. We can help with all aspects of production to distribution – equipment and crew, stock footage sales, packaging and promotion, and worldwide distribution. **Acquisition Contact:** Patricia Mooney

NEW DAY FILMS
90 Route 17M P.O. Box 1084 Harriman NY 10926
Phone: (888) 367-9154 | Fax: (845) 774-2945
curator@newday.com
http://www.newday.com

200 titles. Est. 1972.

New Day Films is a unique member-owned distribution company comprised of more than 100 independent filmmakers. For nearly 35 years, they have worked collectively to distribute their work directly to the audiences that most want and need them. New Day Films specializes in films that move viewers to think deeply about real and often overlooked people, give voice to untold stories of culture and politics, and bring the power of social action to life through artful storytelling.

Subjects: Aging, Arts, Literature & Music, Criminal Justice, Disability, Environmental Issues, Family, LGBT, Gender Issues, Human Rights, Immigration, Labor Issues, Multicultural Perspective, Politics & Government, Religion, Sociology, Women's Issues **Markets:** Theatrical, Nontheatrical, Educational, Home Video, Cable TV, Public TV, Network TV, TV Syndication, Satelitte/DBS **Specialty:** Educational media on social issues **Territories:** U.S. only **Marketing:** Printed Catalog, Web Catalog

Acquisition Information: Acquires Narrative Feature, Doc Feature, Short Narrative, Short Doc, Experimental **Acquisition Method:** Unsolicited Inquiries, Festivals, Markets **Stage:** Finished **Advance:** No.

NEW DIMENSION MEDIA
Parent Company: Questar, Inc.
307 N. Michigan Avenue, Suite 500 Chicago IL 60601
Phone: (312) 642-9400 (800) 288-4456 | Fax: (312) 642-9805
info@ndmquestar.com
http://www.ndmquestar.com

1000 titles. Est. 1978. Principals: Dr. George Holland, Director of Programming and Content;

New Dimension Media provides over 1,000 video titles to school districts, media centers, and ITV stations around the country. NDM produces standards-based original programs and distributes video content in partnership with such distinguished producers as the National Science Foundation, Reader's Digest, A&E, Discovery Channel, Connect with Kids, Marathon (France) & Channel 4 (U.K.).

Subjects: Arts, Literature & Music, Biography, Children's Programming, Environmental Issues, Health & Medicine, History, Human Rights, Immigration, Labor Issues, Nature, Religion, Science, Sociology **Markets:** Educational **Specialty:** Educational media **Marketing:** Web Catalog

Acquisition Information: Acquires Doc Feature **Acquisition Method:** Unknown **Stage:** Unknown **Acquisition Contact:** Dr. George Holland, Director Programming & Content (847) 571-3589 gholland@embarqmail.com

NEW LINE CINEMA
AKA: Fine Line Features, Picturehouse
888 Seventh Avenue, 20th Floor New York NY 10106
Phone: (212) 649-4900 | Fax: (212) 649-4966
http://www.newline.com

500 titles. Est. 1967. Principals: Robert Shaye, Chairman and CEO; Michael Lynne, Co-Chairman and Co-CEO

Founded by Bob Shaye, New Line began as a small distribution company in New York City. Over the past 40 years, New Line has expanded to become a multimedia company with various profitable divisions, having created some of the most successful film franchises in history.

Subjects: Action/Adventure, Animation, Arts, Literature & Music, Children's Programming, Comedy, Criminal Justice, Drama, Environmental Issues, Experimental/Avant Garde, Family, LGBT, Gender Issues, History, Human Rights, Immigration, Labor Issues, Multicultural Perspective, Nature, Politics & Government, Psychology, Religion, Science, Sociology, Sports, Theater, Women's Issues **Markets:** Theatrical, Home Video, Web **Specialty:** Art house and commercial film **Titles:** *He's Just Not That Into You, Ghosts of Girlfriends Past, Journey to the Center of the Earth*

Acquisition Information: Acquires Narrative Feature, Doc Feature **Acquisition Method:** Unknown **Stage:** Unknown **Venues:** Sundance, Cannes, Toronto, Venice, Berlin **Advice:** If you have a completed film or are already underway with production, we would be happy to receive an invitation to view your work at movies@newline.com. Please remember that we are unable to accept unsolicited screenplays or pitches, and that this e-mail address should be used only to invite us to view finished films or production in progress. Any unsolicited screenplays or pitches will be returned without being reviewed.

NEW VIDEO/DOCURAMA
902 Broadway New York NY 10011
Phone: (212) 206-9001 (800) 314-8822 | Fax: (212) 206-9001
info@newvideo.com
http://www.newvideo.com

5000 titles. Est. 1990. Principals: Susan Margolin, COO and Co-Founder

New Video is a leading independent distributor specializing in cutting-edge documentaries, independent films, collectible television series, sports, and classic kids' programming available digitally and on DVD. Home to some of the most prestigious names in entertainment, including A&E, Major League Baseball®, and Scholastic Storybook Treasures, and Docurama Films®, New Video showcases over 5,000 titles in its catalog. Since 1990, the company's mission has been to provide audiences with top-notch special interest programming and to further this goal, New Video has recently expanded into digital distribution developing strategic partnerships with the key outlets including iTunes.

New Video's label, Docurama, is dedicated exclusively to critically acclaimed and cutting edge documentary films for the home entertainment market.

Subjects: Arts, Literature & Music, Biography, Children's Programming, Comedy, Drama, History, Sports, Theater **Markets:** Nontheatrical, Educational, Home Video, Cable TV **Specialty:** Home video and DVD **Titles:** *The Universe, Dr. Quinn, Medicine Woman, Pride and Prejudice, Autism: The Musical* **Marketing:** Web Catalog

Acquisition Information: Acquires Doc Feature **Acquisition Method:** Solicited Only **Stage:** Unknown **Venues:** Sundance, Toronto, DocFest, DoubleTake **Acquistion Contact:** Wholesale sales, acquisitions, and marketing (212) 206-8600 NVG@newvideo.com

NEW YORKER FILMS
Parent Company: Madstone
85 Fifth Avenue, 11th Floor New York NY 10003
Phone: (212) 645-4600 | Fax: (212) 645-4600
info@newyorkerfilms.com
http://www.newyorkerfilms.com

200 titles. Est. 1965. Principals: Dan Talbot, Founder

The company was founded by Daniel Talbot as an outgrowth of his legendary movie house, the New Yorker Theater. Unable to obtain several crucial foreign titles, Talbot was obliged to import them himself. The New Yorker library is now a source for trailblazing works by international women filmmakers.

Subjects: Action/Adventure, Arts, Literature & Music, Biography, Comedy, Drama, Environmental Issues, Experimental/Avant Garde, Family, History, Human Rights, Immigration, Labor Issues, Language/Linguistics, Multicultural Perspective, Sociology **Markets:** Theatrical, Nontheatrical, Home Video **Specialty:** Art house film **Titles:** *Babette*

Acquisition Information: Acquires Narrative Feature, Doc Feature, Experimental **Acquisition Method:** Unknown **Stage:** Unknown

NORTHERN ARTS ENTERTAINMENT, INC.
83 Shays Street Amherst MA 01002
10866 Wilshire Boulevard, #850 Los Angeles, CA 90024
Phone: (413) 268-9301 (310) 481-9911 | Fax: (413) 268-9309
info@NorthernArtsEntertainment.com
http://www.northernartsentertainment.com

60 titles. Est. 1989. 7 employees. Principals: John Lawrence Ré, Chairman; Larry Jackson, President; Anthony Masucci, COO; David Mazor, VP of Distribution; Ava Lazar, VP of Acquisitions

Northern Arts Entertainment, Inc., was founded by filmmakers John Lawrence Ré and David Mazor. In 2000, it expanded to include executive production.

Subjects: Action/Adventure, Aging, Animation, Archival, Arts, Literature & Music, Biography, Children's Programming, Comedy, Criminal Justice, Disability, Drama, Environmental Issues, Experimental/Avant Garde, Family, LGBT, Gender Issues, Health & Medicine, History, Human Rights, Immigration, Labor Issues, Language/Linguistics, Multicultural Perspective, Nature, Politics & Government, Psychology, Regional Profiles & Issues, Religion, Science, Sociology, Sports, Theater, Travel, Women's Issues **Markets:** Theatrical, Nontheatrical, Educational, Home Video, Cable TV, Public TV, Network TV, TV Syndication, Satelitte/DBS, Web, Airline, Foreign **Specialty:** Art house film **Titles:** *Tokyo Decadence* **Marketing:** Web Catalog

Acquisition Information: 3 titles per year. Acquires Narrative Feature, Doc Feature, Short Narrative, Short Doc, Animation, Experimental **Acquisition Method:** Unsolicited Inquiries, Festivals, Markets, Other **Stage:** Treatment, Proposal, Script, Production, Rough Cut, Fine Cut, Finished, Other **Venues:** Cannes, Toronto, Montreal, Sundance, Berlin, Venice **Advance:** Sometimes. **Philosophy:** The company believes in working closely with filmmakers, and that creative marketing and strict cost control is the key to the best possible return for both producer and distributor. **Acquisition Contact:** John Lawrence Ré (323) 422-9099 jlr@NorthernArtsEntertainment.com and Tony Masucci (310) 481-9911 amasucci@NorthernArtsEntertainment.com

OMNI FILM DISTRIBUTION

AKA: Omni Short Film Distribution
11301 W. Olympic Boulevard, Suite 679 West Los Angeles CA 90064
sales@omnifilmdistribution.com
http://www.omnifilmdistribution.com

25 titles.

Omni Film Distribution specializes in short and feature films, foreign language titles, and TV travel.

Subjects: Action/Adventure, Comedy, Drama, Language/Linguistics, Travel **Markets:** Nontheatrical, Home Video **Titles:** *Echo Lake, The Art of the Trash, The Yellow Badge of Courage, Dangerous Toys, Traveling Lite* **Marketing:** Web Catalog

Acquisition Information: Acquires Narrative Feature, Doc Feature, Short Narrative, Short Doc **Acquisition Method:** Unsolicited Inquiries **Stage:** Finished **Advice:** See www.omnifilmdistribution.com/submissions.html

OUTCAST FILMS

P.O. Box 260 New York, NY10032
Phone: (917) 520-7392 | Fax: (845) 774-2945
info@outcast-films.com
http://www.outcast-films.com

20 titles.

Outcast Films is a film distribution company dedicated to the fair and equal representation of media made by or about the diverse lesbian, gay, bisexual, transgender community. Outcast Films outreaches to thousands of teachers, community leaders, activists, policy makers, institutions, and individuals..

Subjects: Gender Issues, LGBT, Women's Issues **Markets:** Educational, Home Video **Titles:** *She's a Boy I Knew, Cruel & Unusual, Rock Bottom, Seeing Red, The Films of Su Friedrich, Pills Profits Protest, Women in Love, Tying the Knot* **Marketing:** Web Catalog

Acquisition Information: Acquires Doc Short, Doc Narratives **Acquisition Method:** Unsolicited Inquiries **Stage:** Finished **Advice for Filmmakers:** Outcast Films is currently seeking films that are socially conscious, progressive, and activist driven. Films must be completed and be of high production value in order to be considered for distribution. If you have a finished film that you think would be of interest to us, please send us a preview tape or DVD of the film, along with a brief synopsis, press kit, promotional material, or any other relevant information to our mailing address. Preview tapes will not be returned unless you supply us with a return envelope and postage.

OUTSIDER PICTURES
1127 9th Street, #104 Santa Monica CA 90403
Phone: (310) 951-0878
info@outsiderpictures.us
http://www.outsiderpictures.us

20 titles.

Outsider Pictures is a motion picture distribution company releasing films in the U.S., Canada and Latin America. It releases 6-8 films per year, building a slate of titles from an acquisitions program and from attaching itself to new U.S. independent features at the pre-production stage.

Subjects: Action/Adventure, Arts, Literature & Music, Comedy, Drama **Markets:** Theatrical **Titles:** *Three Dollars, Buzz, Klimt, London to Brighton* **Marketing:** Web Catalog

Acquisition Information: 6 titles per year. Acquires Narrative Feature **Acquisition Method:** Unsolicited Inquiries **Stage:** Production, Rough Cut, Fine Cut, Finished

PACIFIC ISLANDERS IN COMMUNICATIONS
1221 Kapiolani Boulevard, #6A-4 Honolulu Hawaii 96814
Phone: (808) 591-0059
info@piccom.org
http://www.piccom.org

166 titles. Est. 1991. 10 employees. Principals: Ramsay R. M. Taum, President; Ruth Bolan, Executive Director; Leann Yeung, Director of Operations

Pacific Islanders in Communications (PIC) is a nonprofit organization that tells the stories of Pacific Islanders — the first peoples of Hawaii, Guam, America Samoa, and other Pacific Islands — by supporting, promoting, and developing Pacific Island media content and talent. By funding and distributing film, video, and new media to the broadest possible audience, PIC seeks to generate a deeper understanding of Pacific Island history, culture, and contemporary challenges. PIC also provides scholarships, training, professional development, and community to support media talent.

Subjects: Arts, Literature & Music, Family, History, Human Rights, Multicultural Perspective, Politics & Government, Regional Profiles & Issues **Markets:** Theatrical, Nontheatrical, Educational, Home Video, Public TV, Foreign

Specialty: Film and video by and about Pacific Islanders **Titles:** *Then There Were None, The Hawaiian Sting* **Territories:** Worldwide **Marketing:** Web Catalog

Acquisition Information: Acquires Narrative Feature, Doc Feature **Acquisition Method:** Unsolicited Inquiries **Stage:** Finished **Acquisition Contact:** Ruth Bolan, Executive Director, rbolan@piccom.org and Leann Yeung, Director of Operations, lyeung@piccom.org

PALM PICTURES

76 Ninth Avenue, Suite 1110 New York NY 10001
Phone: (212) 320-3600 212.320.3668 | Fax: (212) 320-3639
cindy.banach@palmpictures.com
http://www.palmpictures.com

220 titles. Est. 1998. 51 employees. Principals: Chris Blackwell, Chairman; David Beal, President; David Koh, Head of Acquisitions and Co-Productions

Palm Pictures, Chris Blackwell's audio/visual entertainment company, produces, acquires, and distributes film, music, and animation projects with a particular focus on the DVD format. Palm Pictures includes the Japanese and international animation company, Manga Entertainment, and the online entertainment destinations, sputnik7 and epitonic. Releasing award-winning films and cutting-edge music projects on the DVD format, Palm has an extensive library including Art house Films, Palm World Voices, The Directors Label Series, and Palm Pictures Video. Each label creates a range of DVDs that are presented with DVD extras and premium added-value pieces.

Subjects: Arts, Literature & Music, Comedy, Drama, Multicultural Perspective **Markets:** Nontheatrical, Home Video **Specialty:** Art house and music film **Titles:** *Sex & Lucia, Dark Days, Scratch, Fulltime Killer, The Cup, Black & White, Lockdown, Basketball Diaries* **Marketing:** Web Catalog

Acquisition Information: Acquires Narrative Feature, Doc Feature **Acquisition Method:** Markets **Stage:** Unknown **Philosophy:** To be artist- and technology-driven. **Advice:** We mostly take projects from agencies and about 20% that is unsolicited. It really helps if you have someone bring the project to someone that they know, giving it an imprima of some sort so that it gets weeded out from the mass of submissions. We are getting an incredible number of submissions because there are fewer and fewer companies that fully finance a project. **Acquisition Contact:** Cindy Banach, Acquisitions, Theatrical, Nontheatrical and Educational Bookings (212) 320-3668 cindy.banach@palmpictures.com and Paul Bain, Direct Sales (212) 320-3631 paul.bain@palmpictures.com

PANORAMA ENTERTAINMENT CORPORATION
125 North Main Street Port Chester NY 10573
Phone: (914) 937-1603 | Fax: (914) 937-8496
panent@aol.com
http://www.panoramaentertainment.com

50 titles. Est. 1987. Principals: Stuart Strutin, President; Steve Florin, VP

Panorama sells, markets, and distributes feature films. It distributes directly to the
U.S. theatrical market, then proceeds to sell home video and all broadcast markets.
Panorama distributes a wide variety of feature products ranging from high concept
adventures, to dramas, comedies, art, family product, and documentaries.
Panorama places pictures in the theatrical, video, foreign, and ancillary marketplace
on a picture-by-picture basis. It releases films city by city, using both national and
local publicists, with intense, carefully constructed grassroots marketing campaigns
keyed to each individual city. This carries over into selling the ancillary markets.
Panorama makes licensing deals with a wide variety of companies with this in
mind.

Subjects: Action/Adventure, Arts, Literature & Music, Comedy, Drama, Family
Markets: Theatrical, Nontheatrical, Home Video, Cable TV, Public TV, Foreign
Specialty: Art house film **Titles:** *Lakeboat, Bang* **Marketing:** Printed Catalog, Web
Catalog

Acquisition Information: Acquires Narrative Feature **Acquisition Method:**
Festivals, Markets **Stage:** Unknown **Philosophy:** We formed the company to
distribute "niche" type product into the marketplace. Our individual film industry
backgrounds were well suited to this philosophy, and we had known each other
prior to forming Panorama. Since we make a conscious effort to limit the number
of films we do distribute at any one time, part of our goal is to establish an
association with the filmmaker. We believe that the film becomes more important
than either the distributor or the filmmaker; thus, our collaborative efforts must
push the product forward.

PAPER TIGER TELEVISION
339 Lafayette Street New York NY 10012
Phone: (212) 420-9045 | Fax: (212) 420-8196
info@papertiger.org
http://www.papertiger.org

340 titles. Est. 1978.

Paper Tiger Television (PTTV) is a nonprofit, volunteer video collective. Through
the production and distribution of its public access series, media literacy/video
production workshops, community screenings, and grassroots advocacy, PTTV

works to challenge and expose the corporate control of mainstream media. PTTV programs analyze and critique issues involving media, culture, and politics.

Subjects: Environmental Issues, Experimental/Avant Garde, LGBT, Gender Issues, Human Rights, Labor Issues, Multicultural Perspective, Politics & Government, Women's Issues **Markets:** Educational, Foreign, Other **Specialty:** Video and television critical of media **Marketing:** Printed Catalog, Web Catalog

Acquisition Information: Acquires Short Doc, Experimental **Acquisition Method:** Solicited Only **Stage:** Unknown **Advance:** No. **Philosophy:** PTTV believes that increasing public awareness of the negative influence of mass media, and involving people in the process of making media, is mandatory for our long-term goal of information equity. **Acquisition Contact:** Maria Byck (212) 420-9045 maria@papertiger.org

PARAMOUNT VANTAGE
5555 Melrose Avenue, Chevalier Building, #212 Los Angeles CA 90038
Phone: (323) 956-2000 | Fax: (323) 862-1212
http://www.paramountclassics.com

30 titles. Est. 1998.

Paramount Vantage is the specialty film division of Paramount Pictures, which is part of the entertainment operations of Viacom, Inc., one of the leading global entertainment content companies.

Subjects: Action/Adventure, Comedy, Drama, Experimental/Avant Garde, Family **Markets:** Theatrical, Foreign **Specialty:** Art house film **Titles:** *A Mighty Heart, Into the Wild There Will Be Blood*

Acquisition Information: Acquires Narrative Feature, Doc Feature **Acquisition Method:** Unknown **Stage:** Unknown

PASSION RIVER FILMS
416 Main St., 2nd Floor Metuchen NJ 08840
Phone: (732) 321-0711 | Fax: (732) 321-4105
http://www.passionriver.com

250 titles.

Passion River Films is an independent film and documentary distributor that provides marketing services for independent films. Utilizing its network of DVD movie wholesalers, mass merchant retailers, and libraries, Passion River Films markets independent films and documentary movies through a variety of traditional and non-traditional film marketing methods.

Subjects: Action/Adventure, Children's Programming, Comedy, Disability, Drama, Family, Health & Medicine, History, Multicultural Perspective, Nature, Politics & Government, Sociology, Sports **Markets:** Theatrical, Educational, Home Video **Titles:** *Apprehension, Tomorrow's Nobody, Dr. Bronner's Magic Soapbox* **Marketing:** Web Catalog

Acquisition Information: Acquires Narrative Feature, Doc Feature **Acquisition Method:** Unsolicited Inquiries **Stage:** Finished **Advance:** No. **Advice:** We welcome film submissions from filmmakers and sales agents. To submit your project, please fill out and send our acquisition form at www.passionriver.com/about-us.php?sub=submissions. We receive hundreds of films every month. Please note that it may take several weeks for your submission to be reviewed.

PERIPHERAL PRODUCE

P.O. Box 40835 Portland OR 97240
info@peripheralproduce.com
http://www.peripheralproduce.com

14 titles. Est. 1996. Principals: Matt McCormick

Peripheral Produce is a video label that started distributing experimental film and video compilations in 1996. Born out of a screening series of the same name, Peripheral Produce currently represents 26 artists and has released 14 titles. Three are multi-artist compilations and the remaining feature the work of one artist or collective. Peripheral Produce was founded in Portland, Oregon by filmmaker Matt McCormick with the intention of creating an outlet for experimental film and video to be purchased and collected by the general public. With small independent record labels serving as a model, Peripheral Produce compiles the work of selected artists and packages it for easy consumption.

Subjects: Animation, Biography, Experimental/Avant Garde, History, Politics & Government, Sociology **Markets:** Nontheatrical, Educational **Specialty:** Underground video **Titles:** *Nest of Tens, The Auto-Cinematic Video Mix Tape, The House of Sweet Magic,* Artists include: Bill Brown, Naomi Uman, Miranda July, Matt McCormick **Marketing:** Printed Catalog, Web Catalog

Acquisition Information: Acquires Narrative Feature, Doc Feature, Short Narrative, Short Doc, Experimental **Acquisition Method:** Solicited Only, Festivals **Stage:** Finished **Venues:** NY Underground Film Festival, PDX Film Festival, CVFF, Sundance **Philosophy:** The company does not want to be confused with the entertainment industry. **Advice:** Know what you are getting yourself into. Know where you are sending tapes. Go to a show, attend an event, buy a tape – before you announce that you want to be involved with the company. **Acquisition Contact:** info@peripheralproduce.com pdxfilmfest@peripheralproduce.com

PICTURE START FILMS
New York NY
Phone: (212) 677-8000 | Fax: (212) 677-3574
ec@picturestartfilms.com
http://www.picturestartfilms.com

40 titles. 50 employees.

At the core of Picture Start Films is director/producer Elliot Caplan whose work includes paintings, drawings and prints, photographs, films, videos, writings, media installations, and theatrical media for music, opera, and dance. Caplan is the creator of acclaimed documentaries ranging from the 90-minute *Cage/Cunningham* to an Emmy Award-winning segment produced for PBS on the completed restoration of the New York Public Library's beautiful Rose Reading Room.

Subjects: Arts, Literature & Music **Markets:** Theatrical **Marketing:** Web Catalog

Acquisition Information: Acquires Doc Feature, Short Doc **Acquisition Method:** Unknown **Stage:** Unknown

PICTURE THIS! ENTERTAINMENT
Parent Company: DW Diversified, Inc.
7471 Melrose Avenue, Suite 7 P.O. Box 46872 Los Angeles CA 90046
Phone: (323) 852-1398 | Fax: (323) 658-7265
acq2008gen@picturethisent.com
http://www.PictureThisEntertainment.com

110 titles. Est. 1984. 6 employees. Principals: Douglas C. Witkins, President/CEO

Picture This! Entertainment specializes in gay, lesbian, bisexual, homoerotic, and coming-of-age features and shorts.

Subjects: Comedy, Drama, Experimental/Avant Garde, LGBT, History, Human Rights, Multicultural Perspective **Markets:** Theatrical, Nontheatrical, Home Video, Web, Foreign **Titles:** *Come Undone, A Love To Hide, O Fantasma, Boys Briefs 1-5* **Territories:** United States and Canada **Marketing:** Printed Catalog, Web Catalog, Direct Mail

Acquisition Information: 9 titles per year. Acquires Narrative Feature, Short Narrative **Acquisition Method:** Festivals, Markets **Stage:** Rough Cut, Fine Cut, Finished **Advance:** Yes. **Philosophy:** A recognized trailblazer in distribution for

almost 25 years, DW Diversified, Inc., through its labels Picture This!
Entertainment and Picture This! Home Video, proudly brings uncompromising
and enlightening motion picture fare to discriminating audiences throughout
North America. Through its slate of films, the company has proven its desire to
push the envelope and disturb the sleeping masses. **Advice:** We are always looking
for gay/lesbian or edgy coming-of-age titles. Send us an e-mail inquiry before
submitting the film. Include excellent still images and any unusual promotional
material you may have. Check out our website and trailers to see what works best
for our company. **Acquisition Contact:** Jason Fox
acq2008gen@picturethisent.com

PLEXIFILM

Parent Company: A Division of Plexigroup, Inc.
61 Greenpoint Ave., #505 Brooklyn NY 11222
Phone: (718) 643-7300 | Fax: (718) 643-7320
distribution@plexifilm.com
http://www.plexifilm.com

35 titles. Est. 2001. 10 employees. Principals: Gary Hustwit, Sean Anderson, Co-
Founders

Plexifilm is an independent DVD label and film production company co-founded
by Gary Hustwit (formerly VP of Salon.com) and Sean Anderson (formerly
Director of DVD Development of The Criterion Collection) in 2001. Plexifilm
produces original films, releases films theatrically, and produces, distributes and
markets DVDs. Its policy is to apply the finest technical and editorial treatment to
every project it releases, from guerilla films to obscure foreign features to
groundbreaking documentaries.

Subjects: Arts, Literature & Music, Biography, Experimental/Avant Garde, History
Markets: Theatrical, Nontheatrical, Home Video **Specialty:** Home video **Titles:**
*Benjamin Smoke, Ciao! Manhattan, Hell House, Helvetica, 13 Most Beautiful... Songs
for Andy Warhol's Screen Tests* **Marketing:** Web Catalog

Acquisition Information: Acquires Doc Feature **Acquisition Method:** Unknown
Stage: Unknown **Philosophy:** Our goals are to expand the variety of films available
on DVD and to champion lesser-known-yet-amazing indie directors. We believe
that the audience for DVDs has grown to the point where it can support non-
blockbuster films and video releases of all shapes and sizes. Our editorial strategy is
simple: we release films that we like. **Acquisition Contact:** dvd@plexifilm.com

POLYCHROME PICTURES
434 Avenue of the Americas, 6th Floor New York NY 10011
Phone: (212) 353-5084 | Fax: (212) 353-5083
info@polychromepictures.com
http://www.polychromepictures.com

60 titles. Est. 2005.

Polychrome Pictures is a home entertainment producer and distributor with an eclectic slate of drama, comedy, urban, music, and special interest titles.

Subjects: Action/Adventure, Arts, Literature & Music, Comedy, Drama **Markets:** Theatrical, Home Video, Web **Titles:** *What We Do, Eddie Black Story, Destination Fame* **Marketing:** Web Catalog

Acquisition Information: Acquires Narrative Feature **Acquisition Method:** Unknown **Stage:** Unknown   acquisitions@polychromepictures.com

PORCHLIGHT ENTERTAINMENT
11050 Santa Monica Blvd., 3rd Floor Los Angeles CA 90025
Phone: (310) 477-8400 | Fax: (310) 477-5555
info@porchlight.com
http://www.porchlight.com

550 titles. Est. 1995. 25 employees. Principals: Bruce Johnson, President; William Baumann, Executive VP, CFO, and COO; Michael Jacobs, SVP of Worldwide Sales; Zac Reeder, Head of Acquisitions

PorchLight Entertainment is one of the world's leading independent suppliers of high quality entertainment to audiences throughout the world. Founded as a production company in 1995 by Bruce Johnson and William Baumann, PorchLight has expanded into several related businesses including worldwide program distribution, DVD distribution, licensing and merchandising, digital media and educational media. A specialist in children's and family programming, the company has produced nearly 400 episodes of animation and over 40 live action movies. A frequent co-producer, PorchLight values creativity, collaboration, and high quality filmed entertainment, working closely with a large number of producers, artists, writers, and creative talent from around the world. PorchLight's distribution library consists of more than 1,500 episodes and 200 movies distributed under three labels: PorchLight, Ocean Park Pictures/Ocean Park Home Entertainment, and PorchLight Inspire.

Subjects: Animation, Children's Programming, Family **Markets:** Theatrical, Nontheatrical, Home Video, Cable TV, Public TV, Network TV, TV Syndication, Satelitte/DBS, Web, Airline, Foreign **Specialty:** Family programs for television

Titles: *Wild Grizzly, John John in the Sky; Ricochet River, Wind River, Heartwood*
Marketing: Web Catalog

Acquisition Information: Acquires Narrative Feature, Doc Feature, Short
Narrative, Short Doc **Acquisition Method:** Unsolicited Inquiries, Festivals,
Markets **Stage:** Production, Rough Cut, Fine Cut, Finished **Venues:** Sundance,
IFP, Heartland, Montreal, Banff TV Fest, Cannes, SXSW, Cinequest, also smaller
fests like Dances with Films, Marco Island **Philosophy:** PorchLight wants to build
the most trusted name in family entertainment. It is a young and aggressive
company that enjoys the challenge of working in a business dominated by the
studios. **Advice:** We are always eager to look at completed films. Please send a VHS
screening cassette or DVD along with a letter describing the budget, format the
film was shot on (eg. 35mm), cast, synopsis, and what rights are available.   Please
see the form at http://www.porchlight.com/submissions.asp; PorchLight is only
considering finished films for acquisition at this time. **Acquisition Contact:** Robert
Yu, Vice President of Acquisitions (310) 477-8400 ext. 269 ryu@porchlight.com

PUBLIC BROADCASTING SERVICE
1320 Braddock Place Alexandria VA 22314
Phone: (703) 739-5000 | Fax: (703) 739-0775
http://www.pbs.org

2000 titles. Est. 1969. Principals: Pat Mitchell, President and CEO; Jacoba Atlas,
John Wilson, Co-Chief Programming Executives

PBS, with its 356 member stations, aims to offer all Americans – from every walk
of life – the opportunity to explore new ideas and new worlds through television
and online content. Each week, PBS reaches more than 65 million people with
programming that expores the worlds of science, history, nature, and public affairs;
expresses diverse viewpoints; showcases premier children's television programming,
and highlights world-class drama and performances. PBS's broad array of programs
has been consistently honored by the industry's most coveted award competitions.
Teachers of children from pre-K through 12th grade turn to PBS for digital content
and services.

Subjects: Arts, Literature & Music, Biography, Children's Programming, Criminal
Justice, Environmental Issues, Family, Gender Issues, Health & Medicine, History,
Human Rights, Multicultural Perspective, Politics & Government, Science,
Women's Issues **Markets:** Nontheatrical, Educational, Home Video, Public TV
Specialty: Educational video and television **Titles:** *The Civil War, Masterpiece: The
Complete Jane Austen Collection* **Marketing:** Web Catalog

Acquisition Information: Acquires Narrative Feature, Doc Feature, Short Doc
Acquisition Method: Unsolicited Inquiries **Stage:** Treatment, Proposal, Finished
Philosophy: Our mission is to inform, to inspire, and to educate. We believe that

the content we develop, fund, and schedule can contribute to a more healthy society and that our programs should encourage the active involvement of citizens to trust, connect, and act collectively to address social challenges. PBS aims to increase awareness, provide multiple viewpoints, treat complex social issues completely, provide forums for deliberation, and strengthen ties between our viewers and their communities. **Acquisition Contact:** Steven Gray, Vice President of Program Scheduling & Editorial Management (703) 739-5295 (fax) and Linda Simensky, Senior Director, Children's Programming (703) 739-7506 (fax)

PYRAMID MEDIA

AKA: Pyramid Film and Video
P.O. Box 1048 Santa Monica CA 90406
Phone: (310) 398-6149 (800) 421-2304 | Fax: (310) 398-7869
info@pyramidmedia.com
http://www.pyramidmedia.com

650 titles. Est. 1960. Principals: Randolph Wright, President; Denise Adams, VP

Pyramid Media is a distributor and producer of films, videos, and interactive media designed to teach, train, and entertain. The company represents established filmmakers as well as student producers. Marketing targets are schools, colleges, universities, libraries, religious groups, nonprofit organizations, and health and medical institutions.

Subjects: Animation, Arts, Literature & Music, Health & Medicine, Psychology, Women's Issues **Markets:** Nontheatrical, Educational, Home Video **Specialty:** Educational media **Titles:** *Beautiful Resistance, Beginning Pediatric Nursing* series **Territories:** Worldwide **Marketing:** Web Catalog

Acquisition Information: 5 titles per year. Acquires Short Narrative, Short Doc, Animation **Acquisition Method:** Unsolicited Inquiries, Festivals **Stage:** Finished **Advance:** Sometimes. **Advice:** If you are a producer with a film or video that you would like Pyramid to consider for distribution, e-mail or telephone us. We will be happy to provide you with information about distribution and the nontheatrical marketplace from our unique perspective as filmmakers and distributors. **Acquisition Contact:** rwright@pyramidmedia.com info@pyramidmedia.com

QUESTAR

AKA: International Video Network
307 N. Michigan Ave, Suite 500 Chicago IL 60601-5305
Phone: (312) 266-9400 | Fax: (312) 266-9523
info@questarhomevideo.com
http://www.questar1.com

200 titles. Principals: Albert J. Nader, Chairman

Questar is a worldwide distributor of television programming.

Subjects: Arts, Literature & Music, Biography, Children's Programming, Family, History, Nature **Markets:** Nontheatrical, Educational, Home Video, Cable TV, Public TV, TV Syndication **Specialty:** Worldwide television and home video **Marketing:** Web Catalog

Acquisition Information: Acquires Narrative Feature, Doc Feature **Acquisition Method:** Unknown **Stage:** Unknown **Philosophy:** Providing timeless and collectible programs that can be watched time and time again.

REEL MEDIA INTERNATIONAL, INC.

4516 Lovers Lane, Suite 178 Dallas TX 75225
Phone: (214) 521-3301 | Fax: (214) 522-3448
reelmedia@aol.com
http://www.reelmediaintl.com

2600 titles. Principals: Tom T. Moore, President and CEO; Shannon Moore, Director of Production

Reel Media International, Inc., is an international, full-service distribution company, supplying video companies, satellite, cable, network, TV stations, DVD manufacturers, and Internet broadcasters worldwide with a wide range of motion pictures, TV series, documentaries, and sports programs. Its classic movie library has over 2,600 movies from the earliest days of silent films to the 1990s. Reel Media International, Inc., also seeks to acquire quality productions for international licensing.

Subjects: Animation, Arts, Literature & Music, Drama, History, Sports **Markets:** Nontheatrical, Cable TV, Network TV, Satelitte/DBS, Web, Foreign **Specialty:** All genres **Titles:** *Death Drug, Tramps, Birds of Passage, Riding the Rails* **Territories:** Internet **Marketing:** Web Catalog

Acquisition Information: Acquires Narrative Feature **Acquisition Method:** Unknown **Stage:** Unknown **Acquisition Contact:** reelmedia@aol.com

REGENT ENTERTAINMENT

10990 Wilshire Blvd., Penthouse Los Angeles CA 90024
Phone: (310) 806-4288 | Fax: (310) 806-4268
info@regententertainment.com
http://www.regententertainment.com

85 titles. Principals: Stephen P. Jarchow, Chairman and CEO; Paul Colichman, President; John Lambert, President of Domestic Distribution and Acqusitions

Regent finances, produces, and distributes award-winning, theatrical and television motion pictures. With offices in Los Angeles, California and Dallas, Texas, the company produces and distributes at least 20 feature films annually. The company acquires films for distribution and maintains a substantial and expanding digitized library of over 3,500 titles. Regent has its own full-service motion picture studio (Regent Studios, LLC), international sales force (Regent Worldwide Sales, LLC), theatrical releasing (Regent Releasing, LLC), and movie theaters (Regent Theaters, LLC). Regent's principle mission involves using its position as a premier producer and distributor of high quality, profitable motion pictures, to build a valuable library of motion picture copyrights and distribution rights.

Subjects: Action/Adventure, Drama, Family, LGBT, Women's Issues **Markets:** Theatrical, Foreign **Specialty:** Feature film **Titles:** *Little Ashes, The World Unseen, 7 Things To Do Before I'm 30, Gods and Monsters* **Territories:** National, International **Marketing:** Web Catalog

Acquisition Information: Acquires Narrative Feature, Doc Feature **Acquisition Method:** Solicited Only **Stage:** Unknown **Venues:** Sundance, Toronto, AFM, MIFED **Philosophy:** Regent's principle mission involves using its position as a premier producer and distributor of high quality, profitable motion pictures, to build a valuable library of motion picture copyrights and distribution rights. **Acquisition Contact:** John Lambert, President of Regent Releasing, LLC; Helene Nielsen Beal, Director of Theatrical Distribution and Marketing, Regent Releasing, LLC

RHAPSODY FILMS
46-2 Becket Hill Road Lyme CT 06371
Phone: (860) 434-3610 | Fax: (860) 434-6201
rhapsodyinc@prodigy.net
http://rhapsodyfilms.com/catalog/

24 titles. Est. 1982. Principals: Bruce Ricker, President; Tim Timpanoro, VP

Rhapsody Films is devoted exclusively to documentary and dramatic films and
videos on music topics (jazz, blues, world, modern, gospel, country) including
performances and portraits.

Subjects: Arts, Literature & Music, Biography **Markets:** Nontheatrical, Home
Video, Web **Specialty:** Documentaries and features on music **Titles:** *Tony Bennett:
The Music Never Ends* **Territories:** Internet **Marketing:** Web Catalog

Acquisition Information: Acquires Doc Feature **Acquisition Method:** Unknown
Stage: Unknown

RHINO ENTERTAINMENT
Parent Company: Warner Music Group
http://www.rhino.com

250 titles. Est. 1978.

Co-founded by Richard Foos and Harold Bronson, Rhino Entertainment began
representing novelty records and eventually expanded into archival reissues and
definitive anthologies and artists' series. In 1985, it established Rhino Home Video
to reach the market for oddball cult films and classic TV programs. In 1991, it
created Kid Rhino to gain a foothold in the rapidly expanding children's
marketplace.

Subjects: Archival, Arts, Literature & Music, Comedy, Drama, History **Markets:**
Nontheatrical, Home Video **Titles:** *The Ramones: It's Alive 1974-1996, Mystery
Science Theater 3000, My Little Pony: The Movie* **Marketing:** Web Catalog

Acquisition Information: Acquires Narrative Feature, Doc Feature **Acquisition
Method:** Unknown **Stage:** Unknown **Philosophy:** We look forward to releasing
CDs and videos – with the same high quality and irreverent attitude that you've
come to expect – for many years to come.

RIALTO PICTURES
45 E 72nd Street New York NY 10021
Phone: (212) 620-0986
rialto.media@verizon.net
http://www.rialtopictures.com

50 titles. Est. 1987.

Rialto Pictures specializes as a reissue distributor.
Subjects: Archival, Arts, Literature & Music, Drama, History **Markets:** Theatrical,
Nontheatrical, Home Video **Specialty:** Classic films and restorations **Marketing:**
Printed Catalog, Web Catalog

Acquisition Information: Acquires Narrative Feature **Acquisition Method:**
Unknown **Stage:** Unknown

RIGEL INDEPENDENT DISTRIBUTION AND ENTERTAINMENT
4201 Wilshire Boulevard, Suite 555 Los Angeles CA 90010
Phone: (323) 954-8555 | Fax: (323) 954-8592
info@rigel.tv
http://www.rigel.tv/index.asp

60 titles. Est. 1993. Principals: John Laing, President and CEO; Kristie Smith, Vice
President of Administration and Worldwide Distribution Services; Sherrie
Guerrero, Vice President of International Sales; Bryan Hambleton, International
Television Sales

Since its establishment in 1993, Rigel Entertainment has specialized in the
production and worldwide distribution of top quality prime time television
programming. Rigel Entertainment has amassed one of the industry's largest
libraries of network-quality movies, series and mini-series, with major international
stars and the most celebrated creative talent in television. To find the best
properties that address the needs of programmers, and the producers who can best
bring them to life, Rigel has set up an aggressive development division to option
new projects and transform them into big-budget, must-see television events.

Subjects: Action/Adventure, Biography, Comedy, Drama, Family **Markets:** Cable
TV, TV Syndication, Foreign **Specialty:** All genres **Titles:** *Max Havoc, 13 Mary
Higgins Clark, Uniersal Soldier II, Blonde and Blonder* **Territories:** Worldwide
Marketing: Web Catalog

Acquisition Information: Acquires Narrative Feature, Doc Feature **Acquisition
Method:** Unknown **Stage:** Unknown **Philosophy:** Rigel Entertainment combines
the accessibility of a boutique with the programming power of a major. The
company looks at broadcasters as partners, and through its years of operation, Rigel

has cultivated successful alliances with broadcasters by paying careful attention to their needs and goals. **Acquisition Contact:** Kristie Smith

RKO PICTURES

1875 Century Park East, Suite 2140 Los Angeles CA 90067
Phone: (310) 277-0707 (212) 644 0600 | Fax: (310) 226-2490
info@rko.com
http://www.rko.com

2000 titles. Est. 1929. 35 employees. Principals: Ted Hartley, Chairman and CEO

With a legacy that includes classic films like *Citizen Kane, King Kong*, and *It's a Wonderful Life*, the modern RKO Pictures produces, finances, and distributes both original entertainment and remakes of its classic films. Led by Chairman/CEO Ted Hartley, RKO exploits its brand and intellectual property assets and develops businesses and entertainment properties for production and distribution. RKO's production strategy includes devoting resources to the repositioning of its famous classic library for current audiences as it develops other businesses and entertainment properties. The company seeks out additional distribution and co-financing ventures for new productions as well as for sequels, remakes, and live stage productions based upon its library of titles.

RKO is also launching its Roseblood Movie Company, which produces scary, youth driven, moderately budgeted genre fare of classic RKO films, including a joint venture with Twisted Pictures, the producers of the highly successful *Saw* franchise.

Subjects: Action/Adventure, Arts, Literature & Music, Comedy, Drama **Markets:** Theatrical, Home Video **Specialty:** All genres **Titles:** *Ritual, Shade, Milk Money, Holiday Affair*

Acquisition Information: Acquires Narrative Feature **Acquisition Method:** Unknown **Stage:** Unknown **Advice:** Send programs through an agent or a lawyer. **Acquisition Contact:** Doris Schwartz, production, marketing, public relations, and corporate communications; and Susan Taigman, financial and business planning, human resources, operations, IT, and office administration

ROADSIDE ATTRACTIONS
421 South Beverly Drive, 8th Floor Beverly Hills CA 90212
Phone: (310) 789-4710 | Fax: (310) 789-4711
info@roadsideattractions.com
http://www.roadsideattractions.com

50 titles. Est. 2003. Principals: Howard Cohen, Co-President; Eric D'Arbeloff, Co-President

Roadside Attractions is an independent film distribution company.

Subjects: Action/Adventure, Comedy, Drama **Markets:** Theatrical, Home Video, Cable TV **Titles:** *The Cove, Battle For Terra, The September Issue* **Marketing:** Printed Catalog, Web Catalog

Acquisition Information: 5 titles per year. Acquires Narrative Feature, Doc Feature **Acquisition Method:** Festivals, Markets **Stage:** Finished **Acquisition Contact:** Howard Cohen howardc@roadsideattractions.com

ROXIE RELEASING
AKA: Roxie Cinema
Parent Company: The Roxie
3125 16th Street San Francisco CA 94103
Phone: (415) 431-3611 | Fax: (415) 431-2822
bill@roxie.com
http://www.roxie.com

10 titles. Est. 1984. 4 employees. Principals: Bill Banning, CEO; Rick Norris, President; Alan Holt; Rachel Hart

Roxie Releasing, an independent film distributor most notably responsible for the 30th anniversary re-release of George Romero's *Night of the Living Dead*. Roxie Releasing currently specializes in documentaries and features, and is associated with the Roxie Theater in California.

Subjects: Action/Adventure, Arts, Literature & Music, Biography, Comedy, Drama, Environmental Issues, LGBT, Gender Issues, History, Human Rights, Politics & Government, Psychology, Women's Issues **Markets:** Theatrical, Nontheatrical, Home Video, Cable TV, Public TV, Network TV, TV Syndication **Specialty:** Art house film (independent, documentary, foreign language) **Titles:** *Forbidden Lie$, Warchild, Rivers and Tides: Andy Goldsworthy Working with Time, Biggie & Tupac, The Days of Nick Drake* **Marketing:** Web Catalog, One Sheets

Acquisition Information: 2 titles per year. Acquires Narrative Feature, Doc Feature **Acquisition Method:** Unsolicited Inquiries, Festivals, Markets **Stage:** Fine Cut,

Finished **Venues:** Cannes, Berlin, Rotterdam, Sundance, Vancouver, Montreal. We have many favorite exhibitors. **Advance:** Yes. **Philosophy:** We only distribute films we absolutely love. **Advice:** It's never too early to begin emphasizing public relations and putting together publicity materials, especially great stills (for one-sheets, newspaper, and web advertising). It never hurts to have a great "hook." **Acquisition Contact:** Bill Banning (415) 431-3611 bill@roxie.com and Rick Norris (415) 431-3611 rick@roxie.com

SAMUEL GOLDWYN FILMS
1133 Broadway, Suite 926 New York NY 10010-7910
Phone: (212) 367-9435 | Fax: (212) 367-0853
info@samuelgoldwynfilms.com
http://www.samuelgoldwynfilms.com/

150 titles. Est. 1979. Principals: Samuel Goldwyn, Jr., CEO; Meyer Gottleib, President; Tom Quinn, VP of Acquisitions

Samuel Goldwyn Films is a major, independently owned and operated motion-picture company. The company develops, produces, and distributes innovative feature films and documentaries, working with both world renowned and emerging writers and filmmakers.

Subjects: Action/Adventure, Comedy, Drama, Health & Medicine **Markets:** Theatrical, Home Video, Cable TV **Specialty:** Art house film **Titles:** *Supersize Me, Brothers at War, The Merry Gentlemen, American Violet*

Acquisition Information: 5 titles per year. Acquires Narrative Feature, Doc Feature **Acquisition Method:** Festivals, Markets **Stage:** Unknown **Venues:** Cannes **Philosophy:** Story is king. We are committed to filmed entertainment offering original voices in uniquely told stories.

SCHLESSINGER MEDIA
Parent Company: Libarary Video Company
7 East Wynnewood Road Wynnewood PA 19096
Phone: (800) 843-3620
submissions@libraryvideo.com
http://www.libraryvideo.com

1000 titles. Est. 1985.

For 15 years, Schlessinger Media's video productions and licensed programs have become staples in schools and public libraries throughout North America. With over 1,000 originally produced and licensed videos, this dynamic programming division of Library Video Company has set the standard for outstanding supplemental learning in and out of the classroom. The Schlessinger Media library focuses on a comprehensive core-curricular collection for grades K-8 as well as grades 9-12. Programs are available on VHS and DVD, and are now available in digitized formats to support digital delivery systems.

Subjects: Children's Programming, Family **Markets:** Educational **Specialty:** Educational media

Acquisition Information: Acquires Doc Feature, Short Doc **Acquisition Method:** Unsolicited Inquiries **Stage:** Finished **Advice:** When submitting a product (Audiobook, DVD, or Video) for consideration in the Library Video Company catalog, we ask that you provide us with the following information: A sample of the completed program and its packaging; product information or sell-sheets describing your program, as well as information about any relevant awards or reviews; the product's availability date; and the suggested retail price (SRP) as well as any other relevant pricing information (please note: We do not include products that are sold at a lower SRP elsewhere and offered to the school and library market at a higher SRP); the production year or copyright date of the program and, when applicable, its running time, format, system requirements, and technical support phone numbers; complete contact information including: name, phone number, fax number, and mailing address.

SCREEN MEDIA FILMS
757 Third Ave., Third Floor New York NY 10017
Phone: (212) 308-1790 | Fax: (212) 308-1791
info@screenmediafilms.net
http://www.screenmediafilms.net

1000 titles. Est. 2001.

Screen Media Films (SMF) acquires rights to high quality, independent feature films for all of the U.S. and Canada. SMF distributes films theatrically, on home video (through an exclusive distribution arrangement with Universal Studios Home Entertainment), and to all television outlets (through its parent company Screen Media Ventures).

Subjects: Action/Adventure, Children's Programming, Comedy, Drama, Family **Markets:** Theatrical, Home Video, Cable TV, Public TV, Network TV, TV Syndication, Satelitte/DBS **Titles:** *I Witness, Bickford Schemeckler's Cool Ideas, Adrift in Manhattan, Noel, One Last Dance, Loverboy, Stoned* **Marketing:** Web Catalog

Acquisition Information: Acquires Narrative Feature **Acquisition Method:** Unknown **Stage:** Unknown

SELECT MEDIA, INC.
190 Route 17M Harriman NY 10926
Phone: (800) 707-6334
http://www.selectmedia.org

50 titles.

Select Media, Inc., produces, publishes and distributes health education materials, mainly targeting youth at-risk. The company provides state departments, community-based organizations, schools, universities, and government agencies with award-winning programs and materials that address major issues such as teen pregnancy, HIV, AIDS, STDs, puberty, drugs, sexual abuse, and dating violence.

Subjects: Children's Programming, Gender Issues, Health & Medicine, Women's Issues **Markets:** Educational **Specialty:** Educational media **Titles:** *The Truth About Sex, Tanisha's Choice, Nicole's Choice* **Marketing:** Printed Catalog, Web Catalog

Acquisition Information: Acquires Doc Feature, Short Doc **Acquisition Method:** Unsolicited Inquiries **Stage:** Unknown **Advice:** If you have a video you would like Select Media, Inc., to distribute, please contact Matthew Martinez at the Marketing Department (800) 707-6334 or send a request by e-mail to sonya@selectmedia.org. **Acquisition Contact:** Matthew Martinez, Marketing Department (800) 707-6334 sonya@selectmedia.org

SEVENTH ART RELEASING
7551 Sunset Boulevard, #104 Los Angeles CA 90046
Phone: (323) 845-1455 | Fax: (323) 845-4717
seventhart@7thart.com
http://www.7thart.com

300 titles. Est. 1994. Principals: Udy Epstein, President

Seventh Art Releasing (SAR) is a U.S. theatrical distributor and foreign sales company founded in 1994 by Jonathan Cordish and Udy Epstein. Seventh Art Releasing conducts domestic and international sales on most of its films. The company specializes in releasing quality documentaries and independent fiction features theatrically and on the festival and educational circuit.

Subjects: Arts, Literature & Music, Disability, Environmental Issues, Family, LGBT, Gender Issues, History, Human Rights, Immigration, Labor Issues, Multicultural Perspective, Nature, Politics & Government, Religion, Sociology, Women's Issues **Markets:** Theatrical, Nontheatrical, Educational, Foreign **Specialty:** Documentaries, Independent Narratives **Titles:** *Steal a Pencil for Me, Daughters of Wisdom, Word Wars, Hell House, The Aggressives, Same Sex America, Balseros* **Territories:** Worldwide **Marketing:** Web Catalog

Acquisition Information: Acquires Narrative Feature, Doc Feature, Short Narrative, Short Doc **Acquisition Method:** Unsolicited Inquiries, Festivals, Markets, Other **Stage:** Rough Cut, Fine Cut, Finished **Advance:** Sometimes. **Philosophy:** Seventh Art Releasing is a full-service, filmmaker-friendly niche distributor. **Advice:** Obtaining distribution is often the most difficult task for filmmakers to accomplish, especially for first-timers. In my experience, 1 out of 100 or 1 out of 200 films make it to distribution. Call them before sending materials. **Acquisition Contact:** Shane Griffin (323) 845-1455 shane@7thart.com

SHADOW DISTRIBUTION
P.O. Box 1246 Waterville ME 04903
Phone: (207) 872-5111 | Fax: (207) 872-5502
shadow@prexar.com
http://www.shadowdistribution.com/

21 titles. Est. 1986. Principals: Ken Eisen, President; Alan Sanborn, VP

Shadow Distribution is a small film distribution company located in Waterville, Maine, dedicated to releasing unusual, specialized films. The company is run by exhibitors, the co-directors of Railroad Square Cinema, which has been bringing unique film programming to central Maine since 1978.

Subjects: Arts, Literature & Music, History, Human Rights, Multicultural Perspective **Markets:** Theatrical, Home Video **Specialty:** Art house film **Titles:** *Under the Sun, Latcho Drom, Windhorse, Carla* **Marketing:** Other

Acquisition Information: Acquires Narrative Feature, Doc Feature **Acquisition Method:** Unknown **Stage:** Unknown **Venues:** Maine International Film Festival and personal contacts **Acquisition Contact:** Ken Eisen (207) 872-5111 shadow@prexar.com

SHORTS INTERNATIONAL
P.O. Box 2514 Toluca Lake, CA 91610
Phone: (212) 370-6077
http://www.shortsinternational.com

3000 titles.

Shorts International is s a full-service short film entertainment company representing over 3,000 films to over 120 international broadcasters across every platform and every medium. The company's catalog includes award-winning titles from film festivals around the world. Their titles are sold through iTunes U.S., U.K., Canada and Germany.

Subjects: Action/Adventure, Animation, Arts, Literature & Music, Comedy, Drama, Family, Science **Markets:** Nontheatrical, Home Video, Web **Specialty:** Short films **Titles:** *Toyland, La Maison en Petits Cubes, Presto, This Way Up, Magnetic Movie, From Burger it Came.*

Acquisition Information: Acquires Animation, Short Doc, Short Narrative **Acquisition Method:** Festivals, Markets, Unsolicited Inquiries **Stage:** Finished **Advice:** If you have a short film that you would like to submit for consideration, complete the form at www.shortsinternational.com/downloads/submission.pdf and send it with either a DVD or VHS copy of your film. Please do not submit any materials other than a screener. **Acquisition Contact:** Linda Olszewski linda@shortsinternational.com

SKYLIGHT PICTURES
330 West 42nd St., 24th Floor New York NY 10036
Phone: (212) 947 5333 | Fax: (212) 643 1208
http://www.skylightpictures.com

20 titles.

For 25 years, Skylight Pictures has been committed to producing artistic, challenging and socially relevant independent documentary films on issues of human rights and the quest for justice. Through the use of film and digital technologies, it seeks to engage, educate, and increase understanding of human rights amongst the public at large and policy makers, contributing to informed decisions on issues of social change and the public good.

Subjects: Criminal Justice, History, Human Rights, Labor Issues, Politics & Government **Markets:** Nontheatrical, Educational, Home Video **Titles:** *The Reckoning, Granito, State of Fear* **Marketing:** Web Catalog

Acquisition Information: Acquires Doc Feature **Acquisition Method:** Unknown **Stage:** Unknown **Acquisition Contact:** Peter Kinoy peter@skylightpictures.com and Pamela Yates pamela@skylightpictures.com

SOLID ENTERTAINMENT
15840 Ventura Boulevard, Suite 205 Encino CA 91436
Phone: (818) 990-4300 | Fax: (818) 990-4320
info@solidpgms.com
http://www.solidentertainment.com

300 titles. Est. 1994.

Established in 1994, Solid Entertainment has grown to represent over 300 broadcast documentary titles. It represents shows created by independent producers as well as network programs created for Discovery Channel, National Geographic Channel, HBO, Cinemax, PBS, TLC, Military Channel, Spike!, and The Travel Channel. It continues to specialize in one-hour and feature length programming in the categories of current affairs, history, military, adventure, science, technology, and wildlife.

Subjects: Arts, Literature & Music, Criminal Justice, Experimental/Avant Garde, History, Human Rights, Immigration, Multicultural Perspective, Nature, Politics & Government, Regional Profiles & Issues, Science, Sociology, Theater, Travel, Women's Issues **Markets:** Theatrical, Home Video

Acquisition Information: Acquires Doc Feature, Short Doc **Acquisition Method:** Festivals, Markets **Stage:** Unknown **Venues:** NATPE, MIP-TV, MIPDOC, MIPCOM, HOT DOCS, IFP, the Realscreen Summit

SONY PICTURES CLASSICS, INC.
Parent Company: Sony Pictures Entertainment
550 Madison Avenue New York NY 10022
Phone: (212) 833-8833 | Fax: (212) 838-8844
http://www.sonyclassics.com

300 titles. Est. 1991. Principals: Michael Barker and Tom Bernard, Co-Presidents of Sony Pictures Classic

Sony Pictures Classics, Inc. (SPC) is an autonomous company of Sony Pictures Entertainment that acquires, produces, and distributes independent films from around the world.

Subjects: Action/Adventure, Arts, Literature & Music, Comedy, Drama, LGBT, Gender Issues, Women's Issues **Markets:** Theatrical, Home Video, Cable TV **Specialty:** Art house film **Titles:** *Crouching Tiger, Hidden Dragon, Run Lola Run, All About My Mother, Pollack*

Acquisition Information: Acquires Narrative Feature **Acquisition Method:** Festivals, Markets **Stage:** Unknown **Philosophy:** The director is the star. **Advice:**

Study the films the company has released. Speak with the filmmakers who have worked with the company. Learn the dynamics of film dealmaking.

STRAND RELEASING

6140 W. Washington Blvd. Culver City CA 90232
Phone: (310) 836-7500 | Fax: (310) 836-7510
strand@strandreleasing.com
http://www.strandrel.com

100 titles. Est. 1989. Principals: Marcus Hu, Jon Gerrans, Co-Presidents

Strand Releasing aims to fuse quality art films with commercial product. Strand has distributed the works of such renowned international artists as Manoel de Oliveira, Lino Brocka, Jon Jost, Terence Davies, Gaspar Noé, Lodge Kerrigan, Cindy Sherman, Nigel Finch, Raoul Ruiz, John Maybury, Ferzan Ozpetek, Jacques Audiard, Benoît Jacqout, Hal Hartley, Nina Menkes, Jon Moritsugu, John Duigan, François Ozon, Lou Ye, Marcelo Pineyro, and John Curran.

Subjects: Drama, Experimental/Avant Garde, LGBT, Gender Issues, Multicultural Perspective, Women's Issues **Markets:** Theatrical, Home Video **Specialty:** Art house and gay and lesbian film **Titles:** *Suzhou River, Wild Reeds, A Single Girl, The Living End, The Cockettes* **Marketing:** Web Catalog

Acquisition Information: Acquires Narrative Feature, Doc Feature, Short Narrative, Short Doc **Acquisition Method:** Solicited Only **Stage:** Unknown **Venues:** Sundance, Toronto, Berlin, Cannes **Acquisition Contact:** Chantal Chauzy, Director of Acquisitions, Home Entertainment, chantal@strandreleasing.com and David Bowlds, Director of Acquisitions, Nontheatrical Sales & Print Traffic, david@strandreleasing.com

SUBCINE

611 Broadway, Suite 616 New York NY 10012
Phone: (212) 253-6273
staff@subcine.com
http://www.subcine.com

32 titles.

SubCine is an artist-run and artist-owned collective of Latino film and videomakers. SubCine specializes in challenging, experimental, and progressive film and video. Its works have been screened on PBS, in the Guggenheim Museum, the Museum of Modern Art, and at the Sundance Film Festival, among others venues.

Subjects: Animation, Arts, Literature & Music, Gender Issues, Human Rights, Immigration, Labor Issues, Multicultural Perspective, Politics & Government **Markets:** Nontheatrical, Home Video, Public TV **Specialty:** Film and video by and about Latinos **Titles:** *¡Palante, Siempre Palante!, The Young Lords, The Sixth Section, The Lost Reels of Pancho Villa* **Marketing:** Web Catalog

Acquisition Information: Acquires Narrative Feature, Doc Feature, Experimental **Acquisition Method:** Unknown **Stage:** Unknown **Venues:** Sundance, Los Angeles International Film Festival **Philosophy:** Our name is meant to evoke our position in relation to both independent film, and to commercial Hispanic film. The edgy, intelligent work produced by independent Latino film and video makers over the past decades has been almost entirely absent from the official history of American independent film. Similiarly, we find ourselves as Independents equally invisible in relation to purely commercial attempts to reach "the Hispanic market." **Acquisition Contact:** staff@subcine.com

SUNDANCE CHANNEL

1633 Broadway, 8th Floor New York NY 10019
Phone: (212) 654-1500 | Fax: (212) 654-4738
feedback@sundancechannel.com
http://www.sundancechannel.com

200 titles. Est. 1996. Principals: Larry Aidem, President and CEO

Under the creative direction of Robert Redford, Sundance Channel is the television destination for independent-minded viewers. Sundance Channel offers audiences a diverse and engaging selection of films, documentaries, and original programs, all unedited and commercial-free. Launched in 1996, Sundance Channel is subsidiary of Rainbow Media Holdings, LLC. Sundance Channel operates independently of the nonprofit Sundance Institute and the Sundance Film Festival, but shares the overall Sundance mission of encouraging artistic freedom of expression. It aims to specialize in programs that are bold, uncompromising, and irreverent.

Subjects: Action/Adventure, Arts, Literature & Music, Biography, Comedy, Drama, Experimental/Avant Garde, History **Markets:** Theatrical **Specialty:** Art house film **Titles:** *Lost Highway, Lost In Beijing, Carny* **Territories:** National, international **Marketing:** Web Catalog

Acquisition Information: Acquires Narrative Feature, Doc Feature **Acquisition Method:** Solicited Only **Stage:** Unknown **Venues:** Sundance **Acquisition Contact:** christian.vesper@sundancechannel.com

TAPESTRY INTERNATIONAL, LTD.

3 Church Street Sea Bright NJ 07760
Phone: (732) 559-1300 | Fax: (732) 559-1309
info@tapestry.tv
http://www.tapestry.tv

1000 titles. Principals: Nancy Walzog President/Founder; Karen Carlson, VP

When Tapestry was first formed, the company tended to seek out social issue documentaries but as the company evolved it has become more involved in series and one-offs made for cable networks. Tapestry is now primarily working in the science, medical, history, and wildlife markets, but occasionally still takes on social issue films. On virtually every project it acquires, Tapestry acts as executive producer, allowing the company to shape and guide projects to make them as sellable as possible. Tapestry focuses its efforts on knowing the market and remaining closely connected to the projects it is involved in throughout the production process.

Subjects: Animation, Arts, Literature & Music, Children's Programming, Criminal Justice, Drama, Family, Nature, Travel **Markets:** Cable TV, Public TV, Network TV, TV Syndication, Other **Specialty:** Documentaries for home video and television

Acquisition Information: Acquires Short Narrative, Short Doc, Animation **Acquisition Method:** Unsolicited Inquiries **Stage:** Rough Cut, Finished **Advice:** Please submit rough-cut, trailer, or finished programs to our mailing address.

TERRA NOVA FILMS

9848 South Winchester Avenue Chicago IL 60643
Phone: (773) 881-8491
tnf@terranova.org
http://www.terranova.org

500 titles. Principals: James Vanden Bosch, Executive Director

Terra Nova Films produces some of the programs that it distributes, as well as distributing hundreds of films from other producers. It uses direct mail, telemarketing, and the Internet to reach its market. Terra Nova exhibits at conferences and conventions. Executive Director James Vanden Bosch is a recognized authority on aging-related audio/visual material. Terra Nova's customer list contains thousands of hospitals, nursing homes, other health care organizations, colleges and universities, schools of nursing, governmental agencies, and many others dealing with aging.

Subjects: Aging, Health & Medicine **Markets:** Educational, Home Video

Acquisition Information: Acquires Doc Feature **Acquisition Method:** Unsolicited Inquiries **Stage:** Finished **Philosophy:** The mission of Terra Nova Films is to foster a greater understanding of life in its later years through the media of film and video. **Advice:** We are always looking for new material to add to our catalog. If you have a video that you think might be of interest to our market, please contact us.

THE FILMMAKERS CHANNEL
9608 Palomita Albuquerque NM 87114
Phone: (505) 349-5951 | Fax: (443) 601-0665
dan@thefilmmakerschannel.com
http://www.thefilmmakerschannel.com

30 titles. Est. 2008. Principals: Dan Latrimurti, Anthony Dellaflora

The Filmmakers Channel specializes in audience direct pay-per-view distribution of independent films and alternative media.

Subjects: Action/Adventure, Aging, Animation, Arts, Literature & Music, Biography, Children's Programming, Comedy, Criminal Justice, Drama, Family, History, Human Rights, Immigration, Labor Issues, Multicultural Perspective, Nature, Politics & Government, Regional Profiles & Issues, Religion, Science, Sociology, Sports **Markets:** Web **Titles:** *Timewave 2012* **Marketing:** Web Catalog

Acquisition Information: Acquires Narrative Feature, Doc Feature **Acquisition Method:** Solicited Only, Festivals, Markets, Other **Stage:** Finished **Advance:** No. **Philosophy:** To lead the way in online, streaming, and pay per view distribution that pays the filmmaker first. **Acquisition Contact:** Daniel Latriurti (505) 349-5957 dan@thefilmmakerschannel.com and Tony Dellaflora (505) 830-9571 TCempire@mindspring.com

THE MUSEUM OF FINE ARTS, HOUSTON
1001 Bissonnet St. Houston TX 77005
Phone: (713) 639-7531 (713) 639-7515 | Fax: (713) 639-7399
film@mfah.org
http://www.mfah.org

25 titles.

The Museum of Fine Arts, Houston runs the oldest repertory film program in Houston, showcasing the best in Hollywood classics, foreign, documentaries, experimental, and shorts.

Subjects: Aging, Biography, Experimental/Avant Garde, Family **Markets:** Other
Specialty: the films of Robert Frank **Titles:** *Pull My Daisy* **Marketing:** Web Catalog

Acquisition Information: Acquires Doc Feature, Short Narrative, Short Doc,
Experimental **Acquisition Method:** Unsolicited Inquiries **Stage:** Finished
Acquisition Contact: Marian Luntz (713) 639-7531 mluntz@mfah.org and Tracy
Stephenson (713) 639-7531 tstephenson@mfah.org

THE VIDEO PROJECT
Parent Company: Specialty Studios
Phone: (800) 475-2638 | Fax: (888) 562-9012
support@videoproject.com
http://www.videoproject.com

200 titles. Est. 1983.

The Video Project aims to provide educational media and documentary
programming to schools, libraries, and educators worldwide. The Video Project
has programs for all ages, including Oscar and Emmy award-winners from over 200
independent filmmakers worldwide. It is the exclusive or primary distributor for
most of the programs in its collection, as well as a major distributor for the
productions of national environmental organizations such as the National Wildlife
Federation, Marine Mammal Fund, League of Women Voters, Union of
Concerned Scientists, and Zero Population Growth, among others. The Video
Project distributes over 10,000 programs every year to a diverse and growing
network that includes thousands of schools, colleges, community groups, public
libraries, churches, businesses, government agencies, and individuals.

Subjects: Arts, Literature & Music, Biography, Environmental Issues, Gender
Issues, Health & Medicine, History, Human Rights, Immigration, Labor Issues,
Multicultural Perspective, Nature, Politics & Government, Psychology, Regional
Profiles & Issues, Religion, Science, Sociology, Women's Issues **Markets:**
Educational, Home Video **Specialty:** environment, science & social issues **Titles:**
*Burning the Future: Coal in America, Crude Impact, Fair Fight in the Marketplace,
Garbage! The Revolution Starts at Home, Life With Principle: Thoreau's Voice in our
Time, One More Dead Fish, Sound of the Soul* **Marketing:** Web Catalog

Acquisition Information: Acquires Doc Feature **Acquisition Method:** Unsolicited
Inquiries, Festivals, Markets **Stage:** Finished **Advice:** Send us a DVD or 1/2 inch
VHS tape (NTSC) and any background information you deem important. This
may include a description, production dates, background on any of the speakers,
quotes from other people that have previewed it, any plans you may have for
producing a study guide and any history of prior distribution including quantities
and pricing. Please feel free to give David Donnenfield a call to discuss your
project. We receive hundreds of submissions each year; a personal contact helps us

to give your project the proper attention. Send to attention David Donnenfield, Managing Director.

THE WEINSTEIN COMPANY

375 Greenwich Street New York NY 10014
Phone: (212) 941-3800 | Fax: (212) 941-3949
http://www.weinsteinco.com

200 titles. Est. 2005. Principals: Harvey and Bob Weinstein, Founders

The Weinstein Company is an independent film production and distribution company started by the founders of Miramax Films, Harvey and Bob Weinstein.

Subjects: Action/Adventure, Comedy, Drama **Markets:** Theatrical, Home Video **Titles:** *The Reader, Crossing Over, Fanboys, Youth in Revolt* **Marketing:** Printed Catalog, Web Catalog

Acquisition Information: Acquires Narrative Feature **Acquisition Method:** Unknown **Stage:** Unknown

THEATRE ARTS VIDEO

174 Andrew Avenue Leucadia CA 92024
Phone: (760) 632-6355 | Fax: (760) 632-6859
admin@theatreartsvideo.com
http://www.theatreartsvideo.com

30 titles. Est. 1988.

Theatre Arts Video has been producing its own professional quality instructional videos for theatre training since 1988. Theatre Arts Video also helps distribute videos for producers with similar topic areas.

Subjects: Theater **Markets:** Educational, Home Video **Titles:** *Play it Safe: Introduction to Theatre Safety* **Marketing:** Web Catalog

Acquisition Information: Acquires Doc Feature **Acquisition Method:** Unsolicited Inquiries **Stage:** Finished

THINKFILM

Parent Company: Captial Films
Bridge House, 63-65 North Wharf Road London W2 1LA
Phone: +44 (0) 207 298 6200 | Fax: +44 (0) 207 298 6201
films@thinkfilminternational.com
http://www.capitolfilms.com

400 titles. Est. 2001.

Boasting seven Academy Award nominations in its short history, THINKFilm is a
distribution and production company originally headquartered in New York and
recently relocated to London as part of the Capitol Films network.

Subjects: Action/Adventure, Arts, Literature & Music, Biography, Comedy,
Drama, Experimental/Avant Garde, History, Multicultural Perspective, Sociology
Markets: Theatrical, Foreign, Other **Specialty:** Art house film **Titles:** *Time Out,
World Traveler, The Dangerous Lives of Altar Boys* **Marketing:** Web Catalog

Acquisition Information: Acquires Narrative Feature, Doc Feature **Acquisition
Method:** Solicited Only **Stage:** Unknown **Venues:** Toronto, Sundance, Cannes,
AFM **Philosophy:** The company is committed to aggressive, strategic release of
high product, representing the best of the independent filmmaking community
worldwide. **Advice:** The company is not interested in developing material. It does
not accept unsolicited work. It acquires films at festivals and markets.

THIRD WORLD NEWSREEL (TWN)

545 8th Avenue, 10th Floor New York NY 10018
Phone: (212) 947-9277 x308 | Fax: (212) 594-6417
distribution@twn.org
http://www.twn.org

500 titles. Est. 1967. 4 employees.

TWN is an alternative media arts organization that fosters the creation,
appreciation, and dissemination of independent film and video by and about
people of color and social justice issues. It supports the innovative work of diverse
forms and genres made by artists who are intimately connected to their subjects
through common bonds of ethnic/cultural heritage, class position, gender, sexual
orientation, and political identification. TWN promotes the self-representation of
traditionally marginalized groups as well as the negotiated representation of those
groups' artists who work in solidarity with them.

Subjects: Aging, Arts, Literature & Music, Environmental Issues,
Experimental/Avant Garde, Family, LGBT, Gender Issues, Health & Medicine,
History, Human Rights, Immigration, Labor Issues, Multicultural Perspective,

Politics & Government, Religion, Sociology, Sports, Women's Issues **Markets:** Nontheatrical, Educational **Specialty:** documentary **Titles:** *Dreams Deferred, Second hand (Pepe)* **Marketing:** Printed Catalog, Web Catalog, One Sheets, Direct Mail, Other

Acquisition Information: 10 titles per year. Acquires Doc Feature, Short Doc, Experimental **Acquisition Method:** Unsolicited Inquiries, Festivals **Stage:** Fine Cut, Finished **Advance:** No. **Philosophy:** TWN has a commitment to developing filmmakers and audiences of color. Today, TWN carries on the progressive vision of its founders and remains the oldest media arts organization in the U.S. devoted to cultural workers of color and their global constituencies. **Acquisition Contact:** Roselly Torres (212) 947-9277 ext. 308 distribution@twn.org and Dorothy Thigpen (212) 947-9277

TLA RELEASING
acquisitions@tlareleasing.com
http://www.tlareleasing.com

200 titles. Est. 2001.

Launched in 2001 by TLA Entertainment Group in Philadelphia, TLA Releasing is dedicated to broadening the choices available to film lovers by specializing in quality independent, international, and gay/lesbian-themed films by distributing them in theaters and on home video. TLA Releasing distributes international and American films in North America and United Kingdom.

Subjects: Action/Adventure, Arts, Literature & Music, Comedy, Drama, LGBT **Markets:** Theatrical, Home Video **Titles:** *Epitaph, Chef's Special, Clandestinos, Schoolboy Crush* **Marketing:** Web Catalog

Acquisition Information: Acquires Narrative Feature **Acquisition Method:** Unsolicited Inquiries, Festivals, Markets **Stage:** Finished **Advice:** TLA Releasing is actively seeking new films for acquisitions. We are principally interested in high-quality American independent cinema, films with gay and lesbian themes, and international genre movies. Films must be no older than 2004 productions. If you are interested in submitting a film for acquisitions consideration, please contact us at acquisitions@tlareleasing.com

TMW MEDIA GROUP
2321 Abbot Kinney Blvd., Suite 101 Venice CA 90291
Phone: (800) 262-8862 | Fax: (310) 574-0886
general@tmwmedia.com
http://www.tmwmedia.com

200 titles. Est. 1989.

TMW Media Group specializes in detailed core-curriculum programming. TMW programs address issues facing teens such as sex, drugs, alcohol abuse, and other subjects.

Subjects: Arts, Literature & Music, Biography, Children's Programming, Criminal Justice, Environmental Issues, Gender Issues, Health & Medicine, History, Language/Linguistics, Nature, Regional Profiles & Issues, Science, Sports, Travel, Women's Issues **Markets:** Educational, Home Video **Titles:** *The Special Kids Learning* series, *Speech & Skill Development* series; *Kids Go To Court; The Teens At Risk* series; *The Simply Painting* series; *The Party's Over: Sex, Alcohol & Pregnancy; The Shakespeare Conspiracy* **Marketing:** Web Catalog

Acquisition Information: Acquires Doc Feature **Acquisition Method:** Unsolicited Inquiries **Stage:** Finished **Philosophy:** As educators through video programming, our goal is stated quite simply: To educate, entertain, and enthrall our audience. **Advice:** We are always on the lookout for new, interesting, or archival material to present to our customers. If you are looking for distribution for a video product or know of a project in development, we would be pleased to offer input. We distribute worldwide to video, television, satellite, institutional markets, and consumers in a variety of languages. For more information e-mail us or write.

TROMA
36-40 11th Street Long Island City NY 11106
acquisitions@troma.com
http://www.troma.com

150 titles. Principals: Lloyd Kaufman, Founder

Troma specializes in cult classics and new releases known for their shocking imagery, overt sexuality, graphic violence, gore and nudity.

Subjects: Action/Adventure, Comedy, Drama, Experimental/Avant Garde **Markets:** Theatrical, Home Video **Titles:** *Toxic Avenger* series, *Class of Nuke 'Em High*

Acquisition Information: Acquires Narrative Feature, Short Narrative **Acquisition Method:** Unsolicited Inquiries, Festivals, Markets **Stage:** Finished **Advice:** If you have a completed film and would like to know if Troma would be interested in distributing it, please send a VHS or DVD (NTSC preferred) to Attention Acquisitions. We can not return any tape or DVD sent to us, so please do not send your only copy!

TRULY INDIE
1614 W. 5th Street Austin TX 78703
Phone: (512) 474-2909
info@trulyindie.com
http://www.trulyindie.com

30 titles.

Truly Indie provides independent filmmakers direct access to all the services of a professional theatrical release. It delivers everything from access to the right theatres in all major markets to custom crafting the marketing, publicity, and advertising campaigns. Truly Indie helps filmmakers act as their own distributor. You choose the theatres.

Subjects: Action/Adventure, Arts, Literature & Music, Biography, Comedy, Drama, Multicultural Perspective, Regional Profiles & Issues **Markets:** Theatrical **Titles:** *Valentino: The Last Emperor, Shuttle, Boogie Man, Lake City, Outsourced* **Marketing:** Web Catalog

Acquisition Information: Acquires Narrative Feature **Acquisition Method:** Unsolicited Inquiries **Stage:** Finished **Philosophy:** Our mission is to find quality films whose filmmakers want to take a new approach to distributing their movies. **Advice:** Contact us at info@trulyindie.com or send a copy of your film to in the mail. Be sure to include your contact information. A Truly Indie representative will contact you promptly to discuss your distribution options. **Acquisition Contact:** Kelly Sanders ksanders@trulyindie.com

UNITED ARTISTS
Parent Company: A Subsidiary of MGM
10250 Constellation Blvd. Santa Monica CA 90067
Phone: 310-449-3000
http://www.unitedartists.com

2000 titles. Est. 2006. Principals: Paula Wagner, Chief Executive Officer; Elliott Kleinberg, Chief Operating Officer; Don Granger, President of Production; Dennis Rice, President of Worldwide Marketing and Publicity

United Artists Entertainment, LLC, was formed under a partnership between Tom Cruise, Paula Wagner, and Metro-Goldwyn-Mayer Studios, Inc. (MGM), with Wagner serving as Chief Executive Officer. The historic United Artists brand was initially founded some 85 years ago by movie greats Douglas Fairbanks, Charlie Chaplin, Mary Pickford, and D.W. Griffith.

Subjects: Action/Adventure, Arts, Literature & Music, Comedy, Drama **Markets:** Theatrical, Foreign **Specialty:** Art house film **Titles:** *Rocky, The Pink Panther, and James Bond* **Marketing:** Web Catalog

Acquisition Information: Acquires Narrative Feature **Acquisition Method:** Solicited Only, Festivals, Markets **Stage:** Unknown **Philosophy:** A filmmaker driven company looking for unique product from a unique perspective.

URBAN HOME ENTERTAINMENT
7744 Union Groove Rd. Lithonia GA 30054
Phone: (888) 254-3822 x107
contacts@urbanhomeent.com
http://www.urbanhomeent.com

50 titles.

Urban Home Entertainment DVD/CD Distribution division, also known as UHE, is an independent distributor of DVDs and CDs in the home entertainment products marketplace. Servicing national music and video retailers, mass merchants, e-commerce, and independent channels, UHE offers niche DVD product inventory to over 7,500 retailers, e-tailers, mobile content providers, as well as digital/streaming providers around the country. In addition, UHE provides distribution and fulfillment services for a growing inventory of videos, CD software, and audiobooks to partners at Blockbuster, Borders, Circuit City, Hollywood Video, Movie Gallery, Musicland Group, Netflix, Target, Tower Records and Video, Transworld Music, Virgin Megastore, and Wal-Mart.

Subjects: Action/Adventure, Comedy, Drama, Family, Multicultural Perspective **Markets:** Home Video **Titles:** *Section 8, Sweet Hideaway, Sweet Spot* **Marketing:** Web Catalog

Acquisition Information: Acquires Narrative Feature **Acquisition Method:** Unsolicited Inquiries, Festivals, Markets **Stage:** Finished **Philosophy:** From day one, it has been the intent of UHE's principle leadership to be the number one niche content provider in the country of quality family frendly content. At the heart of operations lies the commitment to provide production companies and filmmakers alike a trusted means of navigation through the industry. Our goal is to provide a unique experience to reach the bottom line of maximizing all available profit centers. UHE continuously strives to create and acquire programming that is both entertaining and socially responsible and that features Hollywood's biggest new stars. **Advice:** We are always interested in new movie titles. Submit a movie description and contact information, and we will contact you soon. Although we specialize in these genres, other films will also be considered.

V TAPE
401 Richmond Street West, Suite 452 Toronto Ontario M5V 3A8
Phone: (416) 351-1317 | Fax: (416) 351-1509
info@vtape.org
http://www.vtape.org

5000 titles. Est. 1980. 7 employees. Principals: Kim Tomczak, Executive Director; Chris Kennedy, Distribution Director

Founded in 1980, V Tape is an international distribution, exhibition, and resource centre with an emphasis on the contemporary media arts. As a centre for over 900 artists artists, V Tape carries over 5,000 titles. V Tape's in-office facilities include several study carrels for viewing and an extensive library of print materials available to the general public as well as to students, curators, and researchers. In 1994, V Tape began a working partnership with the Aboriginal Film & Video Art Alliance (Ontario) to encourage distribution of Aboriginally produced film and video, publishing a second edition of the catalog, imagineNative, in 1998. Outreach workshops are regularly conducted throughout Ontario to increase awareness of Aboriginally produced media.

Subjects: Experimental/Avant Garde, LGBT, Gender Issues, Health & Medicine, History, Human Rights, Multicultural Perspective, Politics & Government, Religion, Women's Issues **Markets:** Nontheatrical **Specialty:** Video art and documentaries **Titles:** *Twinning Series, Trading the Future, The Guardian, Tomboy, Winona, 100 Stories About My Grandmother* **Territories:** Aboriginal Media Arts Festival, Toronto International Film Festival, art galleries **Marketing:** Web Catalog

Acquisition Information: Acquires Narrative Feature, Doc Feature, Experimental **Acquisition Method:** Unsolicited Inquiries, Festivals **Stage:** Finished **Venues:** Toronto International Film Festival **Advance:** No. **Acquisition Contact:** Kim Tomczak, Restoration & Collections Management Director/Founder (416) 351-1317 kimt@vtape.org and Wanda Vanderstoop, Distribution Director, wandav@vtape.org

V.I.E.W. VIDEO
AKA: Arkadia Entertainment Corp.
34 East 23rd Street New York NY 10010
Phone: (212) 674-5550 | Fax: (212) 979-0266
info@view.com
http://www.view.com

250 titles. Principals: Bob Karcy, President

For over 25 years, V.I.E.W. Video has been committed to producing and distributing quality home video and television entertainment. Its programs have garnered almost 200 awards from a variety of prestigious, international festivals and competitions.

Subjects: Arts, Literature & Music, Criminal Justice, Environmental Issues, Family, Gender Issues, History, Human Rights, Multicultural Perspective, Nature, Politics & Government, Regional Profiles & Issues, Religion, Sports, Theater, Travel, Women's Issues **Markets:** Educational, Home Video, Web **Titles:** *Childbirth from Inside Out, The Magic Flute Story, JFK: The Day the Nation Cried, Healthy Massage* **Marketing:** Web Catalog

Acquisition Information: Acquires Doc Feature **Acquisition Method:** Unsolicited Inquiries, Festivals, Markets **Stage:** Finished acquisitions@view.com

VANGUARD CINEMA
7050 Village Drive, Suite A Buena Park CA 90621
Phone: (800) 218-7888 | Fax: (714) 562-9022
info@vanguardcinema.com
http://www.vanguardcinema.com

450 titles. Est. 1993.

Vanguard is one of the largest direct-to-DVD release studios in the U.S. Vanguard aims to remain true to its original mission of opening doors to the market for new talent on the edge of discovery.

Subjects: Action/Adventure, Arts, Literature & Music, Children's Programming, Comedy, Drama, Family, Multicultural Perspective **Markets:** Home Video, Web **Titles:** *Badland, Broken Windows, The Journey, En Tu Ausencia, Santa and Pete, Over the G.W., Loudmouth Soup, Milagro en la Tierra del Cafe* **Marketing:** Web Catalog

Acquisition Information: Acquires Narrative Feature **Acquisition Method:** Unsolicited Inquiries, Festivals, Markets **Stage:** Finished **Advice:** Vanguard is open to submissions. Currently it is interested in: U.S. independent genre films produced within the last 4-6 years; contemporary international films with high production value, mainstream orientation, and possible festival exposure; current and classic films in Spanish language from Spain, Mexico, Cuba, and Latin America; and classic television programming with emphasis on learning and discovery values for children. See the guidelines at www.vanguardcinema.com/submissions/submissions.html fthor@vanguardcinema.com ibaltezar@vanguardcinema.com

VIDEO DATA BANK

112 S. Michigan Avenue Chicago IL 60603
Phone: (312) 345-3550 | Fax: (312) 541-8073
info@vdb.org
http://www.vdb.org

1500 titles. Est. 1976. 11 employees. Principals: Abina Manning, Director; Brigid Reagan, Distribution Manager

Founded in 1976, the Video Data Bank is a leading resource in the United States for videos by and about contemporary artists. The VDB collections feature innovative video work made by artists from an aesthetic, political, or personal point of view. The collections include seminal works that, seen as a whole, describe the development of video as an art form originating in the late 1960s and continuing to the present. The videos in the VDB collections employ innovative uses of form and technology mixed with original visual style to address contemporary art and cultural themes. Through a national and international distribution service, the VDB makes video art, documentaries made by artists, and taped interviews with visual artists and critics available to a wide range of audiences. Over 1,500 tapes are available for rental or purchase to institutions such as media arts centers, universities and schools, museums and galleries, community-based workshops, public television, and cable access centers worldwide. Some tapes are also available for individual purchase. Fully 75% of the work in the collection is experimental video art and artist-produced documentary, much of it available as part of anthology or curated programs, and 25% consists of interviews with artists.

Subjects: Arts, Literature & Music, Experimental/Avant Garde, Gender Issues, Health & Medicine, History, Women's Issues **Markets:** Educational, Home Video, Cable TV, Public TV **Specialty:** Video by and about contemporary artists **Titles:** Compilations: *Early Video Art, Independent Video and Alternative Media, On Art and Artists* **Territories:** International **Marketing:** Printed Catalog, Web Catalog

Acquisition Information: Acquires Doc Feature, Short Doc, Experimental **Acquisition Method:** Unsolicited Inquiries **Stage:** Unknown **Philosophy:** Organization mission is to make a diverse range of critically acclaimed video art, digital art, and alternative documentary available to museums and galleries, cultural and educational institutions, broadcasters, community organizations, and individuals. We also serve artists by collecting, promoting, distributing, exhibiting, and preserving their work. **Advice:** The viewing committee reviews submissions on an ongoing basis. To submit a film for consideration, send to our address, Attn: Acquistions. We can screen on PAL or NTSC VHS and DVD. Please include information on the work you are sending us, including length, year of production, and a synopsis. Also feel free to include any relevant press materials, along with your resume or C.V. Materials will not be returned. Since we are a not-for-profit with a small staff, our selection process can take quite a while. Please be patient with us. For the same reason, we are unable to enter into a dialogue about submitted work. We look forward to seeing your work. **Acquisition Contact:** Brigid Reagan, Distribution Manager and Dewayne Slightweight, Distribution Associate

VISION MAKER VIDEO
1800 North 33rd Street Lincoln NE 68503
Phone: (402) 472-3522 | Fax: (402) 472-8675
visionmaker@unl.edu
http://www.visionmaker.org

50 titles. Est. 1977. Principals: Frank Blythe, Executive Director

Vision Maker Video, a film funding and distribution service of Native American Public Telecommunications, offers quality Native American videos. Most videos are aired on PBS. Besides distributing to schools, Vision Maker Video offers these videos and others on the Internet through its website.

Subjects: History, Multicultural Perspective **Markets:** Educational, Public TV, Web **Specialty:** Video and television by and about Native Americans **Marketing:** Web Catalog

Acquisition Information: Acquires Doc Feature, Short Doc **Acquisition Method:** Unknown **Stage:** Unknown

VISTA STREET ENTERTAINMENT
8700 Venice Blvd Los Angeles CA 90034
Phone: (310) 280-1184
vistastreet@sbcglobal.net
http://www.vistastreet.com

50 titles. Est. 1975. 3 employees. Principals: Jerry Feifer, Michael Feifer

Vista Street Entertainment represents cult, horror, erotic, and action films.

Subjects: Action/Adventure, **Markets:** Theatrical, Home Video, Cable TV, Satelitte/DBS, Web, Foreign **Specialty:** Genre film of low budget **Titles:** *The Medicine Show, Witchcraft XII* **Marketing:** Printed Catalog, Web Catalog

Acquisition Information: Acquires Narrative Feature, Animation **Acquisition Method:** Unsolicited Inquiries **Stage:** Finished **Advice:** Send tapes, flyers, and screening invitations.

VMS, INC.
AKA: Vocational Marketing Services

805 Airway Drive Allegan MI 49010
Phone: (800) 343-6430
sales@vms-online.com
http://www.vms-online.com

3000 titles. Est. 1986. Principals: Michael S. Walsh, President; Lydia Walsh, Head Buyer

VMS, Inc., distributes books and DVDs for vocational education classrooms. VMS sells to schools, industrial training, home economics, trade and industrial, career and guidance, and business and technical programs. Its primary markets are schools and industry. Many of VMS's sources are industrial training departments and producers who develop a training video.

Subjects: Criminal Justice, Health & Medicine, Labor Issues, Science **Markets:** Educational **Specialty:** Educational training video **Titles:** *Hometime, Taunton Press, John Wiley, Suzuki, Rbt Bosch, Eaton, America's Test Kitchen. Culinary Institute of America* **Territories:** U.S., Canada, limited overseas **Marketing:** Printed Catalog, Web Catalog, One Sheets, Direct Mail

Acquisition Information: 100 titles per year. Acquires Doc Feature, Short Doc **Acquisition Method:** Unsolicited Inquiries **Stage:** Proposal, Script, Production, Rough Cut, Fine Cut, Finished **Venues:** catalogs, trade shows, referrals **Advance:** Sometimes. **Philosophy:** VMS, Inc distributes reasonably priced training products that are suited to classroom use. We focus on materials for skill development. **Advice:** Call to see if your project fits our market. Many projects done for companies as internal training or production installation are very good for their market (if they are not too sales oriented). We are happy to advise if a product can be modified for sale to our market. Visit our web site to view the titles we currently carry. Our market can be very profitable as titles have a very long life. **Acquisition Contact:** Mike Walsh (269) 673-200 mike@vms-online.com

WARNER BROS. ENTERTAINMENT
Parent Company: Warner Bros.
4000 Warner Boulevard, Building 76 Burbank CA 91522
Phone: (818) 954-6430 | Fax: (818) 954-6480
http://www.warnerbros.com

5000 titles.

Warner Bros. Entertainment, a fully integrated, broad-based entertainment company, is a global leader in the creation, production, distribution, licensing, and marketing of all forms of creative content and their related businesses, across all current and emerging media and platforms. The company focuses on every aspect of the entertainment industry from feature film, TV, and home entertainment production and worldwide distribution to DVD, digital distribution, animation, comic books, licensing, international cinemas, and broadcasting.

Subjects: Action/Adventure, Comedy, Drama **Markets:** Theatrical, Home Video, Web, Foreign **Marketing:** Web Catalog

Acquisition Information: Acquires Narrative Feature **Acquisition Method:** Unknown **Stage:** Unknown

WELLSPRING MEDIA
AKA: Winstar TV & Video, Fox Lorber, International Film Circuit
2230 Broadway Santa Monica CA 90404
Phone: (310) 453-1222 | Fax: (310) 453-0074
info1@geniusproducts.com
http://www.geniusproducts.com

125 titles. Est. 1980.

A division of Genius Products, Wellspring is a leading independent supplier specializing in classic, foreign language, and American art house films along with feature documentaries and programming for the mind, body, and spirit. Its unique collection includes films by Jean-Luc Godard, Akira Kurosawa, Rainer Werner Fassbinder, and Eric Rohmer, and authoritative documentaries on Ella Fitzgerald, Muddy Waters, and Henry Darger, as well as enlightening programs by Dr. Andrew Weil, Deepak Chopra, and Joseph Campbell.

Subjects: Arts, Literature & Music, Children's Programming, Health & Medicine **Markets:** Theatrical, Nontheatrical, Educational, Home Video, Cable TV, Public TV, Network TV, TV Syndication, Satelitte/DBS, Web, Airline, Foreign **Specialty:** Art house, performance, and holistic film **Marketing:** Printed Catalog, Web Catalog

Acquisition Information: 10 titles per year. Acquires Narrative Feature, Doc Feature **Acquisition Method:** Festivals, Markets **Stage:** Finished **Venues:** Cannes, Toronto, Sundance, Berlin **Acquisition Contact:** Michael Radiloff, Executive Vice President of Productions and Acquisitions

WOLFE RELEASING
444 N. Norton Ave., #8, Los Angeles CA 90004
Phone: (323) 466-3536
info@wolfevideo.com
http://www.wolfereleasing.com

100 titles. Est. 1985. Principals: Kathy Wolfe, CEO; Maria Lynn, Director & President

Wolfe is one of the oldest and largest exclusive distributors of gay and lesbian feature films. In 2004, Wolfe launched its theatrical distribution arm, which is committed to offering films a full theatrical release in up to 40 North American cities.

Subjects: Comedy, Drama, Gender Issues, LGBT, Women's Issues **Markets:** Theatrical, Educational, Home Video **Specialty:** Gay and lesbian feature films **Titles:** *Brother to Brother, Big Eden, Goldfish Memory, On_Line* **Marketing:** Web Catalog

Acquisition Information: 20 titles per year. Acquires Doc Feature, Narrative Feature **Acquisition Method:** Unsolicited Inquiries **Stage:** Finished **Advice:** We are always looking for new work. Please send a tape or DVD and supporting materials about your film to the following address. **Acquisition Contact:** Jeffrey Winter jeffrey@wolfereleasing.com

WOMEN MAKE MOVIES, INC.
426 Broadway, Suite 500WS New York NY 10013
Phone: (212) 925-0606 | Fax: (212) 925-2052
info@wmm.com
http://www.wmm.com

500 titles. Est. 1972. 11 employees. Principals: Debra Zimmerman, Executive Director

Established in 1972 to address the under representation and misrepresentation of women in the media industry, Women Make Movies is a multicultural, multiracial, nonprofit media arts organization that facilitates the production, promotion, distribution, and exhibition of independent films and videotapes by and about women. The organization provides services to both users and makers of film and video programs, with a special emphasis on supporting work by women of color. Women Make Movies facilitates the development of feminist media through an internationally recognized distribution service and a production assistance program. WMM now distributes more than 500 documentary, dramatic, and experimental films representing more than 400 emerging and established women artists from nearly 30 countries around the globe. WMM films are shown in media arts centers, museums, television, theaters, libraries, and universities and are used by thousands of educational customers and community groups throughout the United States and the world.

Subjects: Biography, Gender Issues, Multicultural Perspective, Women's Issues **Markets:** Nontheatrical, Home Video, Foreign **Specialty:** Independent film and video by and about women **Titles:** *ARUSI Persian Wedding, Club Native, Courting Justice* **Marketing:** Web Catalog

Acquisition Information: 15 titles per year. Acquires Doc Feature, Short Doc **Acquisition Method:** Unsolicited Inquiries, Festivals **Stage:** Finished **Venues:** Sundance **Acquisition Contact:** Debra Zimmerman, Executive Director (212) 925-0606 ext. 301 dzimmerman@wmm.com and Kristen Fitzpatrick Distribution Manager ext. 305 kfitzpatrick@wmm.com

YARI FILM GROUP RELEASING
Parent Company: Yari Film Group
10850 Wilshire Blvd., 6th Floor Los Angeles CA 90024
Phone: (310) 689-1450 | Fax: (310) 234-8975
online@yarifilmgroup.com
http://www.yarifilmgroup.com

30 titles. Principals: Bob Yari, President & CEO

Yari Film Group Releasing is the dedicated domestic distribution affiliate of the Yari Film Group, which finances and produces independent films. It works with both seasoned veterans – such as Lasse Hallström, Paul Haggis, and Sidney Lumet – and first-time writers and directors.

Subjects: Action/Adventure, Comedy, Drama, Family **Markets:** Theatrical **Titles:** *Killing Pablo, Kerosene Cowboys, The Monster of Longwood, The Maiden Heist, Fight or Flight, One Train Later* **Marketing:** Web Catalog

Acquisition Information: Acquires Narrative Feature **Acquisition Method:** Unknown **Stage:** Unknown **Acquisition Contact:** Mike Simon, Domestic Distribution, mike@freestyle.com

YORK ENTERTAINMENT
4565 Sherman Oaks Ave Sherman Oaks CA 91403
Phone: (818) 788-4050 | Fax: (818) 788-4011
york@yorkentertainment.com
http://www.yorkentertainment.com

300 titles. Est. 1990.

York Entertainment is an independent supplier of feature film, television, and new media content for the domestic home entertainment marketplace. York's films are distributed in the traditional DVD format, as well as through new media digital formats and streaming. York's DVD product is available nationally through wholesalers like Ingram Entertainment, VPD, Waxworks, and Baker & Taylor.

Subjects: Action/Adventure, Comedy, Drama, Family **Markets:** Home Video **Marketing:** Web Catalog

Acquisition Information: 50 titles per year. Acquires Narrative Feature **Acquisition Method:** Unsolicited Inquiries **Stage:** Finished **Advice:** Submissions can be sent through our website – print out our submission form and follow guidelines at http://www.yorkentertainment.com/acquisitions.jsp

ZEITGEIST FILMS AND ZEITGEIST VIDEO

247 Centre Street, 2nd Floor New York NY 10013
Phone: (212) 274-1989 | Fax: (212) 274-1644
mail@zeitgeistfilms.com
http://www.zeitgeistfilms.com

160 titles. Est. 1988. 10 employees. Principals: Nancy Gerstman, Emily Russo, Co-Presidents; Ian Stimmler, Director of Video; Shannon Attaway, Video Production Manager; Adrian Curry, Head Designer; Emily Woodburne, Director of Semi-Theatrical Sales; Clemence Taillandier, Director of Nontheatrical Sales

Zeitgeist Films is a NY-based distribution company which includes the home video/DVD division Zeitgeist Video. Zeitgeist has been responsible for the release of over 160 films, including first films by notable directors like Todd Haynes, Christopher Nolan, Francois Ozon, the Quay Brothers and films by other masters of cinema including Abbas Kiarostami, Atom Egoyan, Agnes Varda, Guy Maddin, Jia Jhang-ke, Deepa Mehta, and Nuri Bilge Ceylan. Zeitgeist is also renowned for its collection of ground-breaking documentaries. Zeitgeist Films has won numerous major prizes at film festivals around the world, including the Palme and Camera d'Or in Cannes, Sundance Grand and International Jury prizes, 4 Academy Award nominations and one Academy Award.

Subjects: Arts, Literature & Music **Markets:** Theatrical, Nontheatrical, Educational, Home Video, Cable TV, Public TV **Specialty:** Art house film **Titles:** *Trouble the Water, Up the Yangtze, Tulpan, Examined Life, Stranded, Chris & Don: A Love Story* **Territories:** U.S. & sometimes CANADA **Marketing:** Web Catalog, Direct Mail

Acquisition Information: 56 titles per year. Acquires Narrative Feature, Doc Feature, Animation **Acquisition Method:** Solicited Only, Festivals, Markets **Stage:** Finished **Philosophy:** Zeitgeist acquires its films with the following criteria in mind: passion for the film, its quality and prestige, and its marketability. We still believe in a strong theatrical component to our distribution; *Trouble the Water* played on over 170 screens even before it was shortlisted for an Academy Award! **Advice:** We look at all types of art house films for acquisition but we do not take anything unsolicited. **Acquisition Contact:** Ben Simington
ben@zeitgeistfilms.com

ZENGER MEDIA

Parent Company: A Division of Social Studies School Service
10200 Jefferson Boulevard, P.O. Box 802 Culver City CA 90232
Phone: (310) 839-2436 (800) 944-5432 | Fax: (800) 421-246
access@zengermedia.com
http://www.zengermedia.com

15000 titles. Est. 1965.

Zenger Media, under the wing of Social Studies School Service, has been a leader in educational resources since 1965, searching out the highest quality supplementary learning materials, including books, DVDs, CD-ROMs, videos, laserdiscs, software, charts, and posters. Its experienced editorial staff and teacher consultants carefully evaluate titles from over a thousand publishers, searching for materials that are effective, balanced, easy to use, and reasonably priced. In an ongoing effort to respond to the needs of teachers, Zenger publishes over 30 catalogs a year (focusing on different subject areas and grade levels) that list the best materials for teachers using short, informative, and objective descriptions.

Subjects: Children's Programming, Family, Psychology **Markets:** Educational, Home Video **Specialty:** Educational media **Titles:** *Making Good Choices, American Higher Education Map, Get Organized without Losing It* **Territories:** National, international **Marketing:** Printed Catalog, Web Catalog

Acquisition Information: Acquires Short Narrative **Acquisition Method:** Unknown **Stage:** Unknown **Acquisition Contact:** (800) 421-4246 access@counselorresources.com

ZIA FILM DISTRIBUTION, LLC

369 Montezuma Ave., #320 Santa Fe NM 87501
Phone: (505) 438-9299 | Fax: (505) 438-6137
sales@ziafilm.com
http://www.ziafilm.com

100 titles.

Zia Film Distribution, LLC, is a full-service distribution company representing programming for both the domestic and international marketplace, including cable, satellite, free TV, video-on-demand, broadband, Internet, educational, and home video/DVD. Zia also maintains relationships with theatrical releasing companies both in the U.S. and internationally.

Subjects: Action/Adventure, Children's Programming, Comedy, Criminal Justice, Drama, Environmental Issues, Family, Health & Medicine, Politics & Government, Religion **Markets:** Theatrical, Educational, Home Video, Cable TV,

Public TV, Network TV, TV Syndication, Satelitte/DBS, Web **Marketing:** Web Catalog

Acquisition Information: Acquires Narrative Feature, Doc Feature **Acquisition Method:** Unknown **Stage:** Unknown

Tips on Approaching a Distributor

By Cynthia Close
Executive Director
Documentary Educational Resources

Distributors are inundated with films, so it's important to get your facts straight about the distributor and fine-tune your pitch first. Single yourself out as a professional and get your film noticed by following some advice from this leading distributor.

The first step when seeking a distributor is to do your research first before you make any calls. This book would be a great start in finding companies that match the type of film you are pitching. Then check out the distributor's website. If they do not have a website, then they probably are not worth pursuing. So, taking for granted that every reputable distributor does have a website, that is the next place to go for information. Look at the titles they present. Do they specialize in a particular genre? (In our case we only distribute documentaries, so don't send us your narrative feature starring Ben Affleck – although, if you made a film with Ben Affleck the distribution would likely be all locked up before the film was finished.) Does the distributor have a content focus? (In our case, we lean towards "cross-cultural" films, films about human rights, the environment, and people and places, but not historical docudramas.) Does the distributor address a particular market and is it the same market that you think will buy your film? Do you like the way they present the titles they offer? Does the atmosphere they create on the web look like it would be a good home for your film?

If the answers to all these questions lead you to believe the distributor might be interested in viewing your work, then that's the time to make the phone call. And when you call, be polite. You could start off by saying something complimentary, like "I was so impressed by the list of quality films you offer, and I would love to see my film on that list." Flattery is good if it is informed flattery, and I tend to like filmmakers more who clearly have a high opinion of us as a distributor, and filmmakers who may have come to us on the recommendation of a filmmaker whose work we already distribute. Who you know always counts in this business.

So now we are actually talking, and you've told me a little about your film, and I encourage you to submit a DVD for review. We have guidelines on our website that tell you exactly how to submit. There is a reason why we ask you to send a cover letter and/or press release. We also ask that you make sure the DVD itself is clearly labeled with all your contact information, address, phone, e-mail, and the length of the program! You would be amazed to know how many DVDs we get with nothing but the title scrawled on it with a sharpie. These get tossed in the round file right next to our recycle bin. Then when you call us six months later to find out why you haven't heard from us, and we have no idea who you are, don't be offended, and don't be surprised.

But distributors don't just sit back in their offices all day, waiting for the submissions to pour in. They also attend film festivals, talk to festival curators, and actively pursue films. So getting your film accepted for screening in festivals is a great way to get a distributor's attention and have them chasing you instead of you chasing them. My two favorite festivals for conducting business are HOTDOCS in Toronto (usually in April) and SILVERDOCS just outside of Washington, D.C., (usually in June). I like these events because they include an industry conference that draws all my international colleagues, and I get to negotiate deals as both a "buyer" acquiring films and a "seller" licensing our programs for international broadcast. The actual time I spend sitting in a theater, watching a film in its entirety, as it was meant to be seen, is minimal. It is sad, but true. Therefore the "doc shop" or viewing stations set up mainly for distributors and buyers at these events is a great way to have your film available at times when the distributor can watch it, and hopefully decide to offer you a contract.

There are hundreds, perhaps thousands of film festivals out there and some are better than others. As a distributor, we like to acquire a film early in its festival life, and then we take on the responsibility and cost of promoting it for you. Not all distributors do this. We have an international perspective and relationships with festival curators from Brazil to Beijing. We are more likely to get your film accepted to those festivals than you are because of our knowledge of the proclivities of festival curators. This kind of promotion is essential in building an international audience for your work.

Having your own website for a film is also essential, and it is a great way to build interest, connect with your audience, and provide information. As a distributor, I can get hooked by a well-designed site and a gripping trailer (no more than five minutes long). By the same token, a poorly designed site, where the video doesn't play well, can do more harm than good. Don't have your entire film streaming off your site; that is overkill, and it might actually jeopardize a distribution deal.

Some filmmakers think they need an agent to represent them. I find agents tend to complicate communication and add a layer of unnecessary bureaucracy to the negotiation process. I prefer to work directly with a filmmaker. It is an important aspect of building what can be a successful long-term relationship that may include future work. The relationship between a filmmaker and a distributor is based on trust, and it has to be built over time.

However, not every filmmaker needs or wants a distributor. Some filmmakers are so actively involved with their films, often because they fall into the realm of "advocacy" or are meant to motivate people to take some sort of action to improve the human condition, that they are the best spokespersons for their own work. There are more opportunities today for "self-distribution" than there were just a few years ago, and some consultants have built a whole business around encouraging filmmakers to "go it alone."

But the best situation is when you have a great film, an enthusiastic distributor, and an informed, engaged filmmaker all working collaboratively to find the broadest audience and making enough money to keep everybody happy.

Prepping Your Film for Distribution

By Jason Brubaker

Picture this! By some miracle to end all miracles, born of equal parts luck and blind determination, you've managed to rise above the never-ending barrage of questions from "concerned" friends and family who've always thought your talk about making movies was reckless. You've put together a cast and crew, refined your script, found some financing, and in the process, you've even figured out how to ignore all your significant other's not-so-subtle hints that a career selling life insurance really wouldn't be that bad. To be honest, looking back, even you aren't really sure how you pulled it off. Yet, despite all of the concerns and self doubt, you've somehow managed to make the impossible possible. You've made your first feature film! And, by definition, you're finally a real filmmaker.

So, as your significant other drinks celebratory champagne with your family, friends, and whatever members of your cast and crew are still speaking to you at the wrap party, you and I both know there is one nagging thought still rattling around in the back of your mind. It's the same thought shared by every independent feature filmmaker. You're asking yourself, how am I going to distribute this thing?

As a feature filmmaker, your distribution strategy will fall into one of two categories. Either your movie will be picked up, marketed, and sold through various outlets by one of those distribution companies you read about in the trades, or you will sell it yourself. This is the major difference between traditional distribution and self-distribution. Regardless of which path you take, there are certain fundamental steps you must complete to ensure the film makes a smooth transition from the edit suite to the marketplace.

PREPARING TO FIND A DISTRIBUTOR

When finding a distributor, many filmmakers partner with sales representatives, agents, lawyers, or consultants to help get their movies seen and, hopefully, sold. It is during this time that the representative will often furnish the filmmaker with an extensive checklist of deliverables that include (with some variation): the movie master, talent agreements, high resolution digital photos for use in promotion, a credit lock, talent bios and press kits, a copyright registration form, chain of title, and just about every other legal clearance the distributor can think of to minimize liability. One area where first-time filmmakers often stumble is in properly securing the rights to each and every bit of music included in their flick.

According to Richard Abramowitz of Abramorama, a marketing and distribution consulting firm that specializes in independent films, "Sometimes filmmakers include a song in the background that can't be removed from the dialogue track, or a character sings along to the song in scene. If the music isn't fully cleared, then the filmmaker either has to pay [for the rights] or cut the scene entirely." As you can imagine, finding one of these boo-boos can significantly delay, or even derail, your potential distribution deal.

Because of these surprises and to further mitigate risk exposure, most distributors will require Errors and Omissions insurance. According to Mark Litwak, of the Beverly Hill's based law firm Mark Litwak & Associates, "E&O insurance is malpractice coverage for filmmakers. It protects the insured from liability arising from negligence in not securing the rights, permissions, and clearances needed to exploit the film."

Assuming the movie reaches a deal and all the elements are delivered, the filmmaker's involvement in the project is minimized as the distributor assumes control of the marketing, public relations, packaging, duplication and quality control. From there, the distributor will get the movie into its marketplace pipeline, which may involve anything from movie theatres to any number of straight-to-DVD outlets.

PREPARING FOR SELF-DISTRIBUTION

Distribution as we know it is changing. With models like video-on-demand and fulfillment services becoming more and more integrated with not-so-independent conglomerates like Amazon.com, the options for reaching a global marketplace is wide open. Sooner than you think, all content may very well be available with the push of a button. While the prospect of cutting out the middleman is exciting to the independent filmmaker, as your own distributor, you now bear sole responsibility for both the success of your movie and the safeguarding of your personal liability, should any legal issues arise. To many, this means purchasing E&O insurance, converting the movie website into a sales funnel, capturing leads, creating the DVD cover art, and finding ways to efficiently reach your target audience at a minimal cost.

Stacy Schoolfield, whose film *Jumping Off Bridges* was successfully self-distributed in 2007 after a great festival run, says, "Self distribution provides more control over the film. Where you might only end up with three percent of traditional distribution profits, you could end up with much more through self-distribution."

Stacy, who produced and managed distribution of the film, said her strategy involved showing *Jumping Off Bridges*, ultimately about a group of friends struggling through adolescence, to carefully selected niche audiences, building a mailing list and making the movie readily available on her website. "At our first screening at SXSW [the South by Southwest Film Festival], there were people from the local Teen Suicide Prevention/Mental Health awareness group. They came up to us and said they could use the film in their outreach and education. It was a new idea for us, and after more research, we found out that there were lots of groups like that across the country and we started reaching out to them. You have to know who your audience is and then pull out all the stops to reach them."

Thanks to the Internet, finding the appropriate audience is becoming increasingly more efficient. According to Dana LoPiccolo-Giles, managing director of CreateSpace, which provides filmmakers with direct access to the Amazon marketplace, "Films with a specific focus may see higher sales due to niche audiences and less market competition. Some keys to online sales success are having an attractive, effective cover design that will look professional and interesting as a small thumbnail on web searches. Filmmakers should choose online keywords carefully, and make sure the name of the title will help the film be found in searches. Often a subtitle as part of the name can make it more specific and easily searchable."

Regardless of whether you plan on selling directly to your marketplace or choose to take the time-honored distribution route, getting the appropriate releases, licenses, and clearances during preproduction will only help your movie make a smooth transition from screening room to marketplace. Once everything is ready, then you too can enjoy a little champagne... before getting ready to start the whole process all over again on your next project. Picture that!

Distribution Dealmaking Tips

By Mark Litwak
Attorney
Mark Litwak & Associates

There are several ways to develop or produce a narrative feature film. Beginning with an idea or the movie rights to an existing literary property, a studio can hire a writer to create a script. The studio's development staff works with the writer to craft the story. Note that most of the scripts developed by studios never get produced.

Other movies begin with a script developed outside the studio. Here a writer, working on his or her own or hired by an independent producer, writes a screenplay. After it is finished, it may be packaged (joined) with other elements (e.g., a star or director) and presented to the studio for financing and distribution. The big three talent agencies (CAA, ICM, and William Morris) are responsible for most packaging.

Other films are both developed and produced away from the studio that ultimately distributes them. These independently produced projects are often dependent on investors or pre-sale distribution deals (selling off various foreign distribution rights) to finance production. The producer then enters an acquisition agreement with a distributor for release of the picture. This is called a *negative pick-up deal.*

While the terms of negative pick-up deals vary, the studio/distributor typically pays for all distribution, advertising, and marketing costs. The studio and producer share profits. Because producers take the risk of financing production, they probably can obtain a better definition of net profits than if they made the film with studio financing. Profits may be split 50/50 between the studio and producer without a deduction for a studio distribution fee. Of course, the independent producer takes the risk that if the film turns out poorly, no distributor will want it. Then the producer can incur a substantial loss.

In negative pick-up deals, distributors will often agree to give producers an advance of their share of the profits. Producers can use this money to repay investors. Producers will want to obtain as large an advance as possible because they know they may never see anything on the back end of the deal (i.e., no profits).

The distributor wants to pay as small an advance as possible, and usually resists giving an amount that is more than the cost of production. Its executives will propose, "We'll be partners. We will put up all the money for advertising and promotion. If the picture is successful we will share in its success." Sound good?

Unfortunately, distributors have been known to engage in creative accounting, and profit participants rarely see any return on their share of "net profits" because of the way that term is defined. Consequently, the shrewd producer tries to get as large an advance as possible. He also tries to retain foreign rights and keep them from being cross-collateralized. Cross-collateralized means the monies earned from several markets are pooled. For example, let's say your picture made one million dollars in England and lost one million dollars in France. If those territories were cross-collateralized, and you were entitled to a percentage of the net revenue, you would get nothing. On the other hand, if the territories were not cross-collateralized, you would get your percentage of the English revenues and the distributor would absorb the loss incurred in France.

ORCHESTRATING THE DISTRIBUTION DEAL

The most important advice I can offer to filmmakers seeking distribution is: "Don't brag about how little money you spent to make the picture" before you conclude your distribution deal! You may feel justly proud of making a great-looking picture for a mere $400,000. But if the distributor knows that is all you have spent, you will find it difficult to get an advance beyond that. It would be wiser not to reveal your investment, recognizing that production costs are not readily discernible from viewing a film. Remember, the distributor has no right to examine your books. What you have spent is between you, your investors, and the I.R.S.

Negative pick-up deals can be negotiated before, during, or after production. Often distributors become interested in a film after viewing it at a film festival and observing audience reaction. All the studios and independent distributors have one or more staffers in charge of acquisitions. It is the job of these acquisition executives to find good films to acquire.

It is not difficult to get acquisition executives to view your film. Once production has been announced, don't be surprised if they begin calling you. They will track the progress of your film so that they can see it as soon as it is finished – before their competitors get a shot at it.

From the filmmaker's point of view, you will get the best distribution deal if you have more than one distributor interested in acquiring your movie. That way, you can play them off each other to get the best terms. But what if one distributor makes a pre-emptive bid for the film, offering you a $500,000 advance, and you have only 24 hours to accept their offer? If you pass, you may not be able to get a better deal later. It is possible you may fail to obtain any distribution deal at all. On the other hand, if you accept the offer, you may be foreclosing the possibility of a more lucrative deal that could be offered to you later. Consequently, it is important to orchestrate the release of your film to potential distributors to maximize your leverage.

ORCHESTRATING THE RELEASE

1) **Keep the Film Under Wraps**: Don't show your film until it is finished. Executives may ask to see a rough cut. They will say "Don't worry. We're professionals, we can extrapolate and envision what the film will look like with

sound and titles." Don't believe them. Most people can't extrapolate. They will view your unfinished film and think it amateurish. First impressions last.

The only reason to show your film before completion is if you are desperate to raise funds to finish it. The terms you can obtain under these circumstances will usually be less than those given on completion. If you must show a work in progress, exhibit it on a Moviola or flatbed editing table. People have lower expectations viewing a film on an editing console than when it is projected in a theater.

2) **Arrange a Screening**: Invite executives to a screening; don't send them a videocassette or DVD. If you send a DVD to a busy executive, he will pop it in his player. Ten minutes later the phone rings and he hits the pause button. Then he watches another ten minutes until his secretary interrupts him. After being distracted ten times, he passes on your film because it is "too choppy." Well, of course it's choppy with all those interruptions.

You want to get the executive in a dark room, away from distractions, to view your film with a live audience – hopefully one that will respond positively. So rent a screening room at MGM, invite all the acquisition executives you can, and pack the rest of the theater with your friends and relatives, especially Uncle Herb with his infectious laugh.

3) **Make the Buyers Compete Against Each Other**: Screen the film for all distributors simultaneously. Some executives will attempt to get an early look – that is their job. Your job is to keep them intrigued until it is complete. You can promise to let them see it "as soon as it is finished." They may be annoyed to arrive at the screening and see their competitors. But this will get their competitive juices flowing. They will know that they better make a decent offer quickly if they hope to get the film.

4) **Obtain an Experienced Advisor**: Retain an experienced producer's representative or entertainment attorney to negotiate your deal. Filmmakers know about film; distributors know about distribution. Don't kid yourself and believe you can play in their arena and win. There are many pitfalls to avoid. Get yourself an experienced guide to protect your interests. Any decent negotiator can improve a distributor's offer enough to outweigh the cost of his services.

5) **Investigate the Distributor**: Always check the track record and experience of each distributor. As an entertainment attorney who represents many independent filmmakers, I often find myself in the position of trying to get unscrupulous distributors to live up to their contracts. The savvy filmmaker will carefully investigate potential distributors by calling filmmakers who have contracted with them. I recently read a Standard & Poors report on a distributor and was shocked to learn that the company was $2.3 million in arrears on royalty payments. One can also check the Superior Court dockets in Los Angeles to see if a company has been sued.

CHECKLIST FOR SELECTING A DISTRIBUTOR

1. Amount of advance.

2. Extent of rights conveyed – domestic, foreign, and/or ancillary? Are any markets cross-collateralized?

3. Is there a guaranteed marketing commitment?

4. Does the producer have any input or veto power over artwork and theater selection in the top markets?

5. Track record and financial health of distributor. Visit The Filmmaker's Clearinghouse, for information about specific distributors.

6. Are monthly or quarterly accounting statements required?

7. To what extent does the distributor plan to involve the filmmakers in promotion?

8. Marketing strategy: demographics of intended market, grassroots promotion efforts, film festivals, etc.

9. Split of revenues and accounting of profits: Is there a distribution fee? Overhead fees?

10. Distributor leverage with exhibitors. Can the distributor collect monies owed?

11. Any competing films handled by distributor? Conflicts of interest?

12. Does the producer have the right to regain distribution rights if the distributor pulls the plug early on distribution?

13. Personal chemistry between producer and distribution executives.

Distributor Q&As

CINEMA GUILD

Cinema Guild director of distribution, Ryan Krivoshey, talks about the evolution of independent film distribution.

From *The Independent* September 2008
By Jericho Parms

Much has changed since 1968 when Philip and Mary-Ann Hobel created The Cinema Guild and television was the niche market for all things educational. As award-winning producers of documentary and feature films, including the highly acclaimed *Tender Mercies*, which was nominated for five Academy Awards including Best Picture, the Hobels originally created the company to distribute their own work. Yet, as a natural progression, they began acquiring documentaries from other filmmakers seeking distribution.

Now celebrating 40 years in business, The Cinema Guild is one of the leading distributors of film and video, including documentary, narrative features, and shorts. *The Independent* recently sat down with Ryan Krivoshey, Cinema Guild's director of distribution for the past six years, to discuss the industry's new realities, a distributor's gut instinct, and how "documentary" was once a dirty word.

So, now after 40 years, what does Cinema Guild's collection look like?

We now have just over one thousand documentaries in our collection and take on anywhere between 40 and 60 titles per year. The core of the company, as founded by Philip and Mary-Ann, is rooted in the educational market and we only launched a theatrical division about seven years ago. We'll generally take up to 30 to 50 documentaries for the educational market and release anywhere between four and six films theatrically. But there is some overlap—this year we have three documentaries in theatrical release.

Over the years, how have you seen independent cinema and the distribution of it change?

Just in the six years that I've been here, there has been a noticeable change in the business. Not too long ago, distributors had to look for creative ways to say documentary without actually saying it—as if "documentary" was a four-letter word. But in the past several years, there's been a documentary boom. It's been great for us. It's great for everyone.

What are some of the factors you attribute to this "boom"?

There are always moments when people become more interested in the world around them, whether it was the state of our presidency, or other world events. In the same way that, one of the consequences with 9-11 became people's increased attention to the Middle East. When things spark a fire in people they develop the interest in becoming more aware.

Given some of these changes in the industry, how has Cinema Guild adapted its approach to distribution?

The core of the company has always been documentary, which has left us well positioned. Now, we're able to move beyond what I call the "old-fashioned" documentary towards the films that are winning at festivals like Sundance or Full Frame. We're finding markets for those films now so they can have a life beyond the festival circuit, a life that can maintain even when the Internet takes over.

When the Internet takes over?

Yes, when the Internet takes over, we're all waiting for it to. There is a lot of pessimism going around about the industry—and I don't think it's fully unwarranted—but it's also a really interesting time. Things are changing. The bedrock of distribution is changing. It's a challenge, and any good—any smart—company should be ready to evolve. We've been able to strike strategic partnerships with Internet providers like Netflix, iTunes, and Indieflix, so there are additional revenue streams that are opening up. As the theatrical is shrinking, the Internet will balance some things out. But in the near future, theatrical will be around and despite what many people are saying it's still a viable thing—a viable revenue stream with money to pass along to filmmakers.

Talk about the role of festivals in the evolution of independent film.

It's amazing what has happened with festivals—and if we're talking about changes in the past few years—the festivals have been absolutely great. In a sense festivals make it easier for us to acquire films because now there is so much out there. They also provide an additional thread of revenue; once we've acquired films, we can rent them to festivals, thus generating more for our filmmakers. The bottom line is that festivals provide a great platform, and a film can have an amazing run strictly in the festival circuit alone.

What are some advantages of being represented by a distributor like Cinema Guild?

We are good at finding creative marketing opportunities and initiatives for the projects we pick up. We'd never simply choose a film, throw it on screen in New York, and call it a day if reviews aren't great. Given our access to the various markets, we are able to get a film into theaters and then pursue additional revenue for filmmakers by way of the nontheatrical market, through the universities, the libraries, film festivals, and community organizations. We offer many possibilities.

For a company that receives hundreds of submissions a year, talk a bit about your selection process.

We have a very tailored approach, and we truly believe in every film we pick up. When you can only take on 50 or 60 a year and you receive hundreds and hundreds of submissions, it has to be a tough selection process. Philip and I watch all of the films. Many of our submissions are cold, unsolicited. Every time a festival opens, no matter how large or small, we have someone scour the websites for potential films and request screeners. Most of our theatrical films we'll pick up from Toronto, Sundance—any of the larger fests we attend each year.

How do you work with filmmakers when preparing their films for release?

We work as closely with filmmakers as possible. As a small company we have certain advantages as opposed to the larger players. Distributors are often associated with a bad connotation in filmmakers' minds, so we always try to maintain as open and transparent a relationship as possible, consulting on everything from the beginning of a theatrical release to the selection of what bonus features end up on the DVD. It's proven to be one of our strong suits. Some of the highlights from our 2008 catalog include a handful of new films from previous filmmakers we have worked with. We nurture these relationships.

How do you weigh in on the rise in filmmakers turning towards self-distribution as a means of navigating the industry?

The one issue with self-distribution—it's a very costly and time-consuming process. Of course if a filmmaker has the time and money to invest in becoming their own distributor, then it's a great option and with the Internet and other outlets, it's certainly more doable now than ever before.

Of course I carry a biased perspective here. A distributor can bring a lot to the process, just with established contacts alone. There is a perception that once filmmakers hand their films to a distributor, they relinquish their work and walk away. But we're at the opposite end of that spectrum. The filmmakers we work with are integrally involved in the whole process. If a filmmaker and the distributor can each bring input to the table, I see that as the best option.

How does a film or a filmmaker grab your attention?

First and foremost there has to be a gut reaction to a film. You can belabor the points about market potential all you want, but you have to initially respond to a film on an instinctual level. Once you get that—which can be rare—then we get into questioning market potential, whether there is educational value, if it will appeal to the senses of a general audience, etc. But as a general rule, every film that inspires that gut reaction we'll go after. If it's good, we want to work on it.

What's in store for the next 40 years?

We're having a good run right now and hopefully it will just keep going. Theatrical and nontheatrical are growing, television is great, and we're launching our home video line next year. And, of course, there's the Internet. It's a wide-open plain.

FACETS MULTI-MEDIA

Milos Stehlik talks about how Facets Multi-Media looks for "great films that have fallen through the cracks."

From *The Independent* July 2003
By Jason Guerrasio

What is Facets?

Facets Multi-Media is an arts organization based in Chicago, Illinois. We also have the world's largest and most unique collection of foreign, classic American, independent, experimental, documentary, cult, fine arts, and children's videos and DVDs. The Facets collection represents over 50 thousand individual titles. In addition we also do Facets Cinémathèque, an important Chicago venue for the exhibition of independent cinema, the Chicago International Children's Film Festival, and exclusive theatrical and video distribution lines. A selected number of films exclusively acquired for the Facets Video collection are also released theatrically and in television markets.

When and why was Facets created?

Facets was created in 1975 by Nicole Dreiske and myself as a film exhibition center for international and American art films, alternative children's films, and as a center for the development and performance of experimental theater.

The mission of Facets is...

To develop and find new audiences for important films which are left outside either the commercial or even the mainstream art film circuits. We try to do this at every level—exhibition, distribution, and most importantly, media education for adults and for children.

What types of films do you seek?

Great films that fall through the cracks. Our approach has always been curatorial, in the sense that we are always distressed about the hundreds and thousands of films that are unavailable in any form and should be, deserve to be, and need to be available. It doesn't need to be new or made yesterday. For us it could be a small, quirky, and totally original documentary, or the work of Georges Melies. For example, the history and legacy of the American independent film movement from the fifties, sixties, and seventies, is an area of great concern. All of this work should be on DVD.

Where and how do you find them?

Through all of the major markets, but very often from filmmakers and friends of filmmakers and friends of friends of filmmakers.

How does Facets cater to experimental filmmakers?

We've invested considerable resources in bringing the work of many of the key figures of American experimental film to the home video market, including James Broughton, Barbara Hammer, Scott Bartlett, Larry Jordan, and Paul Glabicki, to name a few. This has expanded to include the work of artists in video as well as feature filmmakers. While finding them is not difficult, marketing is a challenge. American experimental media-makers have to be placed on the same footing, the same level playing field, as independent feature filmmakers. This is what we have attempted to do in giving experimental makers such a full voice in the context of Facets' catalogs and broad-based marketing efforts.

Explain your video distribution lines.

Facets Video hosts three exclusive video lines: Accent Cinema, a world cinema label that has particular strengths in Europe; Cinemateca, a Spanish world cinema label that features films from Spain and Latin America; the Facets Video label, a world cinema label that has particular strengths in Middle Europe, the Middle East, and American independents. Additionally, Facets frequently undertakes exclusive distribution for other independent labels.

How many films do you acquire per year?

We acquire 12-18 films annually for exclusive release on the Facets label; another 20 for exclusive distribution, and 4-5,000 new titles every year for nonexclusive distribution.

How do you work with the filmmakers when preparing their films for release?

This is always a collaborative process, and just how easy or difficult it is depends to a great degree on how much preparation the filmmaker has done in having a film ready for release. This means quality masters and adequate publicity materials, because if we have these then it's less time to dig for them and it allows us to concentrate on the job of distribution and marketing.

At what stage should filmmakers approach you with a film?

When the film is completely finished. That way we know exactly what we're dealing with.

How should filmmakers approach you with their projects?

The best way is just to send a letter with a description/background of the film.

What advice can you give filmmakers seeking distribution?

It's important to find the right distributor that offers the best fit, which can be more important than money. Distributors all have their strengths and weaknesses, and most of them are up front and honest in admitting these. When facing such rejection, accept it as what it is—an admission of the capabilities of that particular distributor. For us, for example, it is very difficult to distribute independent features that aim at a broad, middle-brow audience, and that emulate Hollywood films or television. There are other distributors perfectly capable of moving those films into the marketplace.

What are some issues Facets faces as an independent distributor at the present time?

It is a huge, fragmented marketplace, and make no mistake about it, the major studios and media conglomerates want to own it all. Establishing and finding a home and audiences for challenging films is not for the faint of heart, and we are blessed in the U.S. with hundreds of courageous and brave souls committed to fighting the good fight for independent and art films. The biggest challenge for them, and for us, will be connecting to younger generations.

FILM MOVEMENT

An interview with Larry Meistrich of Film Movement

From *The Independent* April 2003
By Jason Guerrasio

What is Film Movement?

We're a company that matches consumers with deserving filmmakers. We do this in two ways: through theatrical releases and by combining them with a subscription-based service so that people everywhere in the United States and ultimately Canada can get access to the same films as people in New York City, Chicago, or Los Angeles. For example our first film, *El Bola*, opened theatrically on December 10, 2002, and we shipped it to our members nationwide on the same day. If you're in a city that we play theatrically and you're a subscriber, we'll buy your ticket. You go to the website and from the account page you can download a ticket. Even if you go to the theater, you get the DVD as well.

Why was Film Movement created?

I don't live in a city anymore and I have three kids, so for me it's really hard to participate in the films that I want to participate in. They very rarely come to where I live. I wanted to create a platform for people who are educated, sophisticated, and culturally connected no matter where they live, as well as create a marketplace for filmmakers who'll actually be able to make some money on their movies. I think the theatrical release platform model is finished, it's too expensive. We're leading with our subscription business and using our theatrical as a marketing initiative, which takes a lot of pressure off of the film and the filmmaker. We'll play the movie for a year and a half—we don't really care.

How did the subscription idea come up?

Well, I'm a member of the Academy, and two years ago I got a copy of *Harry Potter* when it was still in theaters, which caused quite a stir in my daughter's first grade class. I thought, wouldn't it be great to give everybody that kind of experience, but for good films?

We've also done something different in regards to the financial model for filmmakers. Everybody's on a "true dollar one straight gross." What that means is literally every time someone subscribes, filmmakers get paid.

How large is the subscription base at the moment?

We're not giving out our numbers, but I can tell you we're in over 725 cities and in forty-eight states, so filmmakers are getting true national exposure.

Other than the subscription, how else does Film Movement distinguish itself from other independent distributors?

Quality. There are no horror films. There are no hip-hop films. We're actually trying to lead with our brand and then let the film support that brand. We're trying to stand for something of substance or quality.

What types of films are you seeking?

We're seeking award-winning, well written, well crafted, well performed, well produced independent cinema. It can be documentary. It can be feature. It can be foreign language. It just has to be good.

You guys are doing shorts, too?

Yes, each feature comes with a short.

How do you choose your films?

Our criteria for the films is they have to have been in one of the top seven film festivals (AFI, Berlin, Cannes, New York, Sundance, Toronto, Venice). So far, everything we've bought has won something in those film festivals. We have a panel of curators; Richard Peña from Lincoln Center, Christian Gaines from AFI, Nicole Guillemet, who used to be at Sundance [currently director of Miami International Film Festival], Nate Kohn [director, Roger Ebert's Overlooked Film Festival]— really good professional curators. They have to sign off on the films. They are the best of the festival films. What we're really doing is bringing Sundance to people's houses as well as to people in the theater community.

How many films do you acquire per year?

We acquire 12 per year.

How do you work with a filmmaker in the distribution process?

The filmmaker is truly a partner. They're a marketing partner, a financial partner; we're really doing everything together: trailers, posters, campaigns. I'll play films at film festivals after a theatrical run because I don't really care what my box office numbers are. For example, *El Bola*, which technically had its opening in December, is opening theatrically in New Orleans; then it's playing in a festival in February in San Diego and a bunch of other festivals. The more we're getting a film out there, the more people know about it and about Film Movement. It really takes the pressure off of that opening weekend because very few films have the marketing dollars behind them to be able to open big.

At what stage of post-production should filmmakers approach you? Rough or final, which do you like to get?

So far, we haven't bought anything that wasn't finished, but if something was a fine cut and was really good we would look at it.

What were the lessons you learned at the Shooting Gallery that you think will help make Film Movement a success?

I learned how to market a movie. I'm proud of what we did at Shooting Gallery; the business was very successful. I learned what consumers want and how to reach them. I think the business has changed in the last five to six years. When you have things coming out on eight and ten thousand screens, it really changes the market, because small distributors can't get screens and can't hold screens. It's become a three-day execution. I don't believe in that business model anymore, unless you're a studio; then it works.

What advice can you give to filmmakers who are looking for distribution?

Filmmakers need to pay more attention to marketing. It's one thing to make a movie; it's another thing to know who's going to see your film. Your job isn't done once the film is in the can. Whether it's the producer or the director, someone involved has to have an idea of where the film is going to go when it's done. I think very few filmmakers pay attention to that.

LANDMARK MEDIA

An interview with Joan Hartogs, the co-founder of Landmark Media

From *The Independent* December 2007
By Katelyn Harding

Running a family business. Keeping children's education first. Staying independent through increased corporate consolidation amidst a radical overhaul of the way film and video is distributed. Given all of that idealism, it may seem that educational film and video distributor Landmark Media has its work cut out for it. But it also has 25 years of experience and is driven by a singular focus to provide quality content for kids.

Joan Hartogs co-founded Landmark Media with her husband Michael in 1983. At the time they were both working on Wall Street. Michael was a distributor at Screenscope and when it closed, they decided to start their own distribution company. Her two sons have joined the business and together they have amassed more than 1,000 programs for pre-school through college-aged audiences.

To insure quality to the schools and libraries that purchase Landmark's titles, Hartogs personally reviews then selects about five percent of the films she receives. But budgets are shrinking, and the commercial DVD market has been encroaching on what used to be a self-contained market. Like other distributors, Landmark has evolved with the times, now selling most products on DVD and offering video streaming on request.

The Independent recently caught up with Joan Hartogs and asked her to consider the future of Landmark Media and the educational distribution market at large.

What sets you apart from other educational distributors?

We're very particular about what we sell; we look at it as public service. I spend most of my time looking at films, which could be hundreds and hundreds in a given year. We sign an average of about 70 or so per year, though one year we only signed 10, which is rare.

What are the last three films you have taken on, and how do you think they're going to do?

The last one was called *Animals A-Z* which is a curriculum item, so I think it will do well. We don't usually pick wildlife, but this was so special. There is also *Heads Up* – a 26-part series from Canada directed toward kids between elementary and high school and involves sciences dealing gravity and astronomy. The third one is called *Shattered Dreams* and it features inner city kids in Toronto, Canada, and their life involving guns and violence.

We look at and acquire all types of films but lately we have been taking wildlife for young grades (a little departure for us) and really good films about global warming. However, the film I'm most proud of is titled *Truth Lies and Intelligence* done in Australia about the deception by [President George] Bush, [former British Prime Minister Tony] Blair and [former Australian Prime Minister John] Howard about Iraq.

One never knows how movies will do, but I'm always hopeful. We like cultural programs featuring people from other parts of the world. Children need to understand other counties and how they live. We have a lot of social studies and a lot of science films. We don't produce films, so it's very hard to pick what comes our way.

Have you ever been tempted into making your own films?

There was one film we made ourselves. It was called, *Condoms: A Responsible Option*. It was made in 1986 and as executive producers, we thought it was a very necessary film. There was a lot of publicity about AIDS and STDs at the time, and we did it for high school kids, which was kind of a risk. A lot of schools weren't buying things like that, but the first one we sold was down in the Bible Belt, which was a big surprise.

Were you nervous about taking this risk? And did you make any money from it?

I really didn't care about that; I felt that it was something that needed to be made. STDs were rampant, and I thought if someone wanted to buy it, they would. It was made in good taste. We made a little money because it was a very cheap production. If we had made a fortune off it, we would have made more films.

Would you consider making another film like this today?

The younger generation working here would like to, but right now we have our hands full with marketing, distributing, and selling. It's a money issue – producing is very expensive but I think eventually they'd like to.

How has what sells changed?

There are no patterns I have noticed through the years. In the end it's what schools pick and choose. I'm just offering, and I try to have a variety of different subjects. Ten years ago, you had budgets with people spending a lot of money on films, and you didn't have people going out and buying films for $19.99 at Wal-Mart.

How have shrinking budgets directly impacted your company?

Country-wide, states have lost revenue. There's been a lot of consolidation. One school district could've had 15 different buyers or budgets and now those have been consolidated to maybe eight. I've noticed this since 9/11.

Of course it means that there's less money to spend and less money comes our way. So, we just have to work harder; it's way more challenging than it's ever been. Also, technology has changed a lot. Schools will say, "Oh I'll just let my videos get streamed," which means money goes directly to the producer from schools without us, so that's a challenge to producers as well as us.

Have you tried streaming?

If clients want to stream, we can deliver it. The winners are the people who use it.

How would a filmmaker get a distribution deal with Landmark Media?

Call me up or send me an e-mail and tell me what you have. If I like it, we'll talk, and I'll offer you a contract and you might accept it or not.

What is the contract you sign with filmmakers?

It's pretty typical. We pay royalties against the first sale. Our royalty is 25 percent.

What's your basic approach to releasing a title? How do you market your films?

It's mainly through the salespeople that work directly for us. We have film seminars and preview seminars, we attend film markets, and we have a marketing person to look for inroads everywhere depending on the film. We also have a website and a catalog.

What are the roles of the members of your family?

My husband and I make the decisions—we're the bosses. And my sons basically are employees. They are of course treated as such, with the work ethic here being like a regular company. The difference with having my sons work here is that I listen to them a little more, and they are a little freer, in the sense where sometimes employees won't give you their honest opinion, and my sons are more at liberty to say what they think which is great. It's important to me that no matter what happens, they remain close as brothers. So that's always an issue.

When Richard joined us four years ago, and Peter a year ago they moved the company in different directions. They were willing to be more experimental, trying different things, and finding different ways to do it. Richard brings the technological talent, and Peter brings the marketing talent. Because they have the understanding of newer concepts, (i.e., switching DVD to streaming) they are able to do a lot of things and use more equipment to get it done.

What keeps you going?

I love film. I'm learning all the time. If I had a really good memory I'd be brilliant. Finding a well made film that I think people can learn from and seeing the producer make some money from the sales is really rewarding.

Does anything disappoint you about the business?

Shrinking budgets are very disappointing. I don't feel that America really values our children and education enough. We rank as one of the lowest or possibly the lowest in the western world in educating our children—and we are a wealthy country.

What is one piece of advice for beginning or established independent filmmakers?

My advice would be: use somebody else's money. Talk to distributors. Talk to people. Ask people about your idea who are already in that market before you fund your film. Don't make a film because you're in love with the subject. To distribute in schools, you need to focus on what comes after the premiere. Keep that in mind all the time.

What is the future of independent film distribution in the U.S.?

I don't know. I think about that. We've survived by being flexible, being careful. We're careful with spending. We're careful to try to put money into marketing. We operate pretty much how we operated when we first opened our business. For us, this past year has been a lot better, but I think we've all been through very difficult times. Being independent is very important to us, and hopefully we can stay that way.

OUTCAST FILMS

An interview with Vanessa Domico, founder of Outcast Films, an LGBT distributor

From *The Independent* February 2009
By Nikki Chase

Vanessa Domico was tired of seeing too few LGBT films, so she drew on her expertise as a film distributor and founded Outcast Films.

Outcast Films focuses on politically charged issues, like gay marriage, meth addiction, and intimate explorations of sexual identity and self-acceptance. Since its founding in November 2004 and public launch the following February, Outcast has tackled what Domico says are the most pressing issues in the LGBT community and, in the process, picked up the additional goals of public education and personal activism.

Domico talked with *The Independent* about how Outcast came about, what it represents, and how it stands out from the rest.

How did Outcast Films begin?

While working as the deputy director at another distributor, I saw what I perceived as a gap in LGBT film distribution. I thought I could do it better and I knew I could work with filmmakers in a way that they appreciated and respected.

With four years of experience in film distribution under my belt, not to mention a fairly extensive background in business (30 years and counting) and in film production, I thought I would be able to do a better job of individually marketing the films instead of lumping films together as packages, as most distributors do.

What types of films does Outcast distribute? And how do you go about choosing those films?

Outcast Films is a film distribution company dedicated to the fair and equal representation of media made by or about the diverse lesbian, gay, bisexual, and transgender community. We are also educators and activists and want to be a vehicle for voices that may not otherwise be heard.

Outcast Films seeks films that are socially conscious, progressive, and activist driven. Our first acquisition was the critically acclaimed film, *Tying the Knot*, about gay marriage which, at that time, and unfortunately still is, in the forefront of the news in the U.S. The next film to come along was *Pills, Profits and Protest* about global AIDS activism. Because the LGBT community is marginalized by society, it became clear early on that many films from LGBT filmmakers dealt with activism and social justice, so it was a natural organic fit and one that we wanted to pursue.

How does the distribution project work from start to finish?

What is important to understand is that each film is different and therefore we take very different approaches in marketing and distributing each of our acquisitions.

Outcast Films reaches out to thousands of teachers, community leaders, activists, policy makers and breakers, institutions, and individuals. By doing so, we hope to foster critical discussions around social justice issues, as well as provide the public with a resource of cutting edge films and videos created by and impacting the LGBT community.

What do you think distinguishes Outcast Films from other distributors?

We only pick up the very best of LGBT films. Therefore, we spend time and money on actually marketing and promoting each film, unlike other distributors who will pick up 30-50 films a year and put them in a catalog. After the catalog is published, they move on to another 30-50 films a year.

I like to say that Outcast Films is a custom distributor: we work on each film as if it were our own.

How do you think independent film distribution has changed since Outcast was founded? How has the Internet changed distribution for Outcast Films?

I think the biggest change in indie film distribution in the last five years has been the way in which the Internet has opened up possibilities.

They are so many online communities, and focusing on the ones that you feel are pertinent can be nothing more than trial and error. It's one thing to get the word out; it's another to translate that into sales.

What is the biggest challenge in reaching such a media-saturated audience?

Very simple: standing out among the slew of media that's available. But we tend to form partnerships with other organizations that help us get the word out about the film.

How are the filmmakers involved in the distribution of their films?

Unlike some other distributors, we want to work closely with the filmmakers. Generally, filmmakers spend years making their films and so we believe that as experts of their particular film (and subject), filmmakers can only help in achieving the overall goals of our marketing, publicity, and of course sales expectations.

If the filmmakers have the time, we ask that film festivals invite them to their particular festivals to help promote the film. We will waive any rental fee if the festivals do this for us. That really helps keep the buzz going and ultimately, we hope it translates in to sales (which it has been doing so far)!

Filmmakers also provide insight into their particular subject and offer an expertise that, as distributors, we might not possess. Yet, we have become very savvy with many of these issues over time.

Because we consider our relationships with filmmakers as partnerships, we bring them in on all major decisions and marketing plans.

What are some upcoming Outcast films/filmmakers that we should look out for?

By far, our best-selling titles are from acclaimed filmmaker Su Friedrich. We digitally re-mastered her original 16mm negatives and made a collection of 13 films on five DVDs. A pivotal force in the establishment of Queer Cinema, Friedrich's collection includes her classic works such as *Sink or Swim*, *Hide and Seek* and *The Ties that Bind*.

Also, with recent releases like *Rock Bottom: Gay Men* we are helping to revitalize the dialogue about addiction among gay men and AIDS treatment activism. In addition, at a time when torture has haltingly become part of the national conversation, and when all Americans need to be thinking seriously about the violence in our systems of punishment and detention, *Cruel and Unusual* draws emotionally devastating attention to victims of violence who are persecuted for their stubborn visibility within the penal system but remain invisible to an indifferent world outside.

Our latest acquisition, *She's a Boy I Knew* has been screened at nearly 80 festivals worldwide. This thoughtful film is less a detailing of surgeries and more a meditation on family ties—a mapping of the transitions that take place within blood relationships, friendships, and love over a time of great personal transformation.

We in the LGBT community are literally fighting for our lives. Because film is an incredibly powerful medium, it's the perfect conduit to effect real positive change and to improve the quality of life for millions of people. Outcast Films wants to be a leader in the fight against discrimination.

SAMUEL GOLDWYN FILMS

An interview with Tom Quinn of Samuel Goldwyn Films

From *The Independent* June 2003
By Jason Guerrasio

When and why was Samuel Goldwyn Films created?

In the late 1970s, Samuel Goldwyn, Jr., created the Samuel Goldwyn Company, which then later became Samuel Goldwyn Films. He and our president, Meyer Gottlieb, have been working together since they created the first incarnation of the Samuel Goldwyn Company. We're looking to produce films that net anywhere between $5–10 million. We're also distributing films that range from foreign language to English language -- both our own productions, like *Tortilla Soup*, or acquisitions, like *Raising Victor Vargas*.

The mission of Samuel Goldwyn Films is...

...to produce and acquire films for the U.S. market.

How do you differ from MGM?

We have nothing to do with them. At one time, MGM created a specialty division called Goldwyn Film that had nothing to do with us. The only other relationship is that Sam's father was the first president, so the "G" in MGM is actually related to the family.

Tell me your affiliation with Fireworks Pictures and Stratosphere Entertainment.

We created a distribution partnership, IDP Distribution, with Fireworks and Stratosphere, two other companies that acquire films. We all acquire and fill the pipeline of IDP and sometimes we acquire together. It was basically a much more economical way to have a competitive distribution arm.

What types of films do you seek?

A whole variety. What I'm looking for pretty much runs the gamut of what you will find in specialized film. I think the majority of film that I look for, and Sam is looking for, can pretty much be traced back to his entire slate of films since the early 1980s. That encompasses films as far ranging as *Sid & Nancy* to *The Madness of King George*. I think our slate now reveals the scope of what we can do, between stuff like *The Man from Elysian Fields* to Ingmar Bergman's *Faithless* to *Raising Victor Vargas*. We have not done a documentary in some time, but we are certainly looking to find something [we can market theatrically]. Everything that we buy is theatrical. We do not buy for straight-to-video, and we only buy for the U.S.

Explain what you mean by specialized film.

There are a lot of different types of films that I think qualify as specialized films. One common denominator of what I call specialized film is any release that is 600 prints or under. That's really the only common denominator.

Where and how do you find them?

We track the world quite competitively. We will do Cannes, Sundance, Toronto. We'll also do London screenings when they happen. But on top of that, I will also go to Paris, Guadalajara, Hong Kong. It's a lot of travel during the year. If you can't necessarily have a staff to cover the entire world by virtue of pure labor, I think you will have to go out and make relationships that matter so that you are fairly considered with the other distributors. That's what we try to do. We try to build strong relationships because we are definitely an aggressive buyer, but we're not a volume buyer. On the flip side, the one thing I'm most proud of is that per film, IDP has had an incredible average, and has done far better than other specialized distributors at some of the major studios.

How many films do you acquire per year?

About eight films per year, but that number could go up. Honestly, it's not a quota, and the beauty is if we see something we like, we want to buy it.

How do you work with the filmmakers when preparing their films for release?

It's an open-door policy. You have so many people you can call to get something done. You can call me. You can call our head of distribution. You can call our head of publicity. You can call Sam. You can call our president, Meyer. It may be too open-door policy, but I feel that's the kind of place Sam wants to provide to the filmmakers. We want them to be happy with the release. We want them to be involved. Honestly, we don't want to buy movies where the filmmaker is not going to be involved, because we feel they know the film as well as we do, if not better.

How should filmmakers approach you with their projects?

At any level. If it's the right project, we'll pull the trigger. But since we don't have a quota to fill, it's very much in line with our taste, and we will not compromise that.

What advice can you give filmmakers seeking distribution?

There are certain signs that spell success: It's being at the right festival, being in the right section, having the right materials, having the right word-of-mouth before the movie ever gets screened. Making the movie is, unfortunately, half the process. The other half is marketing it. In marketing a film to an audience, you have to be just as precise, just as passionate, and just as involved. Don't think that you can turn it over to any random producer rep or a sales agent and just sit back and go on to your next movie. You've really got to pay attention, because there's a lot you can do.

What are some issues Samuel Goldwyn Films faces as an independent distributor at the present time?

There were twenty-five plus specialized films released in December, all high-quality films from studios. *About Schmidt*, one of greatest specialized films ever, is really a $5 million indie film, and that is competition. *Punch-Drunk Love*, one of the most expensive art films I've ever seen, is amazing. You've just got to be very smart, you have to be very aggressive, and you've got to make the right choices. And I would say that so far we have been pretty successful.

SEVENTH ART RELEASING

Ten years since their last interview with *The Independent*, co-founder Udy Epstein talks about the changing face of Seventh Art Releasing.

From The Independent June 2009
By Emily Cataneo

Seventh Art Releasing is a distributor and sales company founded in 1994 by Jonathan Cordish and Udy Epstein. The company is known for distributing award-winning documentaries and fiction films, many dealing with Jewish culture, lesbian and gay issues, human rights, music, and popular culture. Exactly a decade since their last interview with *The Independent*, co-founder Udy Epstein talks about the how Seventh Art Releasing has changed over the last 10 years, but more importantly, how its vision has stayed the same.

How would you describe Seventh Art Releasing?

We are basically a full-service independent distributor of mostly documentary films, but we do fiction as well, including non-theatrical films.

Since your last interview with *The Independent* in 1999, how has Seventh Art Releasing changed?

Obviously, the marketplace has changed dramatically in the past 10 years, and not necessarily for the best. The interesting part would be that in terms of size, scope, and areas of interest, Seventh Art has not changed that much. In terms of operations and media, of course, there's a huge difference. But we're pretty much the same size company we were 10 years ago, dealing with similar sized films. We stayed away from the Hollywood game, to the point that people still think we're based in New York, even though we're based in Los Angeles. We devised ways to work and market and distribute in all media. Since we were already thinking that way 10 years ago, it was easier for us to adjust to the changing marketplace, the harder times, the increasing costs. We work a lot with producers, which is probably the most significant change. We still have a fully functional theatrical system with marketing, PR, and all those things that are required to run a theatrical company.

In 1999, you had 30 films in your collection. How many do you have now?

We have many more, but again, it's a combination of feature-length films, one-hour television specials, and shorts. When I said we had 30, I meant full-length films. Our library now is about 10 times that, but a lot of that is shorts. But our library now is somewhere around 300.

Who's working for Seventh Art Releasing these days?

From 10 years ago, a lot has changed. There's myself, James Eowan, Oliver Ike, our head of theatrical sales, and we have Shane Griffin, our head of sales and acquisitions. Those are the more important people.

How have the Internet and new technology changed Seventh Art Releasing over the past 10 years?

Obviously, we use it a lot for research, marketing, and that kind of thing. The big news is that everyone's hoping that the new technology that's already here will revive independent content. Marketing costs in traditional media are such that a lot of sensitive delicate content can't get on mainstream. But everyone in the independent world figures that through streaming and the Internet you can get to whoever is interested in your content. Nowadays with streaming, with download to view, download to burn and all those options, that is in theory smart and the way of the future. But for some reason, that I don't think anyone can explain, it's not quite monetized yet, to the level of filmmakers that we serve. That's an issue that's of great concern to us. And I hear from a lot of companies, bigger and smaller than us, on the video side, on the educational side, that are all saying the same thing. The actual amount that our kind of films generate from new media is not yet sufficient. Having said that, it's not that we don't have any new films from there.

We work with Netflix and iTunes to promote our films, and definitely, that's where the tide is turning and the new media are definitely where we're going with this.

What are some films that you've distributed recently?

We've been working on a documentary called *The Queen and I*. It's about the life of the Shah, the ex-leader of Iran, who was ousted in the Islamic Revolution. He's dead, she's still around, and she speaks about her life. This was the first time she was willing to expose herself. The film's director was another Iranian expatriate.

We also just premiered *Bloody Mondays and Strawberry Pies*, narrated by John Malkovich. It's an essay about the meaning of life and the meaning of time and boredom. It's cerebral, but it's an exciting and invigorating film. Clearly, not a film in the Megaplex near you, but a film for students and people like that, looking into interesting and challenging material. It's a pretty exciting film.

How do you locate films to screen, and how should filmmakers approach you for consideration? What's the process for selecting a film?

We go to a lot of film festivals around the world, and screenings that we're invited to, and we look at stuff that we like, and we follow it from there, and we also get submissions from people we know, and sometimes from people we don't know. We'd rather people tell us what the film is before they send it over to us, and we can save them time and money if it's not suitable. We do accept unsolicited submissions because we're smaller. Once companies are bigger, there are all sorts of legal issues about being able to do that. If you look at a year, we probably look at thousands of films. We also look at works in progress, because of the production work we do. There's a lot to look at, and that's part of the process. It's filtering stuff for that .1 percent that's actually suitable for us, so it's a lot of work, and it's very hard to know where you're going to get your next films from. All you have to do is go to our website, email, and tell us who you are and what you're interested in, and we'll look at it and if we're interested, we'll contact you.

What advice would you give to independent filmmakers who are approaching you with their films?

If you're approaching any company, you need to know a little bit about what they are and what they have done. You need to know what films they've done, get a feel for what it is you're asking of them, if there's a potential fit. Research is very important—and to see what's going on out there, to be involved and in the know about things.

What do you think is the most important social issue being addressed by the independent filmmakers whose works you distribute?

I've been known over the years for being, let's say, a realist, so I don't want to tell the filmmakers to make a film about something just because the subject is important. We're not nonprofit, we're not funded by any state funds. But I can tell you from a personal standpoint, a lot of the films that we're handling right now have to do with the environment. We try to be realistic about what we do, but we're also motivated in our selection by issues, so we're an issue-driven company, for most of our films. But sometimes we take fun films that aren't about a big issue, but are just good films.

What makes Seventh Art stand out from other independent distributors?

I think we blend very interestingly theatrical sensibilities and educational sensibilities. Usually it's very clear-cut. If you're theatrical, you work at a different level. If it's education, it's a whole different ballgame. But we're blending the two. We want to give our films a traditional release, which is a very smart thing to do, but our content is less commercial and more sensitive. Those are two legs, and the third leg is that we're from a production and filmmaking background. It creates something that's at least unique. For that matter, I'll bring another film title into the fold. Family Inc. it's not a theatrical film, but we're helping to finish it, and it's been mostly edited in Hong Kong. It's really a global story that's very hard to explain, to define, but it's sort of a film with Asian-American sensibilities in a global world. So we stand out because of our ability to keep uncompromising content alive in the very, very tough reality that we all face right now. And we, like anybody else, but even more so, definitely feel the economic pinch.

What would you say is the most important issue facing Seventh Art today?

We want to keep doing what we're doing in terms of promoting the same kind of content: mostly socially responsible documentaries. We need to be able to keep our head out of the water and survive this hard economic time.

Where do you see Seventh Art ten years from now?

I don't know. I mean, it's hard to predict. The way I see it now, beside the fact that we want to survive, we don't have any big game plan to grow, to deal with mainstream, big production, Hollywood and all that. Our focus is to stay the course. Of course, there will be a lot of changes: changing economy, changing reality, changing of the new media, all the commercial implications, all of the changes. But in terms of the overall view, it's almost like the more things change, the more they stay the same. We're very confident being where we are. We started this company to service a world-view, and now we're looking back, and it's still there. We want to keep that going.

Anything else you want the world to know about Seventh Art?

We make great coffee here. We have an espresso machine we got on Craigslist. It's probably the best coffee you can get in any distribution office. We don't go to the Evil Empire anymore. We don't work for the man. We make our own coffee.

WELLSPRING MEDIA

An interview with Wendy Lidell and Marie Therese Guirgis, who are looking for that "inherent dramatic arc"– that, and good PR possibilities

From *The Independent* October 2003
By Jason Guerrasio

What is Wellspring Media?

Lidell: It's one of the only independent film distributors that has the capacity to distribute theatrically, on television, domestically, internationally, and on home video. It's the successor company to Winstar and Fox Lorber.

Guirgis: We also have a department that co-produces documentaries between acquisitions and international sales, so basically we raise financing for largely domestic projects by means of pre-selling them to international broadcasters for documentaries, sometimes for series. We haven't done it for fiction films.

When and why was Wellspring created?

Lidell: It was created in the early 1980s. It was initially an international sales company for American independent filmmakers and then it added its home video arm and in 1998, the theatrical. The beauty of the company is that it's so multi-faceted. It can provide one-stop-shopping for the filmmaker, as we can drive revenue in all the different markets. We're not talking about blockbusters. Releasing it in any one market will not pay back the production cost, but if you can combine revenue streams from all those different markets—you make a little bit internationally, you make a little bit theatrically—and combine them then there's something really valuable and enables us to return meaningful revenues to the producers.

Through all the change, has the mission of the company stayed the same?

Lidell: I think it's always been a commitment to the best quality work. I think the way that that's implemented has continued to evolve and gotten better and better.

What types of films do you seek?

Guirgis: We always seek the same kinds of films, which are high end, very independent, high quality, art films, be they fiction or non-fiction. So, they can be films from already famous filmmakers or emerging filmmakers, but they will be films that have a really strong vision and a strong voice that will likely be embraced by the critical community and are likely to stand out from the pack.

How do you find films?

Guirgis: Traditional film festival routes and, because of our reputation, we have relationships with filmmakers and producers overseas as well as in the U.S. For video we work with other distributors who don't have their own video division and we release their films. We also initiate certain projects like *Devil's Playground* that we did with HBO and had at Sundance last year.

What festivals do you attend?

Guirgis: The most important festivals for where we find what we'll release theatrically are Cannes, Toronto, Sundance, and Berlin. Those are the top four.

Are there any second tier festivals that you attend annually?

Guirgis: There are certainly festivals that we don't attend but that we look at: Slamdance, Seattle, San Francisco, and Chicago. Then internationally there's Rotterdam, Hot Docs. We go to Full Frame.

What does a documentary need to have to grab your attention?

Guirgis: For domestic theatrical distribution, I would say a subject matter that people have never seen before, so it generates a lot of press, or a very audience-friendly, uplifting film. It needs to have something that's outstandingly unusual or extremely well-directed because theatrical releasing is so tough for docs.

Lidell: Those that work best theatrically tend to have a dramatic arc and work as a narrative, the same way that a drama does, but it just happens to be reality based. *Harlan County, Capturing the Friedmans, Spellbound, Hoop Dreams*, those have an inherent dramatic arc.

What do you look for on the television side?

Guirgis: For television we look at docs for international television, so it's harder to describe what works. It's easier to say what *doesn't* sell. The political/social docs do not work overseas because they focus on topics that people aren't familiar with— unless it's something really unusual like *Devil's Playground* or some American phenomenon that is so American that it's perceived by people overseas as kind of exotic.

How many films do you acquire per year?

Lidell: For theatrical it's six to eight releases a year.

Guirgis: We know we have to fill those six to eight slots but we might acquire twelve films in a year.

How many of those are documentaries?

Guirgis: Not many for domestic theatrical distribution. We acquire many documentaries to sell internationally.

How should filmmakers approach you with their projects?

Guirgis: The most effective way, especially for domestic release, is to attempt to get into some of the bigger film festivals just because it's hard for us to acquire something, especially if it's an unknown entity, without exposure to a film festival. Also, try to contact producers' representatives; they really help sell films. They can call our attention to a film that we otherwise might not pay that much attention to. A lot of people just submit their films to us, but it's harder that way. We certainly look at everything and get back to people, but we don't pay as much attention to those as we do films that are in festivals.

How do you work with the filmmakers when preparing their films for release?

Lidell: We don't like to be tied contractually, but usually the filmmaker can inspire us to take the film in the right direction. Usually our filmmakers are foreign so suggestions are by phone or e-mail, but at the end of the day I feel I can sell the film better than the filmmaker can. My job is not to portray the film in the way the filmmaker would, but to get as many people into the theater to see the film as I possibly can.

What advice can you give filmmakers seeking distribution?

Guirgis: For American filmmakers: really explore the foreign film festivals because there are a number of cases of American films that were rejected here, but noticed abroad. Sometimes films that are a little more experimental will be appreciated more by foreign festivals and foreign audiences and then they get attention here. *George Washington* is a perfect example of that.

Lidell: I think the mistake that many documentary filmmakers make is to think that they are going to have a theatrical doc so they make it 90 minutes, even though the subject and the material is only good for 30 minutes, or 60 minutes, or 58 minutes, or 45 minutes. Stretching it out in the hopes for a theatrical release will backfire because the film won't be the best it can be.

WOLFE RELEASING

How one of the oldest and largest distributors of LGBT films stays on top of an ever-changing industry

From *The Independent* January 2008
By Michele Meek

A lot has changed since 1985, when Kathy Wolfe started Wolfe Releasing in order to distribute lesbian films on video. For one thing, 20 years ago, the acronym LGBT—which stands for Lesbian, Gay, Bisexual and Transgender—didn't even exist. And words like "gay" and "queer" were still derogatory, not yet taken on as proud emblems. So it's not surprising that LGBT cinema too has grown and flourished in the last two decades, moving beyond a cult following and entering the mainstream culture. And with that, Wolfe's focus has shifted towards representing new award-winning LGBT films from around the world, as well as rescuing classic lesbian and gay films from oblivion.

Now in its 22nd year, Wolfe is the oldest and largest exclusive distributor of gay and lesbian films in the world. *The Independent* recently caught up with Jenni Olson, Wolfe Releasing's director of e-commerce and consumer marketing (and an original co-founder of PlanetOut.com), to learn more about how LGBT cinema has changed over the years and how Wolfe represents independent filmmakers.

When and why was Wolfe created?

Our CEO and founder, Kathy Wolfe, started the company back in 1985 to distribute lesbian films on video. At the time, there were very few lesbian and gay films being made and it was extremely difficult for consumers to get access to them. The company has come a very long way since then, but our primary mission continues to be bringing the best LGBT entertainment to people everywhere.

What is your elevator pitch?

Wolfe is the oldest and largest exclusive distributor of gay and lesbian films in the world. In 2007, we released more than 20 films, from Thom Fitzgerald's epic *3 Needles*, which was selected by the United Nations to be screened on World AIDS Day 2007; to director Katherine Brooks' record-breaking film *Loving Annabelle*; to *Outing Riley* from Project Greenlight winner, Pete Jones; to the Taiwanese lesbian love story *Spider Lilies*, winner of the Teddy Award for best queer film at the 2007 Berlin Film Festival. Wolfe has been a long-standing leader in the video industry and enjoys significant sales with Target, Blockbuster, Hollywood Video,

Amazon.com, Netflix, Wal-Mart and Best Buy to name a few. Traffic to the WolfeVideo.com site now tops one million impressions each month.

How many titles does Wolfe represent?

There are about 100 features and documentaries in our library, as well as several dozen shorts.

How many films do you acquire per year?

Wolfe releases 15-20 features a year, and roughly the same number of shorts.

What is the difference between Wolfe Video and Wolfe Releasing?

Wolfe Video is our long-standing DVD and video label. Wolfe Video also represents the other significant part of our business, which is direct sales to consumers of all kinds of LGBT DVDs, ranging from The L Word to Brokeback Mountain and everything in between. We're proud to be able to help LGBT people from all over North America get the queer movies they're looking for via our website and through our quarterly mail-order catalogs.

Wolfe Releasing handles LGBT features, documentaries, and shorts for festival, nontheatrical, digital delivery, foreign sales, you name it.

How has LGBT cinema and the distribution of it changed since Wolfe started?

Of course it's very exciting that there has been such a boom in LGBT entertainment over this past decade in particular. The landscape has changed so significantly. Consumers have access to more LGBT films and TV shows and other forms of media than ever before. There are so many distribution opportunities now for filmmakers, I think it can be quite daunting.

In addition to the traditional avenues of film distribution that we offer, Wolfe is also fully engaged in the new media space with video on demand and through deals with all the best digital distribution services. This yields new revenue sources and creates new audiences for queer cinema. Consumers can now stream over 50 titles from Wolfe at such destinations as Movielink and Akimbo.

What advice can you give filmmakers seeking distribution?

Get to know the distributors you're considering by talking to them and asking questions. Do they have experience releasing your type of film? Do they have experience with the gay market, the lesbian market? Or perhaps your film should be targeted to other communities as well. Look at the other films the company has released. Does it seem like they will be able to do a good job with your film? Also, talk to other filmmakers who have worked with the distributors you are considering and ask about their experiences. When you start talking about the details of the contract—territories, types of rights, length of the term, royalty percentages, etc. — don't be afraid to ask a lot of questions about anything you don't understand.

Your distributor is your partner. It should work very hard for you to get your film the best exposure and to generate revenue through rental fees, broadcast or foreign sales, and DVD sales. But also remember that nobody loves your film as much as you do! Stay involved in the process all the way through. There is so much work to be done and you are still the person to do it—in particular around getting the media coverage you want and doing grassroots audience outreach.

How do you acquire films and how should a filmmaker approach you?

Our staff attends all the major film festivals looking for films, but we also are happy to have submissions directly from filmmakers. Our acquisitions director is Jeffrey Winter.

We are always looking for new work. Please send a tape or DVD and supporting materials about your film to our address.

Online Distribution

By Michele Meek

Video blogs, vodcasts, YouTube—in many ways it seems that independent filmmakers have taken the Internet by force. But what about independent films picked up for distribution? In many cases, they are notably missing from the online arena. Companies like Zipporah Films, Women Make Movies, and Davidson Films still stick with their tried-and-true model of charging a few hundred dollars per VHS and DVD and have yet to make a switch to online downloads.

In fact, many independent distributors fear the gradual (or dramatic) shaving off of their profits by a move online. This has been an issue for independent filmmakers and distributors for decades—the conversion from film to VHS in the 1980s led to a tenfold retail price cut. As a result, many distributors proceed with trepidation, believing that new technologies may destroy them and that *sharing* profit simply means *less* profit. For many distributors, there is just too little confidence that the market could be expanded. The piece of the pie is fixed—and it's small.

Although exaggerated, their fear is not entirely unfounded. The film industry in general has seen prices continue to drop. Companies like BestBuy and Wal-Mart keep lowering the bar, leaving consumers wondering why they should pay $39.95 for a film no one's ever heard of when they can get the latest James Bond flick for $9.95. Even the educational video market, which has long been a safe-haven for hefty price tags, is feeling pressure from giants like Amazon.com and Discovery Education.

Meanwhile, Hollywood's move online has been hesitant, at best. Apple announced its launch of iTunes movies but even a few months later there are only a few hundred films available. Perhaps even more problematic is the fact that purchases as well as rentals come only in a "locked" format making it difficult to transfer it to non-Apple phones or devices (and even some older Apple devices). Hollywood seems poised to make the same fatal mistake the music industry made—offering an absurdly small selection of titles, charging the same price as physical formats, and then locking buyers into a useless format they can't maneuver as easily as a plain old DVD. And simultaneously, there is already an arsenal of websites and peer-to-peer networks offering pirated downloads with a wider selection of films for cheap (or free) in flexible file formats.

So where does this leave the independent filmmaker and distributor?

They say if you can't beat 'em, join 'em. In fact, now is the time when independents have the real opportunity to win over audiences. As Hollywood falters, online movie sites are more open to independent and off-beat content. And eager audiences await. Why not grab the views when you can? The money will surely follow, right?

It just may be, especially when you consider companies like Movieflix.com's revenues are over $1 million per year—and only 20 percent of that comes from adult films. And EZTakes has noted that when they put a movie online for free with ad-supported viewing, the download-to-DVD sales of those movies increase by an average of 20 percent (ad revenues are shared with rights owners as well). And even companies like Documentary Educational Resources found that when they put their movies online through Google Video their market did expand (although unfortunately Google shifted out of the educational market when they purchased YouTube).

For independent distributors and filmmakers eager to join the online revolution, there are dozens of sites that distribute. So we did some research to figure out which sites you were most likely to come across in your research and what you should know about each.

EZTAKES
Created: June 2003

Elevator pitch: EZTakes lets consumers buy movie downloads that will play on PCs, Macs, DVD players, iPods, Zunes, and just about any other portable device.

Number of films: About 4,000

Source: Mostly from distributors.

Criteria for new films: We look for marketable titles that you don't trip over in Wal-Mart. However, we usually don't take one or two films, unless those films promise to be extremely marketable. Right now, we're looking for catalogs. In the future, we'll also be offering a self-service publishing option that will give smaller publishers an opportunity to sell via EZTakes.

Technical rundown: We require an authored DVD. If the rights holder has art work (cover, label, poster) and meta data (director, producer, plot, etc.) in digital format (e.g., spreadsheet), that's even better. It's also very important to get a good quality trailer when you're selling online. After we get DVDs, they usually start showing up on EZTakes in a few weeks. Some of our distributor partners simply send us shrink-wrapped DVDs as they become available, and we get everything else we need from their website.

Fees: In the "independent" category, downloads run anywhere from free to about $20, but most DVD downloads fall in the $6-7 range. EZTakes also sells physical DVDs which can be mailed.

Payment to filmmakers: Two thirds for the rights holder and one third for us. Plus we give a 50-50 split on ad revenue.

Advice for filmmakers: Don't fall for the lie that Digital Rights Management (DRM) copy protection can do anything for you. Even just one copy of digital content on a file share can be copied an unlimited number of times. All DRM will do is penalize your paying customers by making what you sell much worse than what they can get for free. DRM is pushed like heroin by companies like Microsoft and Apple who only want to lock you and your customers in with proprietary technologies. Once they have you hooked, they can increase switching costs, block competitors, and extract more money from you.

The future of the industry: Like the music industry has already discovered, the film industry will have to learn that customers rule. Successful models will be the ones that create customer value, not the ones designed to protect existing businesses. Once the film industry realizes that, it can begin to make money by exploiting innovative services that cater to consumers.

Author's Take: This seems like the least buggy of the sites. In addition, it's easy to navigate, professionally designed, and prices are easy to see and understand for consumers. Downside is they may not take your film if you are just trying to market one.

Details provided by EZTakes marketing department, www.eztakes.com.

JAMAN

Created: Jaman founder and CEO Gaurav Dhillon has long been a film lover and perhaps most importantly, he loves movies from around the world. He visited Argentina two years ago and saw some extraordinary movies, but when he came back home, he couldn't find them to share them with friends and family. (As you likely know, less than 1% of the world's movies make it to the U.S. theaters). Quality movies are made in every country, but before Jaman, there wasn't an easy place to get them. He founded Jaman to change the way people around the world discover, enjoy, and share movies.

Elevator pitch: Jaman is pioneering entertainment on the Internet by delivering high-definition films to a growing online community of fans and filmmakers. Viewers around the globe can browse and select from the Jaman library of thousands of unique films and then download these movies directly onto their PCs, Macs, televisions and other devices such as AppleTVs and TiVos. Jaman's popular community features provide a forum where people review, discuss, and share world class films with each other. Jaman is based in San Mateo, California, and is backed by luminaries in technology and media.

Number of films: Over 3,500

Source: Mainly distributors, but there are some cases where we've been moved by a particular film and went directly to the filmmaker to get the movie up on Jaman. We go to film festivals and see films; we have a film-loving team at Jaman who is always sniffing out great movies; and we track the buzz of films.

Criteria for new films: Media that matters. We have quality films, many of which have important messages.

Technical rundown: We have a number of film industry folks on staff—they make up a little factory here.

Fees: Most rentals are $1.99 and most purchases $4.99. There are many shorts available for free. Included in this list are the recently added Mira Nair's AIDS Jaago shorts, four dramatic mini-movies that aim to dismantle myths about HIV/AIDS. Additionally, in the near future, a good majority of our films will be made free with advertising (people can opt out of the advertisements and continue to pay the rental or purchase price).

Payment to filmmakers: First dollar gross. [Author's note: First dollar gross means an adjusted gross participation payable from the first dollar of receipts.]

Advice for filmmakers: Yes, there is a big world out there so go global! Jaman's traffic comes from 220 countries, we know that the world is hungry for film and the audience is large.

The future of the industry: Very bright. There is perhaps a change in perspective on this—instead of the goal being to sell films, the Internet provides more of a "democratization of film" where independent filmmakers are in the business of renting our their films. In other words, they own the film and get revenue by leasing it out non-exclusively.

Author's take: Probably the most professional design of all the sites, Jaman has a good selection of mainstream indies like *Italian for Beginners* to personal indies like *Kintaro Walks Japan*. It also has a cool filter to help visitors sort movies. Fees are hard to find but consistent once you're logged in and looking at films.

Details provided by Gaurav Dhillon, founder and CEO of Jaman, www.jaman.com

FILMON.COM

Created: by Alki David in 2006 because he was fed up with being ripped off by distributors.

Elevator pitch: Filmed Entertainment Portal to the Future.

Number of films: 38,000 premium titles aggregated; currently 2,500 online.

Source: Filmmakers and distributors. We have over 60 content partners from Paramount to Granada to Playboy to individual producers.

Criteria for new films: Is it good? Is it legal?

Technical rundown: DVD is sent to London office where it is encoded to a MPEG2 file. Then it is put on the servers and copied to servers in New Jersey, London, Amsterdam, and Hong Kong. It is converted to MPEG4 and available via our proprietary network for distribution. Images and text update from the London office.

Fees: Prices around $2-4 for most movies.

Payment to filmmakers: 50-50 revenue share on all sales. Also, get your own white label for free and you receive 100% of white label revenue.

Advice for filmmakers: Only the obvious: find the portal that suits your market and get on it.

The future of the industry: The future is now. You can build a following through FilmOn's upload service at http://moviebuffs.filmon.com. If you have a serious commercial offering, contact us at info@filmon.com

Author's Take: It's kind of annoying how you have to register before you can even see what movies are available—seems like an unnecessary barrier that might turn users away. Also, some films are not available for download in the U.S. (FilmOn.com is a UK company). Still it seems that they have a lot of films and resources, and they are definitely poised to make a dent in the industry.

Details provided by Alki David, www.filmon.com

MOVIEFLIX

Created: We began in 1999 as place for independent filmmakers to show their work.

Number of Films: We have approximately 4,000 movies as well as over 2.5 million members.

Source: Both distributors and filmmakers. We are always open to submissions from indie filmmakers.

Criteria for new films: It depends really. We just have to like it.

Technical rundown: We receive the film. We capture and then encode the film. Now it's ready to be added to our streaming servers as well as the MovieFlix.com website.

Fees: MovieFlix Plus has a $9.95/month fee for unlimited streaming as well as downloading. The download is download-to-own option. They also have about 1,500 free films.

Payment to filmmakers: We usually do a revenue share. Each agreement is different.

Advice for filmmakers: Read the agreement before submitting your work.

Author's Take: Revenues are impressive. Not sure the "family filter" works properly—I tried turning it on and still got films like *'Tis a Pity She's a Whore*. Not that I have anything against *'Tis Pity She's a Whore*, but it might not be something you want to watch with your mom. Company response was that the film had slipped through and was now added to the filter.

Details provided by Robert Moskovits from MovieFlix, www.movieflix.com

Adventures in Self-Distribution

By Lynn Tryba

Long after they wrap their films, independent filmmakers struggle to get their projects seen by as many people as possible. A distribution deal with a mainstream distribution company is, of course, the Holy Grail. And in the quest for a deal, a filmmaker's family ties will often get strained, their bank accounts will dwindle, and their stress level will surge.

One of the worst parts about the distribution game is that getting your film into a lot of festivals is by no means a guarantee of success. Even a film accepted at Sundance only has about a 5 percent shot of landing a deal.

So what's an indie filmmaker to do? One option – often more of a necessary evil than an alternative lifestyle – is to self distribute your film. This takes hard work, going theater to theater, pleading your case, perfecting your sales pitch, and praying, if you do get a chance to screen your film, that the house will fill before the opening credits role. So we asked three filmmakers fresh off self-distribution success to explain how they pulled it off. Here are their stories.

CASE STUDY 1: *THE SENSATION OF SIGHT*

Filmmaker Buzz McLaughlin wasn't happy with the few distribution offers he received for his film, The Sensation of Sight, *which stars David Strathairn as an encyclopedia salesman in a small New England town. So McLaughlin decided to distribute the film himself in New Hampshire. Could he sell out a theater with more than 900 seats? And even if he could, what would that say about the film's financial viability?*

It's no wonder Buzz McLaughlin feels some pride and relief. His New Hampshire-based film production company, Either/Or Films, just signed a distribution deal for its first movie, *The Sensation of Sight*, during the last week of March. It's been four years since fundraising for the film began and more than four months since the company he founded with *Sensation's* writer, Aaron Wiederspahn, self-distributed the film in New Hampshire.

Monterey Media, one of the biggest outside suppliers of programs for PBS, is now handling the film's limited domestic theatrical release in the U.S. and Canada. Monterey Media's familiarity with *Sensation's* lead actor, David Strathairn, perhaps best known for his Oscar-nominated role in *Good Night, and Good Luck*, was one of the factors leading to the deal, McLaughlin says. The company released another of the actor's films, *Steel Toes*, last year, and knows "Strathairn draws viewers," the filmmaker says.

McLaughlin and Strathairn first worked together in the theater when McLaughlin was an artistic director. The actor loved the *Sensation of Sight* script and was attached to the project from the beginning. This helped with fundraising and attracting other actors such as Ian Somerhalder, Jane Adams, and Ann Cusack.

Expectations were high when the film, shot in the fall of 2005, began making the rounds on the international film festival circuit. *Sensation* made its world premiere at the San Sebastian Film Festival in Spain in September 2006, and its U.S premiere at the Denver Film Festival. It has since screened in 20 festivals on five continents, and is still on the circuit. But the film was not accepted into the few big venues that the distributors attend, like Cannes, Toronto, Berlin, Rotterdam, and Sundance, McLaughlin says. Thus, despite the festival momentum, *Sensation* initially failed to land a credible distribution deal. There were offers, McLaughlin concedes, but he and the other filmmakers always believed they could do better.

In the fall of 2007, the founding partners decided to self-distribute the film in New Hampshire, where it was shot, to see if they could generate some buzz. They knew it was their chance to prove to distributors that the movie could draw an audience. The New Hampshire premiere took place on November 9, 2007, in the 930-seat Colonial Theatre in Keene, a picturesque college town in the southwest corner of the state. The filmmakers promoted the event heavily, which ensured that it sold out on opening night. The movie ran for a few more days in Keene before moving onto Peterborough, the small town where *Sensation* was filmed. Then, it was on to the Red River Theatres in Concord, New Hampshire.

Because of the big turn-out in Keene, the per-screen-average for the film's opening week came in at fourth in the nation, which drew the attention of industry insiders. *Variety* and *Box Office Mojo* published the numbers, and the calls from domestic and international distributors, all of whom were looking for a good sleeper, started to pour in.

"Getting a film distributed is like a golf swing," McLaughlin says today. "We've proven that we can follow through now that our distribution deal is signed and closed. That works tremendously in our favor for our next project."

The bottom line: If your film doesn't get into the major festivals where distributors will be in attendance, you need to do whatever you can to keep momentum going for your project. If you decide to self-distribute—and many independent film producers have no choice—you need to handle it very carefully and make sure people turn out for your movie.

CASE STUDY 2: *BUDDY*

When she couldn't find a distributor for her documentary Buddy: The Rise and Fall of America's Most Notorious Mayor, *a documentary about Buddy Cianci, the colorful mayor of Providence, Rhode Island, Cherry Arnold went to a local art house looking for help. The booker gave her some advice that he meant sarcastically, and that hurt her feelings. But she actually followed it, to great success.*

Cherry Arnold didn't know what she was in for when she started filming *Buddy: The Rise and Fall of America's Most Notorious Mayor*. "If I had known all the work involved...," Arnold says. "Pure ignorance kept me going. I underestimated by months at a time how long each step would take."

The award-winning documentary—which she produced and directed—profiles the charismatic and controversial Buddy Cianci, who served almost 20 years as mayor of Providence, R.I., before being found guilty of conspiracy. Cianci was sent to prison in 2002 and served five years time.

Arnold originally planned to find a director of photography or cameraperson to do most of the filming, but she ended up doing most of the work herself. "The same thing happened every step of the way until the end," she said. And that included distribution.

When her film started racking up awards on the film festival circuit, Arnold thought she could relax—she was so sure her film would be picked up for distribution.

But no one bit. She began making the rounds at television studios in New York City, using her contacts to get the film in front of top decision makers. "They would say it didn't fit the format or it was too long," she said. "It was always something."

For guidance, she turned to one of her mentors, Louis Alvarez from the Center of New American Media. He remained convinced there were people who wanted to see her movie; she just needed to get the film in front of them. He advised her to get the film into local theaters.

Arnold, once again not knowing what she was in for but having no choice, said, "OK."

She started with an art house in Providence. Working with the booker proved difficult and, at one point, he suggested she go talk to the "Redstone people." Arnold realized that he was sarcastically suggesting she talk to the president of National Amusements—Shari Redstone, the daughter of Sumner Redstone who is majority owner of CBS, Viacom, MTV, and other major brands. The chain owns several theaters in Providence. "It was like I'd been kicked in the stomach," Arnold recalls. But then she thought: "What the hell, I'll call."

It took a long time to reach Redstone by phone, but Arnold was finally able to connect with her office and send her a screener. "My expectations were really rock bottom," Arnold said. "I was very much in debt at this point."

National Amusements agreed to show the film in two theaters in Providence, giving Arnold "an unbelievable percentage" of the ticket sales because the booker "knew how much work I was doing," she says.

And as Alvarez had suspected, there was indeed an audience for the film. *Buddy* became the top-grossing movie in the region for four weeks running.

The theatrical run's success gave Arnold the money to make DVDs, which can be ordered online through Amazon.com or purchased at all Borders, Blockbusters, and Barnes & Noble stores in Rhode Island.

Making a film reminds Arnold of entrepreneurs who launch start-ups. "Had they known how hard it would be, they're so glad they don't know it ahead of time."

That being said, Arnold has no regrets. She is proud of the film and grateful to all the people who helped her finish it. She is looking forward to her next project: a cinema vérité film about autism.

The bottom line: Arnold suggests you learn as much as you can about the financial end of things at the beginning of a project. Each type of documentary will have a different business model. Filmmakers always need to have contingency plans. If you aren't flexible at every stage of filmmaking, including distribution, you are making things harder for yourself. Finally, she says, surround yourself with people such as mentors who are passionate about your subject and want to help.

CASE STUDY 3: *ON BROADWAY*

Writer-director Dave McLaughlin and producer-actor Lance Greene took inspiration from their own screenplay: On Broadway *is the story of a working-class Boston man named Jack (played by Joey McIntyre), who writes a play and then has to figure out how and where it might be produced. He ultimately settles on a bar on Broadway, the main drag in South Boston from which the film draws its title. Just as their protagonist showed creativity and tenacity in making sure his artistic vision found full expression, the filmmakers hustled to get* On Broadway *screened in a handful of Boston-area theaters. Along the way, they turned their cause into a community event.*

On Broadway, a movie about a working-class Bostonian's attempt to stage a play in the back of an Irish pub, has received such a good response from film festival audiences around the country that the producers decided to self-release the film in Boston.

The film had more star power than the average indie production: former New Kids on the Block heartthrob Joey McIntyre stars as Joe, the film's playwright protagonist, and Will Arnett of *Arrested Development* fame plays a supporting role.

The struggles of McIntyre's South Boston character to get his play staged echo the methods McLaughlin and Greene used to build buzz for the film. The filmmakers engaged in heavy grassroots marketing, and targeted a surprisingly wide audience. Boston film students came to support a homegrown production, 30-something viewers came with some residual interest in McIntyre, and some more conservative older viewers came to see a heartwarming story that could be a source of pride in the same way that *Good Will Hunting* was to the city years ago.

The box office numbers from theaters in Dedham, Somerville, West Newton, Weymouth, and Sharon, were impressive. The per-screen average for the show's run from March 14 to March 20 was $2,250, and the film grossed about $5,000 in one day at one of the Boston-area theaters.

"Those are studio numbers," boasts Lance Greene, an actor-producer who worked with director and writer Dave McLaughlin to get distribution for the film. Indeed, in three of the five theaters it screened in, *On Broadway* was the top-grossing film of the week, beating out major studio films.

Building on that success, the film opened March 28 in Newport, R.I., and on April 5 in Providence, R.I., earning good reviews in both cities. The filmmakers are now looking to do theatrical runs of at least a week in both New York City and Los Angeles.

The filmmakers signed with Cinetic Media of New York City in fall 2007, and the film then was sent to major players in the home DVD market, such as Magnolia and NetFlix, Greene says. Shoreline Entertainment of Los Angeles markets the film overseas, and the Cannes Film Market (the companion to the Cannes Film Festival) screened the film in May 2008. The plan in April 2008 was to continue to self-release, Greene says, as that will help the filmmakers continue to garner media attention (no kidding) and will prime demand for DVD sales.

The bottom line: Greene observes that film distribution is changing daily, and Web streaming will become a major marketing vehicle in the future. It is essential that first-time filmmakers see the process through to the end. Go to festivals, talk to theater owners, never give up on your project, Greene says. Show that you're passionate about it. The sacrifices you make for the success of a film today will hopefully pave the way for future projects.

Index of Distributors by Subject Area

ACTION/ADVENTURE
Atom Entertainment, Inc.
Bauer Martinez Studios
Castle Hill Productions
Cinevolve Studios
Curb Entertainment
International Corp.
Direct Cinema, Limited, Inc.
EBS World Entertainment
Echo Bridge Entertainment
Entertainment 7
Fabrication Films
Facets Mutlimedia, Inc.
Film Movement
Filmmakers Library
Focus Features
Fox Searchlight Pictures
Freestyle Releasing
Fries Film Group
Genius Products
Harmony Gold USA
Highland Crest Pictures
IFC Films
Image Entertainment
Kino International Corporation
Koan, Inc.
Las Americas Film Network
Leo Film Releasing
Lightning Media
Lionsgate
Magnolia Pictures
Maverick Entertainment Group
Miramax Films
Monterey Media, Inc.
Myriad Pictures
New Line Cinema
New Yorker Films
Northern Arts Entertainment,
Inc.
Omni Film Distribution
Outsider Pictures
Panorama Entertainment
Corporation
Paramount Vantage
Passion River Films
Polychrome Pictures
Regent Entertainment
Rigel Independent Distribution and
Entertainment
RKO Pictures
Roadside Attractions
Roxie Releasing
Samuel Goldwyn Films
Screen Media Films
Shorts International
Sony Pictures Classics, Inc.
Sundance Channel
The Filmmakers Channel
The Weinstein Company
THINKFilm
TLA Releasing
Troma
Truly Indie
United Artists
Urban Home Entertainment
Vanguard Cinema
Vista Street Entertainment
Warner Bros. Entertainment
Yari Film Group Releasing
York Entertainment
Zia Film Distribution, LLC

AGING
Academy Entertainment
AGEE Films
Aquarius Health Care Media
Balcony Releasing
Baxley Media Group
Berkeley Media, LLC
Bullfrog Films
Cinema Guild
Direct Cinema, Limited, Inc.
Documentary Educational Resources,
Inc.
Facets Mutlimedia, Inc.
Fanlight Productions

Filmmakers Library
Human Relations Media
IFC Films
Intermedia, Inc.
Las Americas Film Network
Lucerne Media
Medfilms, Inc.
New Day Films
Northern Arts Entertainment,
Inc.
Terra Nova Films
The Filmmakers Channel
The Museum of Fine Arts,
Houston
Third World Newsreel (TWN)

ANIMATION
Academy Entertainment
Apollo Cinema
Arenas Entertainment
Marketing
Atom Entertainment, Inc.
Bullfrog Films
Canadian Filmmakers
Cinema Guild
Direct Cinema, Limited, Inc.
Documentary Educational
Resources, Inc.
Echo Bridge Entertainment
Facets Mutlimedia, Inc.
Film Movement
Filmmakers Library
Harmony Gold USA
IFC Films
Italtoons
Kit Parker Films
Koan, Inc.
Las Americas Film Network
Leo Film Releasing
Magnolia Pictures
Microcinema International
New Line Cinema
Northern Arts Entertainment,
Inc.
Peripheral Produce
PorchLight Entertainment

Pyramid Media
Reel Media International, Inc.
Shorts International
SubCine
Tapestry International, Ltd.

ARCHIVAL
Academy Entertainment
Canadian Filmmakers
Castle Hill Productions
Direct Cinema, Limited, Inc.
Documentary Educational Resources,
Inc.
Kino International Corporation
Kit Parker Films
Las Americas Film Network
Milestone Film & Video
Northern Arts Entertainment, Inc.
Rhino Entertainment
Rialto Pictures

ARTS, LITERATURE & MUSIC
Academy Entertainment
Acorn Media Group
AGEE Films
Alive Mind
Ambrose Video Publishing, Inc.
Appalshop Film and Video
Avatar Films
Berkeley Media, LLC
Bullfrog Films
Canadian Filmmakers
Canyon Cinema
Capital Communications
Chip Taylor Communications
Choices, Inc.
Cinema Guild
Cinevolve Studios
Criterion Collection
Direct Cinema, Limited, Inc.
Discovery Education
Documentary Educational Resources,
Inc.
Echo Bridge Entertainment
Educational Video Center
Electronic Arts Intermix

Emerging Pictures
Entertainment 7
Fabrication Films
Facets Mutlimedia, Inc.
Film Ideas, Inc.
Film Movement
Film-Makers' Cooperative
Filmmakers Library
Films for the Humanities & Sciences
Films Media Group
Films Transit International, Inc.
First Look Media, Inc.
First Run Features
Focus Features
Fox Lorber
Frameline Distribution
Fries Film Group
Gateway Films/Vision Video
Genius Products
GPN Educational Media
Harmony Gold USA
Image Entertainment
Independent Television Service
Ivy Video
Kino International Corporation
Kitchen Video Distribution Collection
Landmark Media
Las Americas Film Network
Leo Film Releasing
Library Video
Lightning Media
Lonely Seal Releasing
Lucerne Media
Menemsha Films
Microcinema International
Milestone Film & Video
Miramax Films
Monarch Films, Inc./Beatnik Home Entertainment
Monterey Media, Inc.
Museum of Modern Art-Circulating FIlm/Video Library
Mystic Fire Video

National Black Programming Consortium (NBPC)
New & Unique Videos
New Day Films
New Dimension Media
New Line Cinema
New Video/Docurama
New Yorker Films
Northern Arts Entertainment, Inc.
Outsider Pictures
Pacific Islanders in Communications
Palm Pictures
Panorama Entertainment Corporation
Picture Start Films
Plexifilm
Polychrome Pictures
Public Broadcasting Service
Pyramid Media
Questar
Reel Media International, Inc.
Rhapsody Films
Rhino Entertainment
Rialto Pictures
RKO Pictures
Roxie Releasing
Seventh Art Releasing
Shadow Distribution
Shorts International
Solid Entertainment
Sony Pictures Classics, Inc.
SubCine
Sundance Channel
Tapestry International, Ltd.
The Filmmakers Channel
The Video Project
THINKFilm
Third World Newsreel (TWN)
TLA Releasing
TMW Media Group
Truly Indie
United Artists
V.I.E.W. Video
Vanguard Cinema
Video Data Bank
Wellspring Media
Zeitgeist Films and Zeitgeist Video

BIOGRAPHY

Academy Entertainment
AGEE Films
Balcony Releasing
Berkeley Media, LLC
Capital Communications
Direct Cinema, Limited, Inc.
Documentary Educational
Resources, Inc.
Dream Entertainment
Echo Bridge Entertainment
Educational Video Group
Facets Mutlimedia, Inc.
Film Movement
Filmmakers Library
Films for the Humanities &
Sciences
First Run Features
Frameline Distribution
Genius Products
Icarus Films
IFC Films
Independent Television Service
Ivy Video
Kino International Corporation
Las Americas Film Network
Leo Film Releasing
Library Video
Lonely Seal Releasing
Microcinema International
Milestone Film & Video
Monarch Films, Inc./Beatnik
Home Entertainment
Mypheduh Films, Inc.
Mystic Fire Video
National Black Programming
Consortium (NBPC)
New Dimension Media
New Video/Docurama
New Yorker Films
Northern Arts Entertainment,
Inc.
Peripheral Produce
Plexifilm
Public Broadcasting Service
Questar
Rhapsody Films
Rigel Independent Distribution and
Entertainment
Roxie Releasing
Sundance Channel
The Filmmakers Channel
The Museum of Fine Arts, Houston
The Video Project
THINKFilm
TMW Media Group
Truly Indie
Women Make Movies, Inc.

CHILDREN'S PROGRAMMING

Academy Entertainment
Allumination FilmWorks
Alpine Pictures, Inc.
Apollo Cinema
Aquarius Health Care Media
Arenas Entertainment Marketing
Artist View Entertainment, Inc
Arts Alliance America
Atom Entertainment, Inc.
Bauer Martinez Studios
Bullfrog Films
Bureau for At-Risk Youth
Chip Taylor Communications
Choices, Inc.
Cinema Guild
Direct Cinema, Limited, Inc.
Discovery Education
Echo Bridge Entertainment
Educational Productions
Fabrication Films
Facets Mutlimedia, Inc.
Film Movement
Filmmakers Library
First Run Features
Gateway Films/Vision Video
GPN Educational Media
Harmony Gold USA
Human Relations Media
IFC Films
Italtoons
Kit Parker Films

Koan, Inc.
Landmark Media
Las Americas Film Network
Library Video
Lonely Seal Releasing
Lucerne Media
Monterey Media, Inc.
Mypheduh Films, Inc.
National Geographic Television
New Dimension Media
New Line Cinema
New Video/Docurama
Northern Arts Entertainment, Inc.
Passion River Films
PorchLight Entertainment
Public Broadcasting Service
Questar
Schlessinger Media
Screen Media Films
Select Media, Inc.
Tapestry International, Ltd.
The Filmmakers Channel
TMW Media Group
Vanguard Cinema
Wellspring Media
Zenger Media
Zia Film Distribution, LLC

COMEDY
Academy Entertainment
Acorn Media Group
Allumination FilmWorks
Amazing Movies
Apollo Cinema
Arrow Entertainment, Inc.
Artist View Entertainment, Inc
Arts Alliance America
Atom Entertainment, Inc.
Avatar Films
Bauer Martinez Studios
Canadian Filmmakers
Castle Hill Productions
Cinequest Online
Cinevolve Studios
Criterion Collection

Curb Entertainment International Corp.
Direct Cinema, Limited, Inc.
Dream Entertainment
EBS World Entertainment
Echo Bridge Entertainment
Emerging Pictures
Entertainment 7
Fabrication Films
Facets Mutlimedia, Inc.
Film Movement
Filmmakers Library
First Look Media, Inc.
First Run Features
Focus Features
Fox Searchlight Pictures
Freestyle Releasing
Fries Film Group
Genius Products
Harmony Gold USA
IFC Films
Image Entertainment
Kino International Corporation
Kit Parker Films
Las Americas Film Network
Leo Film Releasing
Lightning Media
Lionsgate
Lonely Seal Releasing
Maverick Entertainment Group
Menemsha Films
Milestone Film & Video
Miramax Films
Monterey Media, Inc.
Myriad Pictures
New Line Cinema
New Video/Docurama
New Yorker Films
Northern Arts Entertainment, Inc.
Omni Film Distribution
Outsider Pictures
Palm Pictures
Panorama Entertainment Corporation
Paramount Vantage
Passion River Films
Picture This! Entertainment
Polychrome Pictures

Rhino Entertainment
Rigel Independent Distribution
and Entertainment
RKO Pictures
Roadside Attractions
Roxie Releasing
Samuel Goldwyn Films
Screen Media Films
Shorts International
Sony Pictures Classics, Inc.
Sundance Channel
The Filmmakers Channel
The Weinstein Company
THINKFilm
TLA Releasing
Troma
Truly Indie
United Artists
Urban Home Entertainment
Vanguard Cinema
Vista Street Entertainment
Warner Bros. Entertainment
Wolfe Releasing
Yari Film Group Releasing
York Entertainment
Zia Film Distribution, LLC

CRIMINAL JUSTICE

Academy Entertainment
Ambrose Video Publishing, Inc.
Berkeley Media, LLC
Bureau for At-Risk Youth
Cambridge Documentary Films
Chip Taylor Communications
Choices, Inc.
Cinema Guild
Direct Cinema, Limited, Inc.
Educational Video Center
Facets Mutlimedia, Inc.
Fanlight Productions
Film Ideas, Inc.
Film Movement
Filmmakers Library
Films for the Humanities &
Sciences
Films Media Group

Films Transit International, Inc.
First Look Media, Inc.
First Run Features
Fries Film Group
Genius Products
Icarus Films
IFC Films
Image Entertainment
Las Americas Film Network
Library Video
Maryknoll World Productions
New Day Films
New Line Cinema
Northern Arts Entertainment, Inc.
Public Broadcasting Service
Skylight Pictures
Solid Entertainment
Tapestry International, Ltd.
The Filmmakers Channel
TMW Media Group
V.I.E.W. Video
VMS, Inc.
Zia Film Distribution, LLC

DISABILITY

Academy Entertainment
Aquarius Health Care Media
Berkeley Media, LLC
Capital Communications
Direct Cinema, Limited, Inc.
Documentary Educational Resources,
Inc.
Fanlight Productions
Filmmakers Library
Las Americas Film Network
Lucerne Media
Medfilms, Inc.
New Day Films
Northern Arts Entertainment, Inc.
Passion River Films
Seventh Art Releasing

DRAMA

Academy Entertainment
Acorn Media Group
Alive Mind

Allumination FilmWorks
Alpine Pictures, Inc.
Amazing Movies
Apollo Cinema
Appalshop Film and Video
Arenas Entertainment Marketing
Arrow Entertainment, Inc.
Artist View Entertainment, Inc
Arts Alliance America
Atom Entertainment, Inc.
Avatar Films
Bauer Martinez Studios
Castle Hill Productions
Chip Taylor Communications
Cinequest Online
Cinevolve Studios
Criterion Collection
Curb Entertainment International Corp.
Direct Cinema, Limited, Inc.
Dream Entertainment
EBS World Entertainment
Echo Bridge Entertainment
Emerging Pictures
Entertainment 7
Fabrication Films
Facets Mutlimedia, Inc.
Film Movement
Film-Makers' Cooperative
Filmmakers Library
First Look Media, Inc.
First Run Features
Focus Features
Fox Searchlight Pictures
Frameline Distribution
Freestyle Releasing
Genius Products
Harmony Gold USA
Highland Crest Pictures
IFC Films
Image Entertainment
Independent Television Service
Kino International Corporation
Kit Parker Films
Koan, Inc.

Las Americas Film Network
Leo Film Releasing
Lionsgate
Lonely Seal Releasing
Magnolia Pictures
Maverick Entertainment Group
Menemsha Films
Milestone Film & Video
Miramax Films
Monterey Media, Inc.
Myriad Pictures
National Black Programming Consortium (NBPC)
New Line Cinema
New Video/Docurama
New Yorker Films
Northern Arts Entertainment, Inc.
Omni Film Distribution
Outsider Pictures
Palm Pictures
Panorama Entertainment Corporation
Paramount Vantage
Passion River Films
Picture This! Entertainment
Polychrome Pictures
Reel Media International, Inc.
Regent Entertainment
Rhino Entertainment
Rialto Pictures
Rigel Independent Distribution and Entertainment
RKO Pictures
Roadside Attractions
Roxie Releasing
Samuel Goldwyn Films
Screen Media Films
Shorts International
Sony Pictures Classics, Inc.
Strand Releasing
Sundance Channel
Tapestry International, Ltd.
The Filmmakers Channel
The Weinstein Company
THINKFilm
TLA Releasing
Troma

Truly Indie
United Artists
Urban Home Entertainment
Vanguard Cinema
Warner Bros. Entertainment
Wolfe Releasing
Yari Film Group Releasing
York Entertainment
Zia Film Distribution, LLC

ENVIRONMENTAL ISSUES

Academy Entertainment
AGEE Films
Berkeley Media, LLC
Bullfrog Films
Canadian Filmmakers
Choices, Inc.
Direct Cinema, Limited, Inc.
Discovery Education
Documentary Educational
Resources, Inc.
Echo Bridge Entertainment
Educational Video Center
Environmental Media
Corporation
Facets Mutlimedia, Inc.
Film Movement
Filmmakers Library
Films for the Humanities &
Sciences
Films Media Group
First Run Features
IFC Films
Independent Television Service
Landmark Media
Las Americas Film Network
Library Video
National Geographic Television
New Day Films
New Dimension Media
New Line Cinema
New Yorker Films
Northern Arts Entertainment,
Inc.
Paper Tiger Television

Public Broadcasting Service
Roxie Releasing
Seventh Art Releasing
The Video Project
Third World Newsreel (TWN)
TMW Media Group
V.I.E.W. Video
Zia Film Distribution, LLC

EXPERIMENTAL/AVANT GARDE

Academy Entertainment
Alive Mind
Canadian Filmmakers
Canyon Cinema
Criterion Collection
Documentary Educational Resources,
Inc.
Facets Mutlimedia, Inc.
Film-Makers' Cooperative
Filmmakers Library
First Look Media, Inc.
First Run Features
Frameline Distribution
Fries Film Group
Genius Products
IFC Films
Image Entertainment
Kino International Corporation
Las Americas Film Network
Leo Film Releasing
Microcinema International
Milestone Film & Video
Monarch Films, Inc./Beatnik Home
Entertainment
New Line Cinema
New Yorker Films
Northern Arts Entertainment, Inc.
Paper Tiger Television
Paramount Vantage
Peripheral Produce
Picture This! Entertainment
Plexifilm
Solid Entertainment
Strand Releasing
Sundance Channel
The Museum of Fine Arts, Houston

THINKFilm
Third World Newsreel (TWN)
Troma
V Tape
Video Data Bank

FAMILY
Academy Entertainment
AGEE Films
Allumination FilmWorks
Alpine Pictures, Inc.
Apollo Cinema
Aquarius Health Care Media
Arenas Entertainment
Marketing
Artist View Entertainment, Inc
Bauer Martinez Studios
Berkeley Media, LLC
Castle Hill Productions
Chip Taylor Communications
Choices, Inc.
Cinema Guild
Direct Cinema, Limited, Inc.
Documentary Educational
Resources, Inc.
Educational Productions
Educational Video Center
Facets Mutlimedia, Inc.
Fanlight Productions
Film Movement
Filmmakers Library
Films Media Group
First Run Features
Fries Film Group
Gateway Films/Vision Video
Genius Products
GPN Educational Media
Harmony Gold USA
IFC Films
Image Entertainment
Koan, Inc.
Las Americas Film Network
Leo Film Releasing
Library Video
Lightning Media
Lucerne Media

Microcinema International
Miramax Films
Monterey Media, Inc.
Mypheduh Films, Inc.
National Black Programming
Consortium (NBPC)
National Geographic Television
New Day Films
New Line Cinema
New Yorker Films
Northern Arts Entertainment, Inc.
Pacific Islanders in Communications
Panorama Entertainment Corporation
Paramount Vantage
Passion River Films
PorchLight Entertainment
Public Broadcasting Service
Questar
Regent Entertainment
Rigel Independent Distribution and
Entertainment
Schlessinger Media
Screen Media Films
Seventh Art Releasing
Shorts International
Tapestry International, Ltd.
The Filmmakers Channel
The Museum of Fine Arts, Houston
Third World Newsreel (TWN)
Urban Home Entertainment
V.I.E.W. Video
Vanguard Cinema
Yari Film Group Releasing
York Entertainment
Zenger Media
Zia Film Distribution, LLC

GENDER ISSUES
Academy Entertainment
Alive Mind
Aquarius Health Care Media
Artistic License Films
Balcony Releasing
Berkeley Media, LLC
Bullfrog Films
Cambridge Documentary Films

Canadian Filmmakers
Cinema Guild
Direct Cinema, Limited, Inc.
Documentary Educational
Resources, Inc.
Educational Video Center
Educational Video Group
Entertainment 7
Facets Mutlimedia, Inc.
Fanlight Productions
Film Movement
Film-Makers' Cooperative
Filmmakers Library
Films Transit International, Inc.
First Run Features
IFC Films
Independent Television Service
Las Americas Film Network
Leo Film Releasing
Media Education Foundation
Miramax Films
Monarch Films, Inc./Beatnik
Home Entertainment
National Black Programming
Consortium (NBPC)
New Day Films
New Line Cinema
Northern Arts Entertainment,
Inc.
Outcast Films
Paper Tiger Television
Public Broadcasting Service
Roxie Releasing
Select Media, Inc.
Seventh Art Releasing
Sony Pictures Classics, Inc.
Strand Releasing
SubCine
The Video Project
Third World Newsreel (TWN)
TMW Media Group
V Tape
V.I.E.W. Video
Video Data Bank
Women Make Movies, Inc.

HEALTH & MEDICAL

Academy Entertainment
Ambrose Video Publishing, Inc.
Aquarius Health Care Media
Balcony Releasing
Baxley Media Group
Berkeley Media, LLC
Bullfrog Films
Bureau for At-Risk Youth
Cambridge Documentary Films
Capital Communications
Chip Taylor Communications
Cinema Guild
Concept Media
Direct Cinema, Limited, Inc.
Discover Films Video
Discovery Education
Educational Video Center
Fanlight Productions
Film Ideas, Inc.
Filmmakers Library
Films for the Humanities & Sciences
Films Media Group
First Run Features
Human Relations Media
Icarus Films
Intermedia, Inc.
Las Americas Film Network
Library Video
Lucerne Media
Medfilms, Inc.
Mystic Fire Video
New Dimension Media
Northern Arts Entertainment, Inc.
Passion River Films
Public Broadcasting Service
Pyramid Media
Samuel Goldwyn Films
Select Media, Inc.
Terra Nova Films
The Video Project
Third World Newsreel (TWN)
TMW Media Group
V Tape
Video Data Bank
VMS, Inc.

Wellspring Media
Wolfe Releasing
Zia Film Distribution, LLC

HISTORY
Academy Entertainment
Acorn Media Group
AGEE Films
Alive Mind
Ambrose Video Publishing, Inc.
Avatar Films
Balcony Releasing
Berkeley Media, LLC
Bullfrog Films
Cambridge Documentary Films
Capital Communications
Center for Asian American
Media
Choices, Inc.
Cinema Guild
Cinevolve Studios
Direct Cinema, Limited, Inc.
Discovery Education
Documentary Educational
Resources Inc.
Dream Entertainment
Echo Bridge Entertainment
Educational Video Group
Facets Mutlimedia, Inc.
Film Ideas, Inc.
Filmmakers Library
Films for the Humanities &
Sciences
Films Media Group
Films Transit International, Inc.
First Run Features
Frameline Distribution
Fries Film Group
Guidance Associates
Icarus Films
IFC Films
International Film Foundation
Ivy Video
Kino International Corporation
Landmark Media
Las Americas Film Network

Leo Film Releasing
Library Video
Lonely Seal Releasing
Magnolia Pictures
Menemsha Films
Milestone Film & Video
Monarch Films, Inc./Beatnik Home
Entertainment
Museum of Modern Art-Circulating
FIlm/Video Library
Mypheduh Films, Inc.
National Black Programming
Consortium (NBPC)
New Dimension Media
New Line Cinema
New Video/Docurama
New Yorker Films
Northern Arts Entertainment, Inc.
Pacific Islanders in Communications
Passion River Films
Peripheral Produce
Picture This! Entertainment
Plexifilm
Public Broadcasting Service
Questar
Reel Media International, Inc.
Rhino Entertainment
Rialto Pictures
Roxie Releasing
Seventh Art Releasing
Shadow Distribution
Skylight Pictures
Solid Entertainment
Sundance Channel
The Filmmakers Channel
The Video Project
THINKFilm
Third World Newsreel (TWN)
TMW Media Group
V Tape
V.I.E.W. Video
Video Data Bank
Vision Maker Video

HUMAN RIGHTS
Academy Entertainment

Ambrose Video Publishing, Inc.
Aquarius Health Care Media
Arenas Entertainment
Marketing
Balcony Releasing
Berkeley Media, LLC
Bullfrog Films
California Newsreel
Cambridge Documentary Films
Choices, Inc.
Cinevolve Studios
Direct Cinema, Limited, Inc.
Documentary Educational
Resources, Inc.
Entertainment 7
Facets Mutlimedia, Inc.
Fanlight Productions
Film Movement
Filmmakers Library
Films Transit International, Inc.
First Run Features
Frameline Distribution
IFC Films
Independent Television Service
Las Americas Film Network
Library Video
Maryknoll World Productions
Media Education Foundation
Milestone Film & Video
Monarch Films, Inc./Beatnik
Home Entertainment
Mypheduh Films, Inc.
National Black Programming
Consortium (NBPC)
New Day Films
New Dimension Media
New Line Cinema
New Yorker Films
Northern Arts Entertainment,
Inc.
Pacific Islanders in
Communications
Paper Tiger Television
Picture This! Entertainment
Public Broadcasting Service
Roxie Releasing

Seventh Art Releasing
Shadow Distribution
Skylight Pictures
Solid Entertainment
SubCine
The Filmmakers Channel
The Video Project
Third World Newsreel (TWN)
V Tape
V.I.E.W. Video

IMMIGRATION

Academy Entertainment
Arenas Entertainment Marketing
Berkeley Media, LLC
Bullfrog Films
Direct Cinema, Limited, Inc.
Documentary Educational Resources,
Inc.
Educational Video Center
Facets Mutlimedia, Inc.
Film Movement
Filmmakers Library
First Run Features
Icarus Films
IFC Films
Independent Television Service
Las Americas Film Network
Library Video
Milestone Film & Video
Monarch Films, Inc./Beatnik Home
Entertainment
Mypheduh Films, Inc.
National Black Programming
Consortium (NBPC)
New Day Films
New Dimension Media
New Line Cinema
New Yorker Films
Northern Arts Entertainment, Inc.
Seventh Art Releasing
Solid Entertainment
SubCine
The Filmmakers Channel
The Video Project
Third World Newsreel (TWN)

LABOR ISSUES
Academy Entertainment
Appalshop Film and Video
Berkeley Media, LLC
Bullfrog Films
California Newsreel
Cambridge Documentary Films
Direct Cinema, Limited, Inc.
Documentary Educational
Resources, Inc.
Facets Mutlimedia, Inc.
Fanlight Productions
Film Movement
Filmmakers Library
First Run Features
IFC Films
Independent Television Service
Intermedia, Inc.
Las Americas Film Network
Library Video
Media Education Foundation
Merrimack Films
Milestone Film & Video
Monarch Films, Inc./Beatnik
Home Entertainment
National Black Programming
Consortium (NBPC)
New Day Films
New Dimension Media
New Line Cinema
New Yorker Films
Northern Arts Entertainment,
Inc.
Paper Tiger Television
Seventh Art Releasing
Skylight Pictures
SubCine
The Filmmakers Channel
The Video Project
Third World Newsreel (TWN)
VMS, Inc.

LANGUAGE/LINGUISTICS
Academy Entertainment
Berkeley Media, LLC

Direct Cinema, Limited, Inc.
Discovery Education
Educational Productions
Educational Video Group
Film Ideas, Inc.
Filmmakers Library
Films Media Group
First Run Features
Guidance Associates
Human Relations Media
IFC Films
Independent Television Service
Las Americas Film Network
Library Video
Lucerne Media
Monarch Films, Inc./Beatnik Home
Entertainment
New Yorker Films
Northern Arts Entertainment, Inc.
Omni Film Distribution
TMW Media Group

LGBT
Academy Entertainment
Alive Mind
Aquarius Health Care Media
Artistic License Films
Berkeley Media, LLC
Cambridge Documentary Films
Canadian Filmmakers
Cinema Guild
Cinevolve Studios
Direct Cinema, Limited, Inc.
Documentary Educational Resources,
Inc.
Educational Video Center
Emerging Pictures
Facets Mutlimedia, Inc.
Fanlight Productions
Film Movement
Film-Makers' Cooperative
Filmmakers Library
Fox Searchlight Pictures
Frameline Distribution
IFC Films
Las Americas Film Network

Microcinema International
Miramax Films
New Day Films
New Line Cinema
Northern Arts Entertainment, Inc.
Outcast Films
Paper Tiger Television
Picture This! Entertainment
Regent Entertainment
Roxie Releasing
Seventh Art Releasing
Sony Pictures Classics, Inc.
Strand Releasing
Third World Newsreel (TWN)
TLA Releasing
V Tape
Wolfe Releasing

MULTICULTURAL PERSPECTIVE

Academy Entertainment
Allumination FilmWorks
Ambrose Video Publishing, Inc.
Appalshop Film and Video
Arenas Entertainment Marketing
Artistic License Films
Avatar Films
Balcony Releasing
Berkeley Media, LLC
Bullfrog Films
Bureau for At-Risk Youth
California Newsreel
Cambridge Documentary Films
Capital Communications
Center for Asian American Media
Choices, Inc.
Cinema Guild
Direct Cinema, Limited, Inc.
Documentary Educational Resources, Inc.
Educational Video Center
Emerging Pictures
Entertainment 7

Facets Mutlimedia, Inc.
Fanlight Productions
Film Movement
Filmmakers Library
Films Transit International, Inc.
First Run Features
Icarus Films
IFC Films
Independent Television Service
Las Americas Film Network
Library Video
Lonely Seal Releasing
Maryknoll World Productions
Media Education Foundation
Milestone Film & Video
Monarch Films, Inc./Beatnik Home Entertainment
Mypheduh Films, Inc.
National Black Programming Consortium (NBPC)
New Day Films
New Line Cinema
New Yorker Films
Northern Arts Entertainment, Inc.
Pacific Islanders in Communications
Palm Pictures
Paper Tiger Television
Passion River Films
Picture This! Entertainment
Public Broadcasting Service
Seventh Art Releasing
Shadow Distribution
Solid Entertainment
Strand Releasing
SubCine
The Filmmakers Channel
The Video Project
THINKFilm
Third World Newsreel (TWN)
Truly Indie
Urban Home Entertainment
V Tape
V.I.E.W. Video
Vanguard Cinema
Vision Maker Video
Women Make Movies, Inc.

NATURE
Academy Entertainment
AGEE Films
Aquarius Health Care Media
Berkeley Media, LLC
Bullfrog Films
Choices, Inc.
Direct Cinema, Limited, Inc.
Discovery Education
Documentary Educational
Resources, Inc.
Echo Bridge Entertainment
Environmental Media
Corporation
Film Movement
Filmmakers Library
Films for the Humanities &
Sciences
Films Media Group
First Run Features
IFC Films
Ivy Video
Landmark Media
Las Americas Film Network
Library Video
Milestone Film & Video
Monarch Films, Inc./Beatnik
Home Entertainment
National Geographic Television
New Dimension Media
New Line Cinema
Northern Arts Entertainment,
Inc.
Passion River Films
Questar
Seventh Art Releasing
Solid Entertainment
Tapestry International, Ltd.
The Filmmakers Channel
The Video Project
TMW Media Group
V.I.E.W. Video

POLITICS & GOVERNMENT
Academy Entertainment

Alive Mind
Arenas Entertainment Marketing
Arts Alliance America
Avatar Films
Balcony Releasing
Baxley Media Group
Berkeley Media, LLC
Bullfrog Films
Choices, Inc.
Cinema Guild
Direct Cinema, Limited, Inc.
Discovery Education
Documentary Educational Resources,
Inc.
Echo Bridge Entertainment
Educational Video Center
Facets Mutlimedia, Inc.
Film Movement
Filmmakers Library
Films Transit International, Inc.
First Run Features
IFC Films
Independent Television Service
Las Americas Film Network
Library Video
Lonely Seal Releasing
Magnolia Pictures
Media Education Foundation
Microcinema International
Milestone Film & Video
Monarch Films, Inc./Beatnik Home
Entertainment
National Black Programming
Consortium (NBPC)
New Day Films
New Line Cinema
Northern Arts Entertainment, Inc.
Pacific Islanders in Communications
Paper Tiger Television
Passion River Films
Peripheral Produce
Public Broadcasting Service
Roxie Releasing
Seventh Art Releasing
Skylight Pictures
Solid Entertainment

SubCine
The Filmmakers Channel
The Video Project
Third World Newsreel (TWN)
V Tape
V.I.E.W. Video
Zia Film Distribution, LLC

PSYCHOLOGY

Academy Entertainment
Alive Mind
Aquarius Health Care Media
Berkeley Media, LLC
Bureau for At-Risk Youth
Center for Asian American
Media
Cinema Guild
Direct Cinema, Limited, Inc.
Documentary Educational
Resources, Inc.
Educational Video Center
Fanlight Productions
Film Ideas, Inc.
Filmmakers Library
Films for the Humanities &
Sciences
First Run Features
Icarus Films
IFC Films
Las Americas Film Network
New Line Cinema
Northern Arts Entertainment,
Inc.
Pyramid Media
Roxie Releasing
The Video Project
Zenger Media

REGIONAL PROFILES &
ISSUES

Academy Entertainment
Berkeley Media, LLC
Cinema Guild
Cinevolve Studios
Direct Cinema, Limited, Inc.
Educational Video Center

Film Movement
Filmmakers Library
Harmony Gold USA
IFC Films
Independent Television Service
Las Americas Film Network
Library Video
Lonely Seal Releasing
Northern Arts Entertainment, Inc.
Pacific Islanders in Communications
Solid Entertainment
The Filmmakers Channel
The Video Project
TMW Media Group
Truly Indie
V.I.E.W. Video

RELIGION

Academy Entertainment
AGEE Films
Alive Mind
Aquarius Health Care Media
Arenas Entertainment Marketing
Arrow Entertainment, Inc.
Choices, Inc.
Cinema Guild
Direct Cinema, Limited, Inc.
Documentary Educational Resources,
Inc.
Educational Video Center
Facets Mutlimedia, Inc.
Fanlight Productions
Filmmakers Library
First Run Features
Gateway Films/Vision Video
IFC Films
Ivy Video
Koan, Inc.
Las Americas Film Network
Lonely Seal Releasing
Maryknoll World Productions
Milestone Film & Video
Monarch Films, Inc./Beatnik Home
Entertainment
Mystic Fire Video
New Day Films

New Dimension Media
New Line Cinema
Northern Arts Entertainment, Inc.
Seventh Art Releasing
The Filmmakers Channel
The Video Project
Third World Newsreel (TWN)
V Tape
V.I.E.W. Video
Zia Film Distribution, LLC

SCIENCE
Academy Entertainment
AGEE Films
Alive Mind
Ambrose Video Publishing, Inc.
Bullfrog Films
Chip Taylor Communications
Choices, Inc.
Cinema Guild
Direct Cinema, Limited, Inc.
Discovery Education
Documentary Educational Resources, Inc.
Fanlight Productions
Film Ideas, Inc.
Filmmakers Library
Films for the Humanities & Sciences
First Run Features
GPN Educational Media
Guidance Associates
Human Relations Media
Icarus Films
Landmark Media
Las Americas Film Network
Library Video
Lucerne Media
Monterey Media, Inc.
New Dimension Media
New Line Cinema
Northern Arts Entertainment, Inc.
Public Broadcasting Service
Shorts International

Solid Entertainment
The Filmmakers Channel
The Video Project
TMW Media Group
VMS, Inc.

SOCIOLOGY
Academy Entertainment
Alive Mind
Appalshop Film and Video
Aquarius Health Care Media
Arthur Mokin Productions, Inc.
Balcony Releasing
Berkeley Media, LLC
Bullfrog Films
Bureau for At-Risk Youth
California Newsreel
Cambridge Documentary Films
Center for Asian American Media
Cinema Guild
Direct Cinema, Limited, Inc.
Discovery Education
Documentary Educational Resources, Inc.
Educational Video Center
Fanlight Productions
Film Ideas, Inc.
Filmmakers Library
Films for the Humanities & Sciences
Films Media Group
Films Transit International, Inc.
First Run Features
Icarus Films
Independent Television Service
Landmark Media
Las Americas Film Network
Library Video
Maryknoll World Productions
Media Education Foundation
Milestone Film & Video
Monarch Films, Inc./Beatnik Home Entertainment
Mypheduh Films, Inc.
New Day Films
New Dimension Media
New Line Cinema

New Yorker Films
Northern Arts Entertainment, Inc.
Passion River Films
Peripheral Produce
Seventh Art Releasing
Solid Entertainment
The Filmmakers Channel
The Video Project
THINKFilm
Third World Newsreel (TWN)

SPORTS
Academy Entertainment
Allumination FilmWorks
Arts Alliance America
Chip Taylor Communications
Direct Cinema, Limited, Inc.
Dream Entertainment
Echo Bridge Entertainment
Entertainment 7
Fanlight Productions
Films Transit International, Inc.
IFC Films
Ivy Video
Las Americas Film Network
Library Video
Monterey Media, Inc.
New & Unique Videos
New Line Cinema
New Video/Docurama
Northern Arts Entertainment, Inc.
Passion River Films
Reel Media International, Inc.
The Filmmakers Channel
Third World Newsreel (TWN)
TMW Media Group
V.I.E.W. Video

THEATER
Academy Entertainment
Alive Mind
Bullfrog Films
Choices, Inc.
Direct Cinema, Limited, Inc.

Filmmakers Library
Fox Lorber
IFC Films
Las Americas Film Network
New Line Cinema
New Video/Docurama
Northern Arts Entertainment, Inc.
Solid Entertainment
Theatre Arts Video
V.I.E.W. Video

TRAVEL
Academy Entertainment
Choices, Inc.
Direct Cinema, Limited, Inc.
Echo Bridge Entertainment
Filmmakers Library
Las Americas Film Network
Library Video
National Geographic Television
Northern Arts Entertainment, Inc.
Omni Film Distribution
Solid Entertainment
Tapestry International, Ltd.
TMW Media Group
V.I.E.W. Video

WOMEN'S ISSUES
Academy Entertainment
Alive Mind
Aquarius Health Care Media
Artistic License Films
Balcony Releasing
Baxley Media Group
Berkeley Media, LLC
Canadian Filmmakers
Center for Asian American Media
Choices, Inc.
Cinema Guild
Documentary Educational Resources, Inc.
Educational Video Center
Educational Video Group
Fanlight Productions
Film Movement
Filmmakers Library

Films Transit International, Inc.
IFC Films
Las Americas Film Network
Maryknoll World Productions
Media Education Foundation
Milestone Film & Video
Miramax Films
Monarch Films, Inc./Beatnik
Home Entertainment
New & Unique Videos
New Day Films
New Line Cinema
Northern Arts Entertainment,
Inc.
Outcast Films
Paper Tiger Television
Public Broadcasting Service

Pyramid Media
Regent Entertainment
Roxie Releasing
Select Media, Inc.
Seventh Art Releasing
Solid Entertainment
Sony Pictures Classics, Inc.
Strand Releasing
The Video Project
Third World Newsreel (TWN)
TMW Media Group
V Tape
V.I.E.W. Video
Video Data Bank
Wolfe Releasing
Women Make Movies, Inc.

Index of Distributors by Acquisition Type

ANIMATION
Academy Entertainment
Apollo Cinema
Arenas Entertainment
Marketing
Atom Entertainment, Inc.
Canadian Filmmakers
Distribution Center
Cinema Guild
Direct Cinema, Limited, Inc.
Documentary Educational
Resources, Inc.
Film Movement
Fox Lorber
Harmony Gold USA
IFC Films
Italtoons
Kit Parker Films
Las Americas Film Network
Magnolia Pictures
Microcinema International
Museum of Modern Art-
Circulating FIlm/Video Library
Northern Arts Entertainment,
Inc.
Pyramid Media
Shorts International
Tapestry International, Ltd.
Vista Street Entertainment
Zeitgeist Films and Zeitgeist
Video

DOCUMENTARY
FEATURE
Academy Entertainment
AGEE Films
Alive Mind
Allumination FilmWorks
Ambrose Video Publishing, Inc.
Appalshop Film and Video
Aquarius Health Care Media

Arenas Entertainment Marketing
Arthur Mokin Productions, Inc.
Artistic License Films
Arts Alliance America
Avatar Films
Balcony Releasing
Bauer Martinez Studios
Baxley Media Group
Berkeley Media, LLC
Bullfrog Films
Bureau for At-Risk Youth
California Newsreel
Capital Communications
Center for Asian American Media
Chip Taylor Communications
Choices, Inc.
Cinema Guild
Cinevolve Studios
Concept Media
Direct Cinema, Limited, Inc.
Discovery Education
Documentary Educational Resources,
Inc.
Dream Entertainment
Echo Bridge Entertainment
Educational Video Center
Educational Video Group
Entertainment 7
Fabrication Films
Facets Mutlimedia, Inc.
Fanlight Productions
Film Ideas, Inc.
Film Movement
Film-Makers' Cooperative
Filmmakers Library
Films for the Humanities & Sciences
Films Media Group
Films Transit International, Inc.
First Look Media, Inc.
First Run Features
Fox Lorber
Frameline Distribution
Fries Film Group

Genius Products
Guidance Associates
Harmony Gold USA
Icarus Films
IFC Films
Independent Television Service
International Film Foundation
Ivy Video
Kino International Corporation
Kit Parker Films
Kitchen Video Distribution
Collection
Landmark Media
Las Americas Film Network
Leo Film Releasing
Library Video
Lightning Media
Lonely Seal Releasing
Lucerne Media
Magnolia Pictures
Maryknoll World Productions
Medfilms, Inc.
Media Education Foundation
Microcinema International
Milestone Film & Video
Monarch Films, Inc./Beatnik
Home Entertainment
Monterey Media, Inc.
Museum of Modern Art-
Circulating FIlm/Video Library
Mypheduh Films, Inc.
Myriad Pictures
Mystic Fire Video
National Black Programming
Consortium (NBPC)
National Geographic Television
New & Unique Videos
New Day Films
New Dimension Media
New Line Cinema
New Video/Docurama
New Yorker Films
Northern Arts Entertainment,
Inc.
Omni Film Distribution
Outcast Films

Pacific Islanders in Communications
Palm Pictures
Paramount Vantage
Passion River Films
Peripheral Produce
Picture Start Films
Plexifilm
PorchLight Entertainment
Public Broadcasting Service
Questar
Regent Entertainment
Rhapsody Films
Rhino Entertainment
Rigel Independent Distribution and
Entertainment
Roadside Attractions
Roxie Releasing
Samuel Goldwyn Films
Schlessinger Media
Select Media, Inc.
Seventh Art Releasing
Shadow Distribution
Skylight Pictures
Solid Entertainment
Strand Releasing
SubCine
Sundance Channel
Terra Nova Films
The Filmmakers Channel
The Museum of Fine Arts, Houston
The Video Project
Theatre Arts Video
THINKFilm
Third World Newsreel (TWN)
TMW Media Group
V Tape
V.I.E.W. Video
Video Data Bank
Vision Maker Video
VMS, Inc.
Wellspring Media
Wolfe Releasing
Women Make Movies, Inc.
Zeitgeist Films and Zeitgeist Video
Zia Film Distribution, LLC

DOCUMENTARY SHORT

AGEE Films
Ambrose Video Publishing, Inc.
Appalshop Film and Video
Aquarius Health Care Media
Arthur Mokin Productions, Inc.
Atom Entertainment, Inc.
Baxley Media Group
Bureau for At-Risk Youth
Cambridge Documentary Films
Canadian Filmmakers
Distribution Center
Capital Communications
Chip Taylor Communications
Choices, Inc.
Cinema Guild
Concept Media
Direct Cinema, Limited, Inc.
Discovery Education
Documentary Educational
Resources, Inc.
Educational Productions
Educational Video Center
Educational Video Group
Environmental Media
Corporation
Fanlight Productions
Film Ideas, Inc.
Film Movement
Film-Makers' Cooperative
Filmmakers Library
Films for the Humanities &
Sciences
Films Media Group
First Run Features
Fox Lorber
Frameline Distribution
Fries Film Group
GPN Educational Media
Guidance Associates
Human Relations Media
Icarus Films
IFC Films
Independent Television Service
Intermedia, Inc.
International Film Foundation

Kit Parker Films
Kitchen Video Distribution Collection
Landmark Media
Las Americas Film Network
Library Video
Lucerne Media
Magnolia Pictures
Maryknoll World Productions
Medfilms, Inc.
Media Education Foundation
Merrimack Films
Microcinema International
Milestone Film & Video
Monarch Films, Inc./Beatnik Home
Entertainment
Museum of Modern Art-Circulating
FIlm/Video Library
Mypheduh Films, Inc.
Mystic Fire Video
National Black Programming
Consortium (NBPC)
National Geographic Television
New Day Films
Northern Arts Entertainment, Inc.
Omni Film Distribution
Outcast Films
Paper Tiger Television
Peripheral Produce
Picture Start Films
PorchLight Entertainment
Public Broadcasting Service
Pyramid Media
Schlessinger Media
Select Media, Inc.
Seventh Art Releasing
Shorts International
Solid Entertainment
Strand Releasing
Tapestry International, Ltd.
The Museum of Fine Arts, Houston
Third World Newsreel (TWN)
Video Data Bank
Vision Maker Video
VMS, Inc.
Women Make Movies, Inc.

EXPERIMENTAL

Canadian Filmmakers
Distribution Center
Canyon Cinema
Cinema Guild
Documentary Educational
Resources, Inc.
Electronic Arts Intermix
Film-Makers' Cooperative
First Run Features
Focus Features
Fox Lorber
IFC Films
Image Entertainment
Kitchen Video Distribution
Collection
Las Americas Film Network
Leo Film Releasing
Microcinema International
Milestone Film & Video
Monarch Films, Inc./Beatnik
Home Entertainment
Museum of Modern Art-
Circulating FIlm/Video Library
National Black Programming
Consortium (NBPC)
New Day Films
New Yorker Films
Northern Arts Entertainment,
Inc.
Paper Tiger Television
Peripheral Produce
SubCine
The Museum of Fine Arts,
Houston
Third World Newsreel (TWN)
V Tape
Video Data Bank

NARRATIVE FEATURE

Academy Entertainment
Acorn Media Group
Allumination FilmWorks
Alpine Pictures, Inc.
Amazing Movies

Arenas Entertainment Marketing
Arrow Entertainment, Inc.
Artist View Entertainment, Inc
Artistic License Films
Arts Alliance America
Avatar Films
Bauer Martinez Studios
Castle Hill Productions
Chip Taylor Communications
Cinema Guild
Cinequest Online
Cinevolve Studios
Criterion Collection
Curb Entertainment International Corp.
Direct Cinema, Limited, Inc.
Discover Films Video
Dream Entertainment
EBS World Entertainment
Echo Bridge Entertainment
Emerging Pictures
Entertainment 7
Fabrication Films
Facets Mutlimedia, Inc.
Film Ideas, Inc.
Film Movement
Film-Makers' Cooperative
Films for the Humanities & Sciences
First Look Media, Inc.
First Run Features
Focus Features
Fox Lorber
Fox Searchlight Pictures
Frameline Distribution
Freestyle Releasing
Fries Film Group
Gateway Films/Vision Video
Genius Products
Harmony Gold USA
Highland Crest Pictures
Icarus Films
IFC Films
Image Entertainment
Independent Television Service
Ivy Video
Kino International Corporation
Kit Parker Films

Kitchen Video Distribution Collection
Koan, Inc.
Landmark Media
Las Americas Film Network
Leo Film Releasing
Lightning Media
Lionsgate
Lonely Seal Releasing
Lucerne Media
Magnolia Pictures
Maverick Entertainment Group
Menemsha Films
Milestone Film & Video
Miramax Films
Monarch Films, Inc./Beatnik Home Entertainment
Monterey Media, Inc.
Museum of Modern Art-Circulating FIlm/Video Library
Mypheduh Films, Inc.
Myriad Pictures
Mystic Fire Video
National Black Programming Consortium (NBPC)
New & Unique Videos
New Day Films
New Line Cinema
New Yorker Films
Northern Arts Entertainment, Inc.
Omni Film Distribution
Outsider Pictures
Pacific Islanders in Communications
Palm Pictures
Panorama Entertainment Corporation
Paramount Vantage
Passion River Films
Peripheral Produce
Picture This! Entertainment
Polychrome Pictures
PorchLight Entertainment
Public Broadcasting Service
Questar

Reel Media International, Inc.
Regent Entertainment
Rhino Entertainment
Rialto Pictures
Rigel Independent Distribution and Entertainment
RKO Pictures
Roadside Attractions
Roxie Releasing
Samuel Goldwyn Films
Screen Media Films
Seventh Art Releasing
Shadow Distribution
Sony Pictures Classics, Inc.
Strand Releasing
SubCine
Sundance Channel
The Filmmakers Channel
The Weinstein Company
THINKFilm
TLA Releasing
Troma
Truly Indie
United Artists
Urban Home Entertainment
V Tape
Vanguard Cinema
Vista Street Entertainment
Warner Bros. Entertainment
Wellspring Media
Wolfe Releasing
Yari Film Group Releasing
York Entertainment
Zeitgeist Films and Zeitgeist Video
Zia Film Distribution, LLC

NARRATIVE SHORT
Apollo Cinema
Arrow Entertainment, Inc.
Atom Entertainment, Inc.
Canadian Filmmakers Distribution Center
Chip Taylor Communications
Cinema Guild
Direct Cinema, Limited, Inc.
Discover Films Video

Film Ideas, Inc.
Film Movement
Film-Makers' Cooperative
Films for the Humanities & Sciences
First Run Features
Fox Lorber
Frameline Distribution
Fries Film Group
GPN Educational Media
Guidance Associates
Human Relations Media
Icarus Films
IFC Films
Independent Television Service
Intermedia, Inc.
Kit Parker Films
Kitchen Video Distribution Collection
Landmark Media
Las Americas Film Network
Lucerne Media
Magnolia Pictures
Microcinema International

Milestone Film & Video
Monarch Films, Inc./Beatnik Home Entertainment
Museum of Modern Art-Circulating FIlm/Video Library
Mypheduh Films, Inc.
Mystic Fire Video
National Black Programming Consortium (NBPC)
New Day Films
Northern Arts Entertainment, Inc.
Omni Film Distribution
Peripheral Produce
Picture This! Entertainment
PorchLight Entertainment
Pyramid Media
Seventh Art Releasing
Shorts International
Strand Releasing
Tapestry International, Ltd.
The Museum of Fine Arts, Houston
Troma
Zenger Media

Index of Distributors by Acquisition Method

FESTIVALS
Academy Entertainment
Alive Mind
Allumination FilmWorks
Alpine Pictures, Inc.
Apollo Cinema
Artist View Entertainment, Inc
Artistic License Films
Arts Alliance America
Atom Entertainment, Inc.
Avatar Films
Bauer Martinez Studios
Bullfrog Films
Canadian Filmmakers
Distribution Center
Castle Hill Productions
Chip Taylor Communications
Choices, Inc.
Cinema Guild
Cinequest Online
Cinevolve Studios
Curb Entertainment
International Corp.
Direct Cinema, Limited, Inc.
Documentary Educational
Resources, Inc.
Dream Entertainment
EBS World Entertainment
Echo Bridge Entertainment
Emerging Pictures
Fabrication Films
Facets Mutlimedia, Inc.
Fanlight Productions
Film Movement
Films Media Group
Films Transit International, Inc.
First Run Features
Focus Features
Fox Lorber
Fox Searchlight Pictures
Gateway Films/Vision Video
Highland Crest Pictures
Koan, Inc.

Las Americas Film Network
Lightning Media
Lonely Seal Releasing
Magnolia Pictures
Microcinema International
Miramax Films
Monarch Films, Inc./Beatnik Home
Entertainment
Monterey Media, Inc.
New Day Films
Northern Arts Entertainment, Inc.
Outcast Films
Panorama Entertainment Corporation
Peripheral Produce
Picture This! Entertainment
PorchLight Entertainment
Pyramid Media
Roadside Attractions
Roxie Releasing
Samuel Goldwyn Films
Seventh Art Releasing
Shorts International
Solid Entertainment
Sony Pictures Classics, Inc.
The Filmmakers Channel
The Video Project
Third World Newsreel (TWN)
TLA Releasing
Troma
United Artists
Urban Home Entertainment
V Tape
V.I.E.W. Video
Vanguard Cinema
Wellspring Media
Wolfe Releasing
Women Make Movies, Inc.
Zeitgeist Films and Zeitgeist Video

MARKETS
Academy Entertainment
Alive Mind
Allumination FilmWorks

Alpine Pictures, Inc.
Apollo Cinema
Artist View Entertainment, Inc
Artistic License Films
Arts Alliance America
Atom Entertainment, Inc.
Avatar Films
Bauer Martinez Studios
Bullfrog Films
Castle Hill Productions
Chip Taylor Communications
Choices, Inc.
Cinema Guild
Cinequest Online
Cinevolve Studios
Curb Entertainment
International Corp.
Direct Cinema, Limited, Inc.
Documentary Educational
Resources, Inc.
Dream Entertainment
EBS World Entertainment
Emerging Pictures
Fabrication Films
Facets Mutlimedia, Inc.
Fanlight Productions
Film Movement
Films Media Group
Films Transit International, Inc.
First Run Features
Fox Lorber
Fox Searchlight Pictures
Gateway Films/Vision Video
Highland Crest Pictures
Koan, Inc.
Las Americas Film Network
Lightning Media
Lonely Seal Releasing
Magnolia Pictures
Microcinema International
Miramax Films
Monarch Films, Inc./Beatnik
Home Entertainment
Monterey Media, Inc.
New Day Films

Northern Arts Entertainment, Inc.
Outcast Films
Palm Pictures
Panorama Entertainment Corporation
Picture This! Entertainment
PorchLight Entertainment
Roadside Attractions
Roxie Releasing
Samuel Goldwyn Films
Seventh Art Releasing
Shorts International
Solid Entertainment
Sony Pictures Classics, Inc.
The Filmmakers Channel
The Video Project
TLA Releasing
Troma
United Artists
Urban Home Entertainment
V.I.E.W. Video
Vanguard Cinema
Wellspring Media
Wolfe Releasing
Zeitgeist Films and Zeitgeist Video

SOLICITED ONLY
Allumination FilmWorks
Aquarius Health Care Media
Arenas Entertainment Marketing
Arthur Mokin Productions, Inc.
Cambridge Documentary Films
Capital Communications
Educational Video Center
First Look Media, Inc.
Focus Features
IFC Films
Las Americas Film Network
Lionsgate
Microcinema International
New Video/Docurama
Paper Tiger Television
Peripheral Produce
Regent Entertainment
Strand Releasing
Sundance Channel
The Filmmakers Channel

THINKFilm
United Artists
Zeitgeist Films and Zeitgeist
Video

UNSOLICITED INQUIRIES
Academy Entertainment
Alive Mind
Alpine Pictures, Inc.
Apollo Cinema
Artist View Entertainment, Inc
Artistic License Films
Atom Entertainment, Inc.
Avatar Films
Balcony Releasing
Berkeley Media, LLC
Bullfrog Films
Canadian Filmmakers
Distribution Center
Castle Hill Productions
Center for Asian American
Media
Chip Taylor Communications
Choices, Inc.
Cinema Guild
Cinevolve Studios
Concept Media
Curb Entertainment
International Corp.
Direct Cinema, Limited, Inc.
Discover Films Video
Documentary Educational
Resources, Inc.
Dream Entertainment
EBS World Entertainment
Echo Bridge Entertainment
Electronic Arts Intermix
Emerging Pictures
Facets Mutlimedia, Inc.
Fanlight Productions
Film-Makers' Cooperative
Filmmakers Library
Films Transit International, Inc.
First Run Features
Fox Lorber
Frameline Distribution

Freestyle Releasing
Fries Film Group
GPN Educational Media
Highland Crest Pictures
Intermedia, Inc.
Italtoons
Ivy Video
Kitchen Video Distribution Collection
Koan, Inc.
Landmark Media
Las Americas Film Network
Leo Film Releasing
Library Video
Lonely Seal Releasing
Lucerne Media
Maverick Entertainment Group
Media Education Foundation
Merrimack Films
Monarch Films, Inc./Beatnik Home
Entertainment
Monterey Media, Inc.
National Black Programming
Consortium (NBPC)
New Day Films
Northern Arts Entertainment, Inc.
Omni Film Distribution
Outcast Films
Outsider Pictures
Pacific Islanders in Communications
Passion River Films
PorchLight Entertainment
Public Broadcasting Service
Pyramid Media
Roxie Releasing
Schlessinger Media
Select Media, Inc.
Seventh Art Releasing
Shorts International
Tapestry International, Ltd.
Terra Nova Films
The Museum of Fine Arts, Houston
The Video Project
Theatre Arts Video
Third World Newsreel (TWN)
TLA Releasing
TMW Media Group

Troma
Truly Indie
Urban Home Entertainment
V Tape
V.I.E.W. Video
Vanguard Cinema

Video Data Bank
Vista Street Entertainment
VMS, Inc.
Wolfe Releasing
Women Make Movies, Inc.
York Entertainment

Index of Distributors by Acquisition Stage

Omni Film Distribution
Outcast Films
Outsider Pictures
Pacific Islanders in
Communications
Passion River Films
Peripheral Produce
Picture This! Entertainment
PorchLight Entertainment
Public Broadcasting Service
Pyramid Media
Roadside Attractions
Roxie Releasing
Schlessinger Media
Seventh Art Releasing
Shorts International
Tapestry International, Ltd.
Terra Nova Films
The Filmmakers Channel
The Museum of Fine Arts,
Houston
The Video Project
Theatre Arts Video
Third World Newsreel (TWN)
TLA Releasing
TMW Media Group
Troma
Truly Indie
Urban Home Entertainment
V Tape
V.I.E.W. Video
Vanguard Cinema
Vista Street Entertainment
VMS, Inc.
Wellspring Media
Wolfe Releasing
Women Make Movies, Inc.
York Entertainment
Zeitgeist Films and Zeitgeist
Video

PRODUCTION

Academy Entertainment
Alpine Pictures, Inc.
Cinevolve Studios
Dream Entertainment

Las Americas Film Network
Lonely Seal Releasing
Media Education Foundation
Monarch Films, Inc./Beatnik Home
Entertainment
Northern Arts Entertainment, Inc.
Outsider Pictures
PorchLight Entertainment
VMS, Inc.

PROPOSAL

Dream Entertainment
Fox Lorber
IFC Films
Las Americas Film Network
Monarch Films, Inc./Beatnik Home
Entertainment
Northern Arts Entertainment, Inc.
Public Broadcasting Service
VMS, Inc.

ROUGH CUT

Avatar Films
Direct Cinema, Limited, Inc.
Dream Entertainment
Emerging Pictures
Fox Lorber
Koan, Inc.
Las Americas Film Network
Lonely Seal Releasing
Media Education Foundation
Monarch Films, Inc./Beatnik Home
Entertainment
Northern Arts Entertainment, Inc.
Outsider Pictures
Picture This! Entertainment
PorchLight Entertainment
Seventh Art Releasing
Tapestry International, Ltd.
VMS, Inc.

SCRIPT

Academy Entertainment
Alpine Pictures, Inc.
Dream Entertainment
Harmony Gold USA

Highland Crest Pictures
IFC Films
Las Americas Film Network
Monarch Films, Inc./Beatnik
Home Entertainment
Northern Arts Entertainment,
Inc.
VMS, Inc.

TREATMENT
Dream Entertainment
Fox Lorber
Las Americas Film Network
Monarch Films, Inc./Beatnik Home
Entertainment
Northern Arts Entertainment, Inc.
Public Broadcasting Service

Distributor Submission Form

Please fill out the following form and fax it to Independent Media Publications at 877-513-7400. Fields with * are required. Your information will be included in future editions of *The Independent's Guide to Film Distributors* as well as our distribution database online. You may also submit your entry or corrections online through our website at www.independent-magazine.org/distributor

Name: *			
Description:* (you may attach page)			
AKA:		Parent Company:	
Address:		Address 2:	
City:		State	
Postal Code:		Country:	
Phone:		Phone Other:	
Fax:			
E-mail:		Website:	
Year Founded:		Number of Employees:	
Company Principals:			
Company Philosophy:			
Number of Titles in Distribution*:		Number of Titles in Catalog*:	
Primary Markets:	☐ Theatrical ☐ Nontheatrical ☐ Educational ☐ Home Video ☐ Cable TV	☐ Public TV ☐ Network TV ☐ TV Syndication ☐ Satelitte/DBS ☐ Web	☐ Airline ☐ Foreign ☐ Other
Areas of Specialty*:			
Best Known or Current Titles:			
Formats*:	☐ 35mm ☐ 16mm	☐ DV ☐ DVD	☐ CD Rom ☐ BluRay

	Beta / Beta SP	VHS / S-VHS	Other
	☐ Beta ☐ Beta SP	☐ VHS ☐ S-VHS	☐ Other
Type of Catalog:	☐ Printed Catalog ☐ Web Catalog	☐ One Sheets ☐ Direct Mail	☐ Other
Subject Areas*:	☐ Action & Adventure ☐ Aging ☐ Animation ☐ Archival ☐ Arts, Literature & Music ☐ Biography ☐ Children's Programming ☐ Comedy, Fantasy, Mystery, Thriller	☐ Criminal Justice ☐ Disability ☐ Drama ☐ Environmental Issues ☐ Experimental & Avant Garde ☐ Family ☐ Gay/Lesbian ☐ Gender Issues ☐ Health & Medicine ☐ History ☐ Human Rights ☐ Immigration ☐ Labor Issues ☐ Language & Linguistics	☐ Multicultural Perspective ☐ Nature ☐ Politics & Government ☐ Psychology ☐ Regional Profiles & Issues ☐ Religion ☐ Science ☐ Sociology ☐ Sports ☐ Theater ☐ Travel ☐ Women's Issues
Type of Acquisition: *	☐ Narrative Feature ☐ Doc Feature	☐ Short Narrative ☐ Short Doc	☐ Animation ☐ Experimental
Method of Acquistion:*	☐ Solicited Only ☐ Unsolicited Inquiries ☐ Festivals ☐ Markets		☐ Other
Stage to View Work: *	☐ Treatment ☐ Proposal ☐ Script	☐ Production ☐ Rough Cut ☐ Fine Cut	☐ Finished ☐ Other
Pay advances:			
Acquisitions/ Year: *			
Venues:			
Offers Filmmakers:	☐ Commission Projects ☐ Coproduction ☐ Financing	☐ Producer Representation ☐ Outreach Campaign Assistance ☐ Fiscal Sponsorship	
Advice for Filmmakers:			

Acquisitions Contacts:

Name:		Secondary Name:	
Phone:		Secondary Phone:	
E-mail:		Secondary E-mail:	

Made in the USA
Charleston, SC
08 January 2011